ALSO BY BRUCE WEBER

As They See 'Em: A Fan's Travels in the Land of Umpires

Savion!: My Life in Tap (with Savion Glover)

Look Who's Talking: An Anthology of Voices in the Modern American Short Story (ed.)

LIFE IS A WHEEL

LOVE, DEATH, ETC., AND A BIKE RIDE ACROSS AMERICA

❧

BRUCE WEBER

SCRIBNER

New York London Toronto Sydney New Delhi

Scribner
A Division of Simon & Schuster, Inc.
1230 Avenue of the Americas
New York, NY 10020

First Scribner hardcover edition March 2014

SCRIBNER and design are registered trademarks of The Gale Group, Inc.,
used under license by Simon & Schuster, Inc., the publisher of this work.

For information about special discounts for bulk purchases, please contact
Simon & Schuster Special Sales at 1-866-506-1949 or
business@simonandschuster.com.

The Simon & Schuster Speakers Bureau can bring authors to your
live event. For more information or to book an event contact the
Simon & Schuster Speakers Bureau at 1-866-248-3049 or
visit our website at www.simonspeakers.com.

Maps © copyright 2014 by Jeffrey L. Ward

Jacket design by Darren Hagger
Jacket photographs: Wheel © hudiemm/E+/Getty Images; Background © Diane Cook
and Len Jenshel/Stone/Getty Images; Biker © Alexander Fortelny/E+/Getty Images

Manufactured in the United States of America

1 3 5 7 9 10 8 6 4 2

Library of Congress Control Number: 2013040182

ISBN 978-1-4516-9501-4
ISBN 978-1-4516-9503-8 (ebook)

For Andrew and Sharon Joseph,
Rebecca and Julia Rohrer, Hayley Gibson,
and Jacob Weber. Keep pedaling. Wear a helmet.

Contents

PART ONE

The West

1

_⌒∽⊙∽⌒_

Everything Up to the Beginning

Sunday, July 10, 2011, New York City

*L*ike you, I'm growing old. It's harder to remember things, espe-cially good things, the things I want to remember, not so much because my mind is diminishing (hold the jokes, okay?), but because they happened longer ago than they ever did before.

Days seem more alike than they used to, probably because there is an ever-mounting total of them and it's hard to keep them distinct. This happens to everyone, I know, but I think it's worse for people who work at a newspaper, as I do, because our work product greets us each day, steady as a metronome, with the date plastered across the top of the front page. *Tick. Tick.* It's relentless—Monday, Tuesday, Wednesday, etc., week after week; July 9, July 10, July 11 . . . 2010, 2011, 2012. . . . Egads. How long can this go on?

This week is my twenty-fifth anniversary at the *New York Times*. Twenty-five years! And, as it happens, for the last three of them I've been writing obituaries. Every day, thinking about . . . well, you know.

So, here's what I'm doing about it. Eighteen years ago this summer, I rode a bicycle, solo, across the United States and wrote about it for the newspaper. Starting next weekend, when I fly from New York to Portland, Oregon, and turn back around on two wheels, I'll be trying to do it again.

I say "trying." This is not modest so much as careful, certainly a function of being fifty-seven, my age now, and not thirty-nine, as I was when I embarked the last time, blithely certain of myself and without any of the qualms that are now weighing down the saddlebags in my mind. In short, I had no concept of the length and arduousness of what lay in front of me. Every challenge—climbing the Rockies, for example, or persisting through the shadeless, sunbaked plains of South Dakota, or rattling over the cold-heave cracks along highways in Idaho and Minnesota that made riding a bike as comfortable as sliding down a miles-long washboard on my ass—was essentially a surprise, and perseverance is, after all, easier for the poorly informed. This time I know exactly how hard I'm going to be working. Does that make me nervous? Sure.

Excited, too. Among other things, assuming I do persevere, I'll be spending a summer and part of a fall largely outdoors, something New Yorkers in general (and obituary writers in particular) rarely get to do. But mostly it'll be a chance to relive—well, maybe that's the wrong word—to revisit an adventure I'd thought, at the time, was a once-only, last-chance, now-or-never thing.

I suppose I can conclude that I'm younger than I thought I'd be at this age. Still, a lot has happened since I last did this, and I expect the trip will give me the opportunity to mull things over. Experiential bookends like this encourage you to take stock, don't they? Add up the life details?

Off the top of my head, here's a quick summary: Both of my parents died. My brother had a son. I survived some bad episodes of depression and anxiety, but eventually ended twenty years of therapy and felt better for it. I moved to Chicago and back to New York. I spent four years as a theater critic. I wrote a book—two, actually, if you count the short one for kids. Much to my surprise, I developed an affinity for country music. I traveled on a bicycle in Costa Rica, New Zealand, Italy, Ireland, France, and Vietnam—where I was arrested and spent a night in jail. A handful of sincere and serious love affairs began and ended. I renovated my apartment. Twice.

So what do you think? How am I doing?

*   *   *

Partly because of my job, partly by inclination, I'm far better traveled within the United States than outside it. I've actually crossed the country a number of times by means other than a bicycle, the first time in 1973 as a hitchhiker, just for the hell of it, after I'd dropped out of college. In 2006, while I was working on a book about umpires in professional baseball, I drove from Florida to Arizona during spring training and, when the major league teams (and the umpires) dispersed to start the season, back to New York. Not long ago, I went to a conference in California and, instead of flying back, I rented a car and retraced much of the bicycle route I took in 1993. One satisfying highlight: the Bates Motel, in Vale, Oregon, near the Idaho border, where I couldn't resist staying overnight back then—I even took a shower!—was still there. (Need I explain to younger readers that a fictional Bates Motel—Anthony Perkins, proprietor—was the scene of the crime in Alfred Hitchcock's *Psycho*?) The cross-country trek has always appealed to me because as a New Yorker with a New Yorker's bias—and even worse, a Manhattanite's—I find much of America exotic.

After all, New York may be the nation's greatest city, but it isn't representative. You don't need me to count the differences, but an especially pertinent one is that New York is a vertical place and America isn't. To travel on the ground from sea to sea is to have a proud encounter with its horizontality.

Even in a car, each crossing of a state border is a singular triumph because the passage through the previous state has been earned. At ground level you measure a state's actual breadth with your tires, you roll over its topography and live in its weather. When you click past the far border, you put the experience of the state in your pocket for safekeeping and reference. Of course, crossing the country by bicycle is to feel these things in the extreme, and the absorption of long distances on the road has always felt, to me, like the qualifying exam for some enhanced form of citizenship. Even if you wanted to, you couldn't really avoid landmarks and cultural shrines—on my last trip across I hit

Yellowstone National Park; Little Big Horn; Devil's Tower, the remarkable rock formation in Wyoming that was featured in *Close Encounters of the Third Kind*; the Badlands; the Judy Garland museum in her hometown, Grand Rapids, Minnesota; De Smet, South Dakota, where Laura Ingalls Wilder spent her teenage years and set five books of her Little House series; Highway 61, the Minnesota highway along Lake Superior that inspired a Bob Dylan song; the Mt Shasta restaurant on the Upper Peninsula of Michigan, where much of the great Otto Preminger movie *Anatomy of a Murder*, the forerunner of so many courtroom thrillers, was filmed; Niagara Falls; the Finger Lakes; Cooperstown, New York, home of the National Baseball Hall of Fame & Museum on the shores of Lake Otsego, a.k.a. Glimmerglass, the region inhabited by James Fenimore Cooper's Deerslayer; and Hyde Park, Franklin Roosevelt's hometown—not to mention the Bates Motel.

An impressive list, right? I haven't considered before the string-of-signifiers aspect of these long rides. But it's true, you pedal and pedal and every now and then—more often than that, really, intermittently and unexpectedly—you find yourself in a place where something has happened, something of interest beyond itself, that has made a distinct mark in history or geography or culture, that helps describe the country, the known world, in some small but crucial way. Connect the dots on a bike ride the way I did then, the way I'm looking forward to doing again in the coming weeks, and you feel like the owner of a tiny, private slice of it all.

Partly for that reason, one of the strongest lingering memories of my last trip was how it fired up my patriotic instinct. You can't gobble up the nation, mile by mile on your own power, without assimilating a sense of its greatness.

You can't pass through the Badlands on a bike in ninety-five-degree heat, for example, and not feel some sense of proprietorship: you're proud of yourself and proud of the place, too. It really is a weird landscape—the Badlands, I mean—like another planet come to rest on earth with the spectacular cones and spirals of ancient sediment deposits rising from the prairie. You think, or at least I did, Cool beans! I crossed that sucker! It's mine!

And you can't encounter other Americans living lives completely different from your own without being reminded of what you share. A conversation I had in Canby, California, has stuck with me. Canby is in Modoc County in the northeast corner of the state on a plateau of rolling ranchland fitted among mountain ranges to the east, west, and south, and a desert to the north. I'd ridden through the pine-forested Sierras to get there, and it was probably the first time, of many that would follow, that I was taken by how much space there sometimes is between actual places (places you'd find people, that is) and by the marvelous vistas that the few who lived in the region lived with. I remember thinking, as I pulled into town after twenty miles of early-morning riding, that whereas I see water tanks on the tops of buildings every day from my bedroom window, the quotidian backdrop of the lives of Modoc residents features deep black lakes, grass, and scrubland stretching toward foothill, and, in the distance, the snowy peak of Mount Lassen. (I've come to think of the water-tank view as the screensaver of my life; now there's a metaphor that I didn't have at my disposal in 1993.)

I stopped for breakfast at the Canby Hotel, whose sign featured the carved outline of a steer's head. A photo I found online recently shows the hotel and sign are still there, with the addition of a hand-drawn wooden placard leaning against a telephone pole and declaring the place to be the home of the world-famous Modoc-burger. Anyway, I remember the meal I had—pork chops and eggs—and the proprietor, a man named Charlie who looked like the old actor Melvyn Douglas as he appeared in the movie *Hud*.

"Pretty country," I said to him.

"Yeah, well, country's all we got," he replied. He spoke in a resigned, low-volume growl that I recognized; he could have been a city cab-driver complaining about crosstown traffic.

Canby, California—that's another point. Entertaining the idea of a cross-country bike trip, most people think about the length of it, and because of that the endless stretches of empty road spanning vast swaths of the country, especially in the West, the distances between places instead of the places themselves. But there are towns, too, so many towns along the way; you can't believe how many towns, dozens for sure, maybe hundreds, and each one you pass through represents dozens, maybe hundreds of others you don't get to see. Each leaves a trace of itself in your memory. A lot of them make an effort to do so. The welcome signs that greet visitors to many, many places in this country are touching testaments to local pride. Nyssa, Oregon, for instance, on the Idaho border (not far from the Bates Motel, actually), calls itself rather dully the "gateway to the Oregon Trail," but also more colorfully, the "Thunderegg Capital of the World." (Thundereggs are geologic formations, most of them about the size of baseballs, that look like rocks on the outside but sliced open reveal intricate patterns of agate.) In Michigan, Onaway is the state's sturgeon capital, Atlanta is its elk capital, Fairview the wild turkey capital.

I should have made a list of the towns I passed through last time. (I will this time.) But I remember a lot of them—well, some of them: Wagontire, Oregon, population two, for instance, on the high desert in the southeast quadrant of the state, maybe eighty-five miles from the closest town of any size. (That would be Lakeview, to the south, which is known for its elevation—4,798 feet—as the "Tallest Town in Oregon," and, with 7,000-foot promontories outside of town, as a hangout for hang gliders.)

Wagontire had a motel, café, general store, and, across the road, a dirt runway with a windsock and a sign reading WAGONTIRE INTERNATIONAL AIRPORT. Local recreational pilots would land on the airstrip, taxi across the two-lane highway, and fill up at the gas station.

A couple named Bill and Olgie Warner owned the whole place when I went through (they were the population), and after seven years there they were ready to retire, buy an RV, and visit other places, presumably not as isolated as Wagontire. I was glad to have met them before they left—they were engaging folks with a good act, affecting an amiable, henpecked husband–weary wife routine, and they fed me very well. In 1998, they were evidently still there. Interviewed by the *Medford (OR) Mail Tribune*, Bill identified his wife as the mayor and chief of police. "Maybe I'll run next year," he said.

On the TripAdvisor website, I found a customer's restaurant review of the Wagontire Café from 2003: "Good home-style food and good service in a dumpy-looking little café in the middle of nowhere." And I found another article in the *Mail Tribune* from 2005 that identified a different couple as the town's owners, saying a general spiffing-up of the place was in the offing. Not too long ago, though, I passed through Wagontire again—in a car—and everything was closed up. I stopped and poked around. The buildings were still standing, a little the worse for wear but not too terribly run-down. The airport sign was still there. No more windsock, alas.

About thirty miles down the road from Wagontire is a town called Riley, whose population in 1993 was six. The guy who owned the café and gas station that made up the town was actually named Riley—Rich Riley—though he said he hadn't named it after himself; it already had the name. (I looked it up later. Apparently the name has been around since the nineteenth century; Amos Riley was a local rancher back then.)

Rich Riley, who looked to be in his thirties, had been a truck driver in a previous professional incarnation, and he explained to me that passing through town once, years earlier, on his route, he had stopped to eat and a waitress in the café was rude to him. It stuck in his craw. So he returned at some point and bought the place, planning to put her out of work. She was gone by the time he got there, he said, but when I met him he said he was still hoping she'd apply for a job.

He did acknowledge that he liked the idea of owning a place that already had his name on it. He moved his family in; that was the population: six. After I ate in his café—I'm pretty sure it was pancakes—he gave me a souvenir: the rattle off a rattlesnake that had bitten him two years earlier. I still have it.

I didn't stop in Riley on my recent drive through the area, so I don't know if Rich Riley is still there. The café and post office are. One addition is a billboard just beyond them, reading: WHOA! YOU JUST MISSED RILEY!

Bicycling makes you wonder about places like these in a way you wouldn't otherwise. When you drive through a place, the windshield is a barrier against its reality, the speed of the car a defense against memory. Hemingway, of all people, once made that point: "It is by riding a bicycle that you learn the contours of a country best," he wrote, "since you have to sweat up the hills and coast down them. Thus you remember them as they actually are, while in a motorcar only a high hill impresses you, and you have no such accurate remembrance of country you have driven through as you gain by riding a bicycle."

On a bike, the same thought crosses my mind often as I go through a town, mundane but nonetheless mind-boggling. All the time I've been living my life in New York City, people have been going about their business here, living theirs.

The options in the world! The size of this country and what's in it!

New Yorkers tend to think of Americans elsewhere as provincial, but we have a hard time recognizing our own provinciality. That's something else I learned on my previous cross-country ride. We share the country but not much else. It's amazing, isn't it, how so many of us can have a collective experience and see it differently? To put it another way, Americans may disagree about what it is that makes the country we share so fabulous, but we do seem to agree on its fabulousness.

I embark this time with a little less delight and a little more concern over all this. We are a more polarized populace now, with hostility hovering as our default national emotion.

The big political issue in June 1993 was gays in the military. The official Don't Ask, Don't Tell policy was enacted just a few months later. Now, of course, it seems just about ready to be overturned* and we're carrying on about same-sex marriage, though why it bothers anyone—except maybe a jilted lover—that anyone else wants to marry someone is beyond me. Issues evolve, but it's hard to account for the evolution of our national temperament, with a ratcheted-up

---

*Don't Ask, Don't Tell was repealed in September 2011, while I was bicycling through Wisconsin.

vehemence and implacability that strikes me (and a lot of other people, too) as poisonous.

When I pulled into little towns like Canby and Wagontire in 1993, looking for a diner, a motel, a milkshake, or a cold beer, not necessarily in that order, I was received, most often, with curiosity and warmth. And now? How well will a complete stranger on two wheels be welcomed in places he's never visited before? It's telling, I think, that this time I've had many people ask me if I'm carrying anything for protection. In the world I'm used to living in, the implication has generally meant a condom. At this point, I don't think that's what they mean. For the record, I'm not carrying a knife or a gun or mace or any other weapon—or any form of contraception, for that matter.

What else might be different? In 1993, neither cell phones nor personal computers were the ubiquitous human appendages they are today. The GPS was yet to be invented; I stopped at dozens of 7-Elevens along the way for local maps, which turned into a significant budget item. The stories I wrote for the newspaper about once a week were scribbled longhand in a notebook—then I called them in from a motel room or a roadside phone booth, reading them aloud into a tape recorder to be transcribed by a typist and passed along to an editor.

Quaint, right? The newspaper's recording room doesn't exist anymore. Among other things, this process kept me at a remove from the people who were reading my work, not to mention from my friends and family. The series generated more mail than anything I'd written before for the newspaper, but I had no idea of it until I found the stack of letters on my desk when I got back. People really liked the idea of the trip; they found it romantic—and I think they were amused, learning where I was popping up from week to week—but I didn't know that while it was happening. Aside from other cyclists I encountered on the road occasionally and the people I interviewed along the way, I pedaled along in pretty much total isolation until the technology of the day—television—intervened.

After a handful of my newspaper columns were published, the *Today* show on NBC sent a crew—a producer, a cameraman, and a driver—to meet me in Rapid City, South Dakota, and we spent a sweltering day cruising side by side through the Badlands, I on a bike, they in a van, the cameraman leaning out of an open door and taking endless film of my churning feet.

Some three weeks later, *Today* broadcast its piece, which included a live roadside interview with me on the outskirts of Atlanta, in north-central Michigan, conducted by Katie Couric. (On screen they spelled my name wrong, it turns out, but that was another thing I didn't know until I got home.) Twenty minutes or so after Katie signed off, I was pedaling along when a station wagon passed me and screeched over to the shoulder of the road, blocking my path. A woman got out tugging her small son, six or eight years old, by the arm, and slung him toward me. "May I take a picture of him with you?" she asked.

I was still mulling over the meaning of this when I stopped for breakfast at a restaurant in the next town. I walked in carrying my helmet, and the diners began applauding.

For this trip, I'll be blogging regularly on the *Times*'s website and sending out brief updates on Twitter, my first ever venture into social media. We'll see how that goes; like most reporters from the Pleistocene era, I'm curious about and fearful of this in equal measure, not sure what I'll be inviting. The whole reader-friendly aspect of online journalism is something that reporters often discuss. We get a lot of helpful stuff from readers who, with the convenience of email, now write to us, and overall the close scrutiny of our readership keeps us well warned about ever growing lazy, but we're also heaped with a lot of scorn, disparagement, and complaint from those who live to play gotcha, decry the incompetence or bias of the media, or simply send maledictions into the world. Certainly one unexpected consequence of the cyber age is how much unprovoked venom it has let loose. Pandora lives on the web.

*   *   *

Like last time, I'm starting in the West for two reasons—because the prevailing wind blows west to east (though expecting the wind to assist you is foolish) and because home is such a compelling destination. The idea of celebrating the finish by putting my feet up on my own coffee table is irresistible.

In 1993, I started in Marin County, California, just north of the Golden Gate Bridge (which I actually crossed the day before, just to be able to say I did); this time I'm pushing off farther up the Pacific Coast, riding initially in Oregon and Washington. The plan is to stay north, mostly because it'll be cooler, and because the only state I've never set foot in is North Dakota; I want to fix that. (Full disclosure: My only trespass in Hawaii was in the Honolulu airport. I'm counting it.) For some reason, I'd like to visit Lake Itasca, in Minnesota, the source of the Mississippi River. After that, we'll see.

One concession I've made to my age is a new bicycle, which I had custom-built to my precise dimensions and for the precise purpose of this journey. It cost about as much as a good—very good—used car. Not to be coy: the price was about $8,000.

As for other FAQs:

- I'm estimating the trip to take three months, which will bring me back to New York in time for the World Series. The last trip took seventy-five days; I'm giving myself an extra day for each year older I've gotten.

- The plan is to average three hundred miles a week, or fifty miles a day with one day off. A very doable schedule, though there is a relentlessness to it that I'm certain will become mentally as well as physically taxing. I averaged about sixty-five miles a day last time.

- I'll be sleeping indoors. Against the possibility that I'll be stuck without a roof a time or two, I'll be carrying a sleeping bag and a tent, but if I never ever sleep on the ground again, on this trip or afterward, I'll have gotten my wish. The theory is that if you carry an umbrella it won't rain.

Yes, I have thought about the obvious physical question: Can my body handle this?

Here's my self-assessment: I'm in reasonably good health and reasonably good shape—for someone getting close to sixty. I get to the gym most mornings. (In my opinion, given the amount of time I've spent exercising over the years, I should have a much better physique than I do.) I drink a little too much—bourbon is my chief vice—but I don't eat many sweets. A year ago, I rode a rigorous tour in New Zealand, somewhere north of three hundred miles in six days, including some pretty vertical terrain, so I'm not starting from a place of utter weakness or ineptitude. I'm six one, and I weigh just about 190, precisely my weight when I began my trip in 1993. (I finished at 176.)

All that is mostly to the good. So is the fact that I quit smoking three months before the 1993 trip, but it has been ten years this time.

On the other hand, my knees aren't great; they haven't been since I tore an anterior cruciate ligament playing basketball in grad school. I've long since given that up. Tennis, too. Don't even play much softball anymore.

I have gout, a couple of episodes a year for the last ten or so, though medication keeps the severity down.

A tendon in my right foot is degenerating, and about half the time it hurts when I walk.

Last year, tendinitis in my left elbow kept me from straightening my arm for about a month.

I have tinnitus—persistent ringing in my ears—the result of some ill-advised scuba lessons in the Caribbean a couple of winters ago.

I now take medication daily for acid reflux, which caused an irritation in the back of my throat that gave me a persistent, and occasionally debilitating, cough off and on for more than a year.

Three years ago, I had surgery to reattach the retina in my right eye and a subsequent laser procedure to repair a tear in the retina in my left; we caught that one before it detached. My eyesight has never been much to brag about and it is now fuzzier than ever. I've worn glasses for nearsightedness since I was six and once had an optometrist try to persuade me to wear contact lenses and glasses at the same time.

This spring I was diagnosed with cervical spinal stenosis—a narrowing of the spinal cord in my neck, which pinched a nerve and sent throbbing pains into my left shoulder and upper arm. It was treated with steroid injections—cervical steroidal epidurals, in medical parlance—and, knock on wood, it feels better.

The standard joke is that I'm both perfectly healthy and falling apart, and my doctors have pretty much confirmed this. The eye surgeon told me that nearsighted people are seriously at risk for retina detachment after fifty.

I asked the doctor who helped me with my neck problems what caused them. Gravity, he said. Most men my age are at risk for stenosis. He's exactly my age and he has it, he said.

Last month I went to my long-time internist for a full physical, just to make sure a cross-country bike trip was only a little crazy, not entirely insane. I said I thought I'd had an unusual string of irritating problems, and she laughed.

"It's a short list," she said. "Believe me."

What about the bike trip? Did she want to talk me out of it? Would she?

She laughed again. No such luck.

Before I go, I need to mention two people who have been close to me for decades but who have only recently, and with startling urgency, become part of the story of this trip.

The first is Jan Benzel, whom I met in the *Times* newsroom twenty-five years ago, but who is now, remarkably, suddenly, my girlfriend. I guess it happened over a long time—you know what I mean by *it*—but it also happened all at once, on a trip to Provence (yes, on bicycles) that we took together in May. I can't believe my luck.

The second is my oldest friend, Bill Joseph, whom I've known since we were ten-year-old Little Leaguers and who is dying of cancer. I went to see him last week in Los Angeles, where he is being cared for by his ex-wife and suffering in front of his young children. I can't believe his luck.

Sigh. I suppose every midlife reckoning story is implicitly about the idea of impermanence and teeters between the poles of love and death. I didn't plan mine to be literal in that regard, but I'll be bringing both Jan and Billy with me, of course.

"Don't do it," Billy said to me last week about the trip. Everyone who's known him forever still calls him Billy. "You did it once," he said. "You don't have anything to prove."

"It's too dangerous," he said.

For her part, Jan just wishes she could come along, though she knows even if she could arrange it, I wouldn't let her.

"I know, I know," she said the other night, though she added a good point, that we're getting started late, that we've already had our time apart.

Tick. Tick.

Tuesday, July 12, New York City

A bicyclist not in possession of his bicycle is at sixes and sevens. Mine, brand-new, custom-made, after only about sixty-five miles of test driving here in New York City, is now winging its way, via FedEx, to Portland, Oregon, where I'll pick it up on Monday. In the meantime, like a bereft parent missing a child, I'm happy to tell you about it.

First of all, it's red, rather dashingly so, though with a boxy profile, not terribly sleek. It doesn't look like an aerodynamically contemporary machine, which was a bit disappointing to me, but it's what I asked for, durability before aesthetics, and anyway, the more I look at it, the better I like its simplicity, its unadorned form. There is something tanklike about it; it emanates sturdiness. On a ride through the city the other day my friend Bobby Ball, riding behind me, reported that it remained uncommonly erect on the road, with none of the angling away from upright to the right and left, back and forth, that most bikes effect as their riders stroke their pedals. Even so, compared with the bike I rode across the country eighteen years ago, it's a featherweight. Before the addition of a rack, handlebar basket, lights, water bottle cages, bike computer, or any luggage, it weighed just a shade over twenty pounds.

I'm an experienced cyclist, though not an expert one. Or maybe a better distinction is that I'm an experienced rider but not a fully committed cyclist—that is, one of those people who lives in Bikeland, who proudly declares himself with the ugly spandex apparel, who speaks in the lingo of brand names and component parts. I love bicycles when I'm on one, not generally otherwise—okay, I'm a dilettante—meaning I can sense when something is wrong but generally can't fix it. Change a tire, restore a slipped chain, or tighten a brake cable? Sure. Replace a spoke, true a wheel? Uh-uh. I know what a headset and a derailleur are, I think, but I'm not going to risk my credibility by trying to prove it.

When I decided to give myself the advantage of a custom-built bike for this trip, I put myself in the hands of the erudite specialists at NYC Velo, a shop located in the East Village of Manhattan and also deep in Bikeland. The proprietor, Andrew Crooks, measured and interviewed me for over an hour—the first of several conversations—before the bike was designed, the frame built, and the components chosen.

The crucial info: I wanted straight-across handlebars—well, didn't want them, exactly, but promised my physiatrist I'd get them. (*Physiatrist*, what a word! So exotic-sounding I'm almost proud to need one—a nerve, muscle, and bone specialist who treats injuries.) He was worried about the pinched nerve in my neck and didn't want me spending weeks with my head tilted back and my neck contracted. Andrew also brought up the idea that I was going to spend a lot of money on this bike and that I would want it to be, very likely, the last one I ever bought. When the trip was over, he said, I wouldn't want to be riding a bike that was built only for long-distance touring and carrying extra weight and that couldn't be a little bit frisky on a casual ride.

NYC Velo worked with Independent Fabrication, a frame builder in Newmarket, New Hampshire, and together they decided on titanium as the best material for the frame, a compromise between hardiness and handling. The straight-across handlebars, highly unusual for a touring bicycle, mean that the top tube—the frame's horizontal beam connecting the seat post to the steering column—has to be slightly shorter than normal; and to keep me sitting at least semi-upright, the head tube—essentially the steering column, the vertical tube that the front fork passes through—is slightly longer.

Once I rode a few miles, I brought it back to the shop for some adjustments. The handlebars were so wide and keeping me so upright that on my first couple of trial rides, I felt like a sailboat sail, my body's breadth working against me. So Andrew lowered the bars slightly and cut an inch off each end. I also had him add bar ends—grips affixed perpendicular to the handlebars—to give me alternative hand positions.

Unlike the wheels on many new bikes, mine are made from separate components—hub, rim, spokes—which adds durability. (Prebuilt wheels tend to be a smidgen lighter in weight.) Each wheel has thirty-six spokes, rather than the standard thirty-two, another strengthening element. And the tires are touring specific and essentially flatproof, with a layer of puncture-resistant foam between the outer rubber and the inner seal, though with the extra armor you don't roll with maximum alacrity.

"The bike is unique," Andrew said. "It's expected to do dual duty, to get you across the country loaded with a certain amount of gear, in as fine a fashion ergonomically as possible. For the trip we wanted to balance the need to be lightweight, to be durable, and to be comfortable. But you're also going to use it for other rides, so we wanted to make sure you had a bike that wasn't singular in function."*

---

*I'm a little embarrassed by how little I know about bicycle design, bicycle components, and bicycle repair, and as I knew they would, a fair number of readers have chastised me for being a mere tourist in Bikeland, someone without a real grounding in bicycle mechanics who doesn't want his hands greasy. I accept their scorn, but that doesn't mean I'm going to discuss the elements of bicycle building. For those who wish to read about that, I suggest *It's All About the Bike: The Pursuit of Happiness on Two Wheels*, a 2010 volume by an accomplished English rider, Robert Penn, who discusses, in largely readable prose, the design and construction of his perfect bike. That said, for my gearhead readers, here is a components inventory:

This morning, before I took it back to Andrew for packing and shipping to Portland—he's got a pal who owns a bike shop out there where I can pick it up—I took a final test ride, about thirty-five miles, up the West Side bike path and over the George Washington Bridge into Fort Lee, New Jersey.

I spent the ride thinking ahead, trying to imagine living on this bicycle for three months and more than four thousand miles, alert to the slight irritations of the moment that can balloon into future pain. The bike is comfortable and perfectly sized, but the repetitive motion of pedaling hasn't yet worn a groove in my psyche, and the various body parts that work together on a ride, the muscles and joints for which every bike is a different solar system, haven't yet described their orbits. I'm still getting used to wearing bike shoes, locking into the pedals, and at each stop clipping out again; the aggressive twist of the ankle needed to release the shoe from the lock feels peculiar and unnatural.

Frame (titanium) and custom paint: Independent Fabrication
Fork (steel): Independent Fabrication
Headset: Cane Creek
Brake levers: Paul Component Engineering (short-reach flat bar)
Brake calipers: Paul Component Engineering (touring)
Shift levers: Shimano (10-speed flat bar)
Front derailleur: Shimano Ultegra
Triple rear derailleur: Shimano Ultegra
Long cage chain: Shimano Ultegra
Cog set: Shimano Ultegra 11-28
Crank set: Shimano Ultegra
Triple bottom bracket: Shimano Ultegra
Stem: Ritchey WCS
Seat post: Ritchey WCS
Handlebar: flat bar
Hubs: Shimano XT
Rims: Mavic A719
Spokes: Phil Wood (custom)
Tires: Schwalbe, Marathon 700 x 32
Tubes: Q-Tubes 700 x 32
Rim strips: Velox 17 mm
Saddle: Terry

For twenty years I've been riding with sneakers and toe clips, just sliding my foot back out of the clip as I coasted to a stop; I'm sure an awkward fall from a standing position is in my future.

I had chosen a seat with some gel padding to it, for additional initial comfort, rather than a Brooks leather seat, which molds to your ass after a few hundred miles and would probably be better in the long run; I didn't want to start out any more uncomfortably than I had to. In spite of a recent article in the *Times* about the benefits of a noseless seat, which allegedly relieves pressure on the perineum and is said to prevent a numbness in the genitals, along with a host of other discomforts that many riders are familiar with, mine has a rather long nose. The proof will be in the pedaling, and I won't be averse to changing along the way; a saddle is easy to replace.

It was a steamy day, and I was more worn at the end than I wanted to be—or should have been. I haven't trained enough, and with no extended hills on the ride, I still found myself pedaling comfortably only in lower gears. So one mistake I know I've made already is that I bought the bike too late (or that I'm departing too soon). I won't have broken it in before I begin the long trek. I'll be starting out with a stranger and not an old friend.

Sunday, July 17, 35,000 feet above the Midwest

High above America, somewhere between JFK and Portland International, I'm thinking it's going to take me six hours to get across the country east to west and ninety days or so to come back the other way. Why am I doing this again?

Well, okay, one reason is that as a writer I tend to think in storytelling terms, and a long bike ride is a good long story, after all. Since I finished the baseball book two years ago I've been waiting for another subject to seize me, and this seems like a natural. In fact, I've thought about a bicycling book, a cross-country bicycling book, since the last time I made the trip, though something told me back then that I wasn't prepared to write it, that the story I wanted to tell hadn't fully percolated. I know now, of course, that that's because the story I was contemplating was my own.

Bicycling, the way I think of it, is solitary, and if it's going to stand for anything in a narrative, it might as well be the solitary experience of being alive. That's a bit of high and mighty ambition, I guess. But why not? I've now got almost twenty more years of living and twenty more years of thinking about it.

There's another thing, too: For the past three years I've been writing obituaries, each morning arriving at work and trying to condense the life of someone else into a coherent, meaningful—and interesting—story. Sometimes I succeed and the dead come alive—I say that fully aware of the wordplay—or are at least recognizable to the people who knew and loved them. But sometimes either the details don't coalesce into a whole or they don't add up to much more than a résumé and a list of grieving survivors. I'm feeling both challenged and ready now to focus that task inward, especially without the pressure of a daily deadline, and the cross-country journey as a narrative spine, as a controlling metaphor, strikes my writer self as worthy. In other words, in one sense I'm doing this again to consider why I'm doing this again.

Here's something that's already different from the last trip and that has me both surprised and curious. People are already checking in, both in the comments on the newspaper's website and in emails to me personally, with some rather forceful opinions, and I'm finding myself provoked by them, inclined to respond.

How should I react to the feedback to what I'm writing while I'm still writing it? How deaf should I be to compliments and complaints? Say I listen to good ideas and accommodate them or take criticism to heart and adjust my thinking. I wonder: Is using readers this way, as editors before the fact, interesting? Is it good for the book? Is it kosher?

Anyway, here I am still at the very beginning—before the beginning—but I can already start to parse my readership and, like a politician scanning the polls, begin to recognize where my sympathizers and critics come from. The readers who accept what I'm saying at face value—about myself, the trip, my bike—seem compelled to applaud and offer sincere advice.

Matters of uncertainty for me have included where, exactly, to begin pedaling and in what direction. Tips have been pouring in on these issues, and my volunteer counselors are divided. Some say head east from Portland up the Columbia River gorge to Hood River, then cross the Columbia into Washington and ride in the direction of Walla Walla. Others tell me the Washington side of the Columbia is preferable. Another option: I could go south into central Oregon and then turn east toward Bend. Or I could begin by going in the wrong direction altogether, west toward the coast to dip a tire symbolically in the Pacific. I've had this last one in mind all along, but one cool thing about a trip like this is it doesn't really matter. It'll be new and eye-opening whatever I choose. On the other hand, it's the beginning: Is any part of a journey—or a narrative—more important?

I've been impressed by—flattered and touched by, too—the encouragement and generosity that the majority of readers have expressed. I've had offers of meals and lodging in Washington, Idaho, Minnesota, Wisconsin, Illinois, Ohio, West Virginia, and Maine, and I hereby acknowledge that I am not too proud to ignore such hospitality (though Maine isn't exactly on the itinerary). Several readers have already alerted me to cross-country cyclists already on the road, among them a group of students from St. Paul's School in New Hampshire, who are riding to raise money for the rehabilitation of wounded American soldiers, and a woman who on her blog is keeping a body count of animal roadkill. I've been advised to carry Good & Plenty candy (licorice is reputedly therapeutic for acid reflux) and to take full advantage of technology.

"Loneliness is the biggest problem," David Goodrich, a 58-year-old cyclist wrote to me from Sumpter, Oregon, 3,800 miles into an east-west cross country trip that he's also blogging about. "Stay in touch through these remarkable gadgets. You will have a down place; use your friends to help you get over it."

Pretty sound counsel, I'd say.

Of course, I'm hearing from others, too, those who simply know better than I do—about bicycling and bicycles, certainly, but about life in general as well. From them I'm already hearing snorts of derision.

Like most people, I think, I tend to be more wounded by criticism than buoyed by praise, and I'm nervous enough as it is. "You're a total Fred," one guy wrote, scorning my new bike as badly thought through, foolishly designed, and overpriced. I don't know what a Fred is, but surely not anything good.

An online debate has ensued regarding my choice of straight-across handlebars; many reader/riders seem to think it a big mistake that I'll regret when I face the inevitable headwinds or when my wrists and shoulders stiffen because I won't have the alternative handholds and riding positions offered by drop bars. Also, they say, I haven't trained enough, I haven't planned my route adequately, I bought the wrong saddle, and my rear cassette is too small; a larger one, with more cogs that would make for easier pedaling uphill, a grannier granny gear, is something I'm going to wish I had. (Actually, I'm pretty sure that's true.)

A certain amount of resentment has accrued to the cost of the bike, and this has pissed me off a bit. I'm convinced most of the attitude has come from people who own cars—I don't—that cost a lot more than $8,000. And why does anyone care how I spend my money?

And then there is a truly dyspeptic character from Arizona—he calls himself Thus Spake the Dancing Scorpion—who just shat on the whole idea. "Nah, I wasn't one of those readers who encouraged this aging *New York Times* obit writer to pedal across the wide dangerous spaces of a nation busily devouring itself these days," he wrote. "My suggestion, Webber [sic], is that you stop acting out and return to work as soon as possible. Don't you have a girlfriend or OTB to keep you distracted? By the way, clinical professionals don't have a lot of nice things to say about someone backing into a frenetic past indulgence to find meaning. Learn to be calm and you will always be happy. Most men pursue pleasure, like this stunt, with such breathless emotion that they hurry past it."

What a reaction to someone else's essentially harmless adventure! There's a lot to pique my curiosity in that, not least Mr. Scorpion's apparent misanthropy. Why does he care so much about what I'm doing that he took the time to craft such a crabby critique, not just of my work, but me?

Anyway, he's probably right. If I could only learn to be calm I'd always be happy. Just typing that makes me giggle.

I should clarify something. I'm hardly a person you'd describe as spiritual. God? Nah. For one thing, there's been too much misery too close to home. (I'll no doubt get back to that later.) I've never been a yoga devotee—a girlfriend once attempted to get me interested, but as much as I liked her, it didn't take. I haven't explored enlightenment through Eastern philosophy or, for that matter, sought it through mind expansion. My one LSD trip, in college? A disaster. It was sleeting outside and I ended up losing my hat, scarf, and gloves. I whined through the whole thing, didn't sleep for three days, and got a terrible cold.

That said, to my mind a long bike ride comes close to being transcendental. For one thing, no matter how many people you're traveling with, cycling is a consuming enterprise, one in which you are communing all at once with your body and your bike and the road and the weather and the traffic and the scenery—in other words, the whole world as it pertains to you. The relentless pedaling is the cyclist's version of chanting or prayer.

This isn't the same as being contemplative, by the way; to the contrary, cycling is not especially conducive to brooding or pondering or weighing your options.

People often ask me what I think about on a long bike ride, as if all I have to do while tootling along is to meditate on grand themes, and as if part of the challenge is filling empty hours with fruitful cogitation. I tell them I think about the bike ride. I listen for the sound of my chain in its orbit: Is it gritty and grinding? Does it need oil? I pay attention to the keening in my thighs, the strain in my quadriceps and hammies and glutes as I pump uphill or into the wind: Should I slow my stroke? Gear down? Gear up? I keep tabs on my fuel level and hydration; cycling when you're hungry or thirsty is an agony. I monitor my progress, watching my odometer/speed gauge/clock for info and entertainment as though it were a television set, checking on mileage, the distance to the next turn or the next town, the hours until I rest for the night. None of this amounts to thinking so much as release from thought.

The point is that big thoughts don't happen on the bike. The contemplation stuff—that will mostly happen at night. Though maybe not; then I'll be packing and unpacking, seeking and eating a substantial dinner, planning the next day's route, obsessively tracking the weather.

No, biking across the country for the second time is a thing I'm doing to have important things to think about afterward.

Tuesday, July 19, Astoria, Oregon

The novelist Richard Ford was a teacher of mine long ago, and among the things he said that I've remembered is that a novel has no place in the world except the one it makes for itself. In fact, I stole the thought from him when I began my first cross-country trip in 1993.

"Novelists will say that one reason their work is so agonizing is that no one out there is waiting for what they do; they have to create their own welcome in the world," I wrote then.*

Then I added, "A cross-country bicyclist feels the same way."

---

*I don't want anyone to think I'm apologizing here or coming clean for borrowing from Ford without attribution twenty years ago. But what goes around comes around. Many years ago, when I was a high school English teacher, I told Ford, who is still a friend, a story about one of my students who, in a paper, referred to the competitive environment of a high-level prep school as "a doggy-dog world." That phrase subsequently showed up in a Ford short story, and when I confronted him about it—this was mock indignation, you understand—Ford looked off vaguely into the atmosphere, shrugged his shoulders, and said, "Well, we find fiction everywhere."

I'm not a novelist and this isn't a novel (though I'd argue that because I'm generating the plot as I go along, not as the writer but as the main character, it amounts to something pretty similar). In any case the parallels between riding and writing are actually substantial; it seems so, at least, for someone engaged in both of them.

Like a writer beginning a book, a cyclist has a long way to go before he can envision the end. Both push off in a specified direction with hope and uncertainty. Both make wrong turns, both are prone to whimsy, serendipity, and sudden inspiration. Both come up with ideas they didn't know they had and encounter surprising characters who change the course of things. Trying to effect and negotiate a compelling path from beginning to end, both confront potential disaster, succumb to misleading optimism, experience hubris and self-doubt, anguish and delight. Indeed, sitting down to begin a piece of writing and climbing aboard a bicycle to begin a long journey are both daunting prospects, equally likely to induce procrastination. I know something about that, too.

To wit: I haven't gotten anywhere yet. In fact, I've traveled one hundred miles in the wrong direction.

On Monday morning—jeez, was that only yesterday?—I picked up my bike from Erik Tonkin, who owns Sellwood Cycle Repair in Portland. A former racer who, like a lot of cycle shop owners (and like a lot of people who work in or just hang around in cycle shops) he is a promoter of bicycling in any form. Bicycling accommodates a subculture of true believers, that's for sure, and Erik was a warm and enthusiastic counterbalance to my cynical correspondents.* He and a coworker, Julie

---

*Several months later, I wrote to Erik and asked him if he was surprised that I'd made it. I thought I'd come across to him like a novice—it's certainly how I felt—and I could only imagine that he and Julie were shaking their heads at my folly when they left me. He wrote back that he wasn't in the least surprised: "I didn't think of you as a novice, either. Life experience can carry the day. Even if I had, I would've admired the courage it takes to do something new. When I teach bike riders the sport of cyclocross, for example, I'm always impressed by

Kramer, got on bikes and rode with me from the shop along the Spring-water bike trail on the Willamette River. They led me over the Haw-thorne Bridge and deposited me downtown where, for the first time, I was left alone, thousands of miles from home, on my new bicycle. I was sorry to see them go.

Since then I've done some shopping; I bought a tent and a sleeping bag at the local REI, things I hadn't bought (or owned) in years. I've never been especially good at the minutiae of camping, which includes matching tent pegs to eyelets, but I'd assumed that during the time since I'd last tried to put up a tent on my own, the ingenuity of tentmak-ers had solved the ineptitude problem embodied by the likes of me and that you could pretty much just snap your fingers and the thing would stand up by itself, with the tent flap invitingly unzipped and maybe a wood-burning fire cozily ablaze inside.

Not so, it turns out. I tried setting up the new tent in my hotel room last night, and a Chaplinesque scene unspooled. At one point I managed to catch a tent peg in the lamp cord and pull out the plug. At another I snagged my foot on a tent flap and tumbled over the back of the sofa. After an hour or so I finally got the thing erect, with the rain tarp slung over it and my new sleeping bag inside, though, alarmingly, there was a collapsible pole with an elastic band strung through it lying extrane-ously on the bed. Yet another reason to hope I never have to sleep on the ground.

This morning I packed and repacked my panniers and shipped home some clothes I already knew I wouldn't need, or at least wouldn't miss. And then I loaded up the bike and rode around town for a couple of hours, getting used to handling the extra weight, maybe thirty-five pounds, on the rear. It was raining, and the road surfaces were slick. I was a little wobbly. Gulp.

I knew before I arrived, of course, that Portland is about a hundred

---

their bravery. Yes, some part of that bravery is misinformed by ignorance, but who cares? I'm there to help. I often wonder if I'd be so brave if the roles were reversed."

miles inland from the Pacific coast, and that Astoria, at the mouth of the Columbia River, is a traditional launching site for cross-country cyclists. But for reasons I'm not sure of, I didn't do much thinking about how I would get from there to here and what route I would set off on once I did.

I considered pedaling here, but two days heading in absolutely the opposite direction I wanted eventually to go was a little too psychologically onerous for me, so I decided to put myself and my bike on a bus. Then last night I had dinner with Laura Guimond of the Portland travel bureau, and she brought along a television reporter—a young woman—and a cameraman from a station in the Czech Republic who, on a limited budget, were in town to do a travel story about the American Northwest. We made a deal; they'd drive me to Astoria, and I'd give them an interview when we got here. Their English was textbook good, though slangier idioms left them looking puzzled. At one point I said I was bushed, and their reference point was the former president; I made a mental note to speak on camera as literally as I could. They wanted to shoot me doing the dipping-a-wheel-in-the-Pacific thing.

We left Portland the next afternoon. They were nervous on American highways, so I drove their van to Astoria, listening all the way to the voice of their GPS giving me directions in Czech. Astoria is pleasant and weatherworn, a fishing and tourist hub that is not actually on the Pacific, but on the Columbia, a few miles upriver. (Don't tell the Czechs.) It's not exactly a pretty place, but it has an aura of admirable longevity; it is, in fact, old. Founded by John Jacob Astor as a fur-trading outpost in 1811, it was the first enduring American settlement west of the Rockies, none of which I knew until I got there, three weeks before the city's bicentennial celebration, just in time to miss it. I have a newsman's timing, don't I?

Anyway, the Czechs set up a shot beneath the Astoria-Megler Bridge, a gorgeous, steel-girdered viaduct that dramatically spans the river from Oregon to Washington. I spoke into the camera, declaring my love for the beauty of America and my nervousness and excitement at the beginning of such an arduous journey. And we did three or four takes of a departing shot, with me riding along the wooden boardwalk in Astoria and disappearing from sight, ostensibly in the direction of New York.

Then I bought them dinner. They were earnest and sweet-tempered. Probably not yet thirty, they seemed very young to me, and a little unnerved to be on their own in an out-of-the-way corner of a foreign country, though they surprised me a little. After we ate I excused myself, saying we all must be tired, and the young woman reporter smiled. "Bushed," she said.

Wednesday, July 20, before dawn, Astoria, Oregon

I'm lying in bed as I write this, consciously watching my fingers on the wireless keyboard I bought to go with my iPad. It's not surprising that I can't sleep. In a couple of hours I have to begin living up to all the bravado of my newspaper stories and begin riding a fucking bicycle across the United States.

Despite Astoria's status as a bike mecca, there is no consensus on the best way to get out of town. U.S. Route 30, which follows the Columbia and heads toward Portland, accommodates bicycles, but it's a busy highway without a consistent shoulder. The bridge across the river to Washington is rideable, I'm told, but terrifying—it certainly looks terrifying from underneath—with minimal bike room, traffic that buzzes by at high speed, and the possibility of buffeting winds high above the water. So I've decided to go south, down U.S. 101, another heavily used road, though it is officially designated as part of the Oregon Coast Bike Route.

It would be nice to get started without route anxiety, but oh well. Trying not to think about that, I'm thinking about writing instead—at this hour anxiety looms wherever your mind goes—which is why I'm concentrating on my fingers as the words seem to squirt out of them onto the page. It's so weird, isn't it?

Anybody who has ever written anything has had that sensation, I think, the feeling—whether you're writing with a pencil, a typewriter, or a computer—that between the time thoughts are born in the brain and the time they escape from your fingertips onto the page and take coherent form some kind of alchemy happens. How and where do those thoughts gestate? Do they swim through the bloodstream and take their nourishment? Are they fired to life as they are transferred from nerve ending to nerve ending? Is an idea an idea, a thought a thought before there is language for it? And what is the role of your hands, really, in shaping the language?

Writers know that in every mind there is a chamber, an awful, dark place where sentences retreat in order not to be written, a safe house where the perfect verb, the clever and poignant metaphor, the incontrovertibly brilliant coinage is always hiding, avoiding revelation. Often, as I watch myself typing, I imagine my hands reaching into that chamber and feeling around, straining, my fingers waving like tentacles, fishing desperately for the absolute best way to say what I want to say.

Which brings me to my fingers, specifically: as it happens, I was born with two missing from my right hand.

Granted, it's the kind of handicap that is not a handicap so much as a conversation starter. Fortunately, or maybe consequently, I'm left-handed. I can't play the piano or the clarinet. I use a baseball glove that would be well-suited to a Little Leaguer, my right arm is a little attenuated so my overall strength isn't quite what I'd like—pull-ups have always been a misery—and on all of my bicycles (I own five at the moment, including the new one) I've had the rear brake, the controlling brake, switched to the left-hand side, where my grip is better. Almost every time I use a borrowed bike I forget about this and during the ride squeeze the left brake, making the front wheel seize, threatening to toss me over the handlebars.

All that said, my right hand is an okay hand, a little small but reasonably functional; I'm a better-than-adequate typist, for instance, hunt-and-peck variety. The hand is smooth in profile, not stumpy or ugly. I have a thumb, a middle finger, and a ring finger, and the overall shape is that of a talon.

When I look at pictures of myself, I think my hand makes me look slightly off balance. Other people, though, tend not to see it at all, unless we have occasion to shake hands, which I always do firmly, with conviction. (Is this meant as a macho statement? A subconscious declaration: I'm as much a man as you are, even though I have only eight fingers? Reasonable hypothesis.) Then their faces tend to register briefly that something is amiss and they are seized by a conundrum of etiquette. Say something? Or just plunge forward, maybe with a stammer or a blush?

Kids are better; they're curious, of course, and don't much bother with manners. Sometimes they think I'm pulling an adult prank on them, as if I've got a couple of fingers in my wallet that I'll screw back on in a minute or two. A few incidents—a handful?—have been especially memorable. Once at work a colleague introduced me to his six-year-old son. We shook hands and the kid freaked.

"He's a monster!" the kid wailed, horrifying his father, who continued to apologize for days afterward, until I got tired of trying to placate his guilt, and, really, we could no longer be friends.

That was a while ago, and as an event it didn't mean much. I'm insecure about a lot of things, but not my hand, though I had a therapist who thought otherwise and I admit that in a lot of photos of me my right hand is in my pocket; I've just noticed that recently. I attribute my general equanimity about it to a few childhood influences, among them a grandmother who knitted me three-fingered gloves that would always be returned when I lost them; and a junior high school friend who cheerfully nicknamed me Claw and initiated the practice of greeting me with a particular handshake, two fingers extended and the ring finger and pinky folded against the palm, a ritual that, among my remaining acquaintances from that time, persists to this day.

Anyway, a few years after the "monster" business, I was walking with a friend's eight-year-old child—it was Sharon Joseph, Billy's daughter, actually—and I took her hand as we crossed the street. On the other side, she didn't let go right away and instead was doing some exploring, feeling around a bit. After a moment or two, she stopped on the sidewalk—we were in a crowded neighborhood in Hermosa Beach, California—and placed her hands theatrically on her hips. "Three fingers!" Sharon announced. "That's extraordinary!" and repeated the phrase, or versions of it—maybe she'd just learned the word—several times as we proceeded down the street. Heads swiveled. "That's just extraordinary!" she declared. "Really extraordinary!"

It was funny. Her father and I grew hysterical. But the incident has stayed with me because the idea of what is ordinary and, by extension, extraordinary is interesting to me, and at this stage of my life even profound. I wonder if missing fingers are relevant to character. Did my unusual hand, a physical feature I was born with, mark me in some way as distinctive? Watching my fingers skitter across the keyboard in the unique eight-fingered way they do, I can answer yes to that.

Then there is the grander, more general question. Am I an ordinary guy? I think I am, but is this something to be proud of or disappointed by?

Another feeling everyone has had, I think (or maybe not), is of not fitting in, of being in a school or a group or an office, of being at a party or a dance or in a bar, and being unable to make contact with other people, feeling left out, not knowing the secret password and being somehow excluded or cut off, like an unwanted runt from the herd. Part of the agony of this sensation—for me, anyway—is the ambivalence that accrues to it, the absolute inability to decide whether you want in or whether you're better off on your own.

If only those people would open their ranks and accept me, you think, they'd discover I'm just like them. But is that what I want? They're all so, I don't know, indistinguishable, and as a result not very interesting, so maybe I'm better off just hanging out here, fending for myself, enjoying my own company, waiting for another opportunity in a place where I'll feel more at home, among other people, more extraordinary people, with whom I'd feel more ordinary. On the other hand, while I'm waiting, I'm just so lonely.

To put this another way, finding a context for yourself is one of life's great projects. And this brings me to my cross-country bike rides—ample undertakings to be sure, but hardly the sort of epic or frontier-crashing journeys that, by their Odysseus-like scope or Lindberghesque daring, are compelling by definition and make readers want to read about them. The origins of the modern bicycle date to the early nineteenth century, and people have been riding across the United States on their bicycles for more than a century, since the 1890s at least. Between 1894 and

1895, a Boston mother of three named Annie Cohen Kopchovsky most likely became the first woman to cross the country on a bicycle.*

By now hundreds, maybe thousands, of people do it every year, and in fact, if you want to know more about them, there's a website called crazyoldguyonabike.com that serves as a forum for hundreds of bicycle diaries. The year after my first trip, a reporter for the *Los Angeles Times*, David Lamb, wrote a book about his own cross-country ride as a middle-aged man. *Over the Hills* it was called. Yuk yuk. Eighteen years ago, after my first trip, I heard from dozens of people who congratulated me for completing a fine feat but who wanted to let me know that their own trips were longer and faster and accomplished under much more difficult circumstances.

This spring, on the cycling tour in Provence during which Jan and I fell in love, one of our guides was a slender, banjo-playing Breton named Gwendal who idolized Clint Eastwood and had a similarly wry, implacable demeanor. He had spent the previous winter—winter!—crossing Siberia on a bicycle in the snow. By himself. Siberia. Next February, Gwendal said, he would go to Sweden. I asked him why. I think what I actually said was: "Why the fuck?" "I want to cross the Arctic Circle on a bicycle in winter," he said with a shrug.

Over three weeks every July, the Tour de France guys race more than two thousand miles through the Alps and the Pyrenees, often in gulps of more than a hundred miles a day, averaging about twenty-five miles per hour. This kills me, and whether they're juicing or not, it's still amazing. An *average* of 25 miles per hour! Occasionally I get going that

---

*Kopchovsky, who was also known as Annie Londonderry, made her crossing in two parts. In fact, she claimed to have ridden around the world, and though she did circumnavigate the globe, evidently a good deal of her overseas journey involved alternative transportation. However, she did cycle from Boston to Chicago and back east to New York City, and later from San Francisco to Los Angeles, El Paso, Denver and finally to Chicago, where her arrival was reported in *The New York Times*. A full account of her adventure is available in *Around the World on Two Wheels: Annie Londonderry's Extraordinary Ride* (2007) by Peter Zheutlin.

fast on a long downhill. It hasn't escaped me that as I begin my long, slow journey, this year's Tour is coming to its end.*

But forget about them: Jure Robic, a soldier in the Slovenian army, was the five-time winner of something called the Race Across America, in which leading riders make it from sea to sea in less than nine days. During one race, Robic set the world record for distance cycled in twenty-four hours: 518.7 miles. Extraordinary. (My personal record is 138 miles in fifteen hours.) As it happened, last fall, Robic was careening downhill on a training ride near his home in Slovenia when he ran smack into an oncoming car and was killed. I wrote his obituary.

In such company my poor little rides don't bear mentioning. And yet here I am mentioning them—writing about them at length, in fact— because in the context of men and women who wouldn't contemplate such a journey they are arguably distinguishing feats. I didn't realize it at the time, but I can see now that yes, my first transcontinental ride in 1993 was an act of some conceit, a bold project I conceived simply because I imagined I could do it and then wear it like a notch on my belt. I don't doubt for a second that I was partly (wholly?) motivated by self-elevation, by wanting to feel extraordinary among my millions of ordinary peers.

In my final piece for the *Times* about that ride, I wrote that there are two kinds of people, those who understand such a journey and those who don't. People who don't, I said, wanted to know why I would do such a thing, what the point was, their idea being that it was an immense effort in pursuit of an essentially intangible reward; after all, what would I get out of it but a sense of completion? I'd cross the George Washington Bridge, ride my bike to my apartment door, and, with great relief, stop riding. That being the case, one of my relatives said to me, I could just as well stay home and bang my head against the wall, and when I stopped I'd feel the same thing.

---

*A thirty-four-year-old Australian, Cadel Evans, won the 2011 Tour de France, which ended on July 24; that day I rode from 8:00 a.m. until nearly sunset, covering 53.2 miles up the Columbia River gorge to Hood River, Oregon.

Of course, trying to explain the appeal to that relative and people like him was pretty much impossible. I usually said something like "Well, it's fun!" and that would generally make them shake their heads and go away. By the same token, for people who intuitively got it, there was no need to explain at all. They just thought it was cool, or amazing, or inspiring. (Not that they were deserved, but I never got tired of the admiring adjectives people threw at me.)

This doesn't explain why I feel the need to do it again, of course. I'm not trying to reclaim past glory. I don't think so, anyway; that would be a glum errand. To experience again an exhilaration that I associate with youth—yes, that's part of it. But at this juncture, writing about the ride is just as important. Writing of any kind is, after all, an act of self-aggrandizement. Putting words on paper is a declaration: "I have something to say." It's a louder declaration if you mean them to be published, downright hubristic if you're writing in the first person: "Listen here! I have something to say about *myself*!"

To try and do it well, to succeed at doing it well—that's what I would call extraordinary now.

2

The Geyser Effect

Wednesday, July 20, Tillamook, Oregon

*T*he proverbial journey of a thousand miles that begins with a single step . . . That step is both daunting and exciting. Oh, please! Blah, blah, blah. Get rolling, man!

This morning, I did.

For a departure ceremony, Michael Claussen, the engaging manager of the Commodore Hotel in Astoria, where I spent my restless night, snapped my picture in front of the hotel.

"I do this a lot," he said, though by the evidence his gift is hospitality, not photography. It was drizzling, a cool gray morning, not bad for cycling but far from cheery, and in the photo I look pudgy and unhappy.

Nonetheless, I took off through the streets of the city, along the old waterfront and past a crowded marina, under the bridge, and, picking up U.S. 101, across Youngs Bay on a long causeway.

For the first twenty-five miles or so the road was easy, relatively flat, the drizzle unthreatening. I passed through a couple of towns—Seaside, where I had excellent pancakes for breakfast, and Cannon Beach, where the ocean came splendidly into view.

It was a fine beginning; the whole day was fine, in fact, except for a handful of hazardous spots—especially one, inside a narrow tunnel, where a couple of logging trucks sped by close enough to make me wobble. I'd never come across this before: entering the tunnel, cyclists are urged to stop in order to press a roadside button, setting off a light signal above the entrance that is supposed to warn drivers of our presence. It struck me as a good idea until I was actually in the tunnel, where the shoulder had dwindled to maybe six inches up against a curb and the traffic seemed to have taken advantage of the alert to take aim at me.

Directly out of the tunnel was the day's longest climb, maybe a mile without a bend in the road, a trying, steady incline, woods on either side, a steep slope up across the road to the east and a sense of the ocean far below to the west.

Halfway up, I passed two cyclists taking a break, my first encounter with two-wheeled road colleagues. Both of them were standing just off the shoulder astride heavily loaded, clunky-looking old bikes, wearing sandals and faded jeans. Both of them were bearded and smoking hand-rolled cigarettes. (Maybe they were joints; my sense of smell isn't all that reliable on that score anymore.) They said they'd ridden to Yakima, Washington, from somewhere in New Mexico and now they were going home. I couldn't make out exactly where that was; they were mumblers. And their attitude was cloaked in suspicion as if they suspected me of threatening to pilfer their stash, or maybe to arrest them and confiscate it. Anyway, they didn't remind me of anyone I'd ever met on a roadside on a bike before; I left them smoking and ground on.

At the top of the hill, just north of Manzanita, there was a small car park, where I took a break and was rewarded by a striking view through the pines overlooking the ocean and a beach curving south into the distance. I was amazed at how high I'd climbed and the perspective I'd gained with the altitude. For some reason, going up it always feels like you gain elevation faster than you think you do and going down you lose it more slowly.

At the rest stop, I met Kevin and Jennifer Hart, a young couple from Battle Ground, Washington, who were on the eleventh day of a trip down U.S. 101 from the Canadian border to California. Their bikes were piled high with stuff. They'd done a lot of camping along the way and, unlike me, were carrying cooking gear and food. Neither Kevin, a firefighter, nor Jennifer, a nursing student, has ever traveled by bicycle before, but they are hooked, they said, and they think it is exceptionally cool that I am at the start of a cross-country jaunt to New York, even though it seems to puzzle them that I'm heading, at the moment, toward Los Angeles.

We rode the last thirty miles of the day together, to Tillamook (yes, home of the cheese), their intended destination for the day. Me, I hadn't expected to make it that far—63.7 miles, according to my odometer— so Day 1 turned out to be a good test and a bit of a triumph. I owe the Harts for pushing me. Appropriately, the sun was shining when we pulled into town about four thirty in the afternoon.

I made it in acceptably good shape physically, though I had all the symptoms of a first-day rider. My wind was short. My control of the bike, loaded with gear, was a little tentative, especially on long downhills, during which I nervously rode my brakes more than I usually would. (I'm not the most intrepid downhill rider in the world under any circumstances.) My behind got good and sore. The last couple of hours, I watched my odometer obsessively. Before I left, when people asked if I was in shape for a cross-country trip, I blithely said I'd be in better shape for it after two weeks. I certainly hope I was right.

I met the Harts for dinner at a restaurant across the road from our motel. They were taking the night off from canned and freeze-dried food and from sleeping on the ground. Naturally I asked them the question that I'm constantly asking myself. They didn't have any better explanation than I did.

"We just had a wild hair to do this," Kevin said.

They don't have unlimited time; they'll stop in Crescent City, in northern California, several days from now, rent a car, and drive home, but they're already planning to return by car to Crescent City next year and complete the southward journey to Mexico.

"Then we'll do what you're doing," Jennifer said to me, with what sounded like complete conviction.

"What?" her husband said.

Thursday, July 21, McMinnville, Oregon

Jan is nine time zones away, so figuring out how to communicate with her is one of my unanticipated problems. I'd like to call her now, but it's 5:00 a.m. in Paris, and I'll be asleep by the time she gets up in an hour. She says I can wake her up anytime, but I find I can't do that just to say "Hey, I'm lonely" or "Hey, what have I gotten myself into?"

This was a tough day, my second day. It rained all morning and I got soaked, first as the Harts and I continued south on U.S. 101, and then, after fifteen miles, when I said good-bye to them and turned east toward New York for the first time on the Nestucca River road, a route suggested to me by Erik Tonkin, the bike store owner in Portland. It was stunningly pretty, a winding path through the forest that, during the intervals the rain wasn't falling, was shrouded in mist.

In the early afternoon, the sun came out, but I hit a couple of climbs that defeated me—long but otherwise endurable slopes that tilted up suddenly and severely in the last quarter mile, as though the road graders had miscalculated and realized at the last minute that at the angle they'd laid out the road wouldn't reach the top. I had to dismount a couple of times, sit down on a rock, catch my breath, and wait for my thighs to stop quivering; the second one found me pushing the bike for a couple of hundred yards, up over the summit. Damn.

Now, here's something I already knew. Part of long-distance cycling, a big part, actually, and a rewarding, even pleasurable part, has to do with enduring discomfort and pushing through it to enjoy—and deserve—a cold beer, a good dinner, and a happy sleep. It's perverse, of course, working harder than you might wish to in order to feel worthy when you're done—a kind of self-loathing that lays the groundwork for self-esteem. If you understand that particular perversion, you might well be a cyclist, or maybe you should be one.

I knew all that. And still, on Day 2 of a long haul you don't want that to be the lesson. You don't want the specter of your walking uphill following you on Days 3 and 4, and you really don't want to wake up in the morning on Days 3 and 4 thinking there's some uphill walking in your very near future. Every cyclist eventually makes the psychic discovery that you can climb only one hill at a time, but for some reason that's something that slips your mind a lot, especially at the beginning.

This, I thought, was bad. I still think so. These weren't even especially brutal hills, and mountains, real mountains, are ahead. By the end of the day, and it was a shorter day than yesterday, fifty-five miles—I was crippled with exhaustion, my hamstrings sore and throbbing, my quads seemingly worn to threads, and my ass so truly uncomfortable that I thought about eating dinner standing up. By the time I got here, to this undistinguished motel on an undistinguished commercial strip, I was the picture of a guy who had bit off more than he could chew, someone who hadn't been careful what he'd wished for.

The news got better. The motel clerk suggested I try the local brew pub, but it was a mile away, too long a walk, and I'd had too long a day in the saddle, so I went next door to the Tequila Grill. It looked tacky; the building that housed it was once a competing motel, now mostly shuttered. I was seated in a booth in what had been the lobby, and the waitress pointed out the window to the site of the former swimming pool. But the tortilla chips and salsa were fresh, the chicken fajitas attractively prepared, and the frozen margaritas perfectly tart. I had three of them. I suppose that's partly responsible for why I'm too tired to wait and call Jan.

So I'm thinking about my girlfriend and I'm thinking about how I ended up in a motel in McMinnville, nine time zones away from her, with a sore ass, tired legs, and four thousand miles to go. I know I'm repeating myself, but why did I want to do this again? Here's today's answer: a shift in perspective, maybe a lasting one.

When Jan and I went cycling in southern France in the spring, it was my first time out of the country in several years, and my first time out of New York for more than a day or two in several months.

Strange word to use, *girlfriend*, at this age, but it has the advantage of intimating the relationship is youthful and fresh, which this one is. Well, fresh, anyway. In any case it's a better word than the gender-neutral and stodgily unsexy *companion*, or the literal yet somehow aggrandizing *lover*, even though it carries a suggestion of impermanence.

We'll see about the permanence—for once, I have hopes—but we can't do anything about that right now. We're just getting started, and Jan isn't quite divorced yet. This bothers her college-age kids a little bit—funny how the generations determine what is seemly—and, to my surprise, a few of her female friends, too.

Anyway, Jan has been living in Paris for a couple of years now, and she wasn't my girlfriend *until* we went on the cycling trip; I'll tell you more about that later, maybe, but the point is by now she's used to seeing the U.S. in general and New York and the life she lived there in particular from a distant perspective. She thought it was funny how goggle-eyed I was about the very fact of being in France, even though it wasn't my first, or even second or third, visit there.

"Traveling abroad," I said to her, in what became a running joke. "How come nobody ever thought of this before?"

But the moment I landed in Paris, I felt my worldview expand to what I like to think of as its natural state—the one where I'm not wearing self-imposed blinders—as if someone had tapped me on the shoulder and pointed out that I was looking through the wrong end of the binoculars. It was a powerful feeling of release; I'd been unaware of the box I'd been living in, its walls the circumscribing routine of existence for a single, middle-aged man in Manhattan. I'd worn ruts in the sidewalk from my apartment to the gym and to the office and to the Knickerbocker, the local bar that feels, at this point, a lot like my living room.

It was only by escaping to a different environment that I understood how easily our habits take control of us and how thoroughly mine had. You settle into a life where familiarity is everything, and yikes! Before you know it, you haven't been to a museum in a year and a half, you're treading the same aisles in the same supermarket twice a week, you can't remember the last time you made a friend, you're not trying any new restaurants (or even eating lunch anywhere but the company cafeteria), and you find yourself watching soporific reruns of favorite television shows—some episode of the *Law & Order* franchise seems to be on at any given moment of the day—merely to pass the time. I often feel lately as though I'm not learning anything anymore, that I can't, nothing that sticks in my memory, anyway. What I glean in a day's work is forgotten the following morning, what I knew last week is what I know today, what I knew six months ago is what I knew last week, what I'll know tomorrow is—well, you get it. For example, I had a great time in Paris and Provence, where I marveled at the medieval hill towns, Roman ruins, and thrilling landscapes mixing the domesticity of vineyards and olive groves with the natural drama of stony cliffs and fields smeared luridly with orange-red poppies and stalks of lavender. I'm a more worldly fellow as a result of seeing these things and being able to describe them, though if I thought my high school French would improve after ten days in France, I was wrong.

Okay, this is pessimistic hyperbole, but even though I'm probably better informed than I was in 1993, I do feel a good deal less receptive and, as a result, relatively speaking, less intelligent. But I digress. (Sorry, I do that.) The point is that as late middle age encroaches on middle age, the impulse to absorb new things or to view old things in a new way grows dormant and needs a jump start. Doesn't it? Just as you have to work harder at the gym to stay in the same shape, you have to think harder to stay just as smart. My last cross-country bicycle trip changed my perspective on things—I felt smarter when I got back. Of course, that's mostly a sensation, a belief born of enlightening experience, but here's a tangible example of what I mean.

I spent more than a decade, from 1992 to 2003, writing about the theater, but at the beginning of that time I was pretty much a novice, and when I took off across the country for the first time I'd been at it less than a year. During the trip I rode into Yellowstone Park, my first ever visit there, so of course I wanted to see Old Faithful, the famous geyser that erupts with such predictable regularity that the park posts a schedule. When I arrived, it was about thirty minutes from an eruption, so I stood around with a gathering crowd, curious tourists like me who had heard so much about a celebrated attraction that they couldn't be nearby and not take it in—the natural world's equivalent of *Cats*. Anyway, the thing went off, bubbling up slowly and eventually spewing an impressive column of water and steam into the air, the wind sending a sheen of spray across the flat rocks, and then gradually, over the course of a minute or so, dwindling to a gurgle before it disappeared again underground.

Almost on cue, everyone watching began to applaud, and they applauded for a while, twenty seconds or so. At the time I thought this was merely funny, a harmless illustration of human folly: Who are they applauding for? Do they expect a curtain call? But later, when I was back in New York and going to the theater again every night, I realized I had a new idea about the nature of applause and audiences, that applause is at least as much a gesture of self-expression as it is of generosity or approval. People applaud for themselves, in other words, to register their presence. Over the last several years, many theater writers (and other theatergoers) have acknowledged that the standing ovation is now such a common occurrence that it no longer confers extraordinary reward on a performance; it merely signifies the end of the show. The geyser effect, I call it.

Sunday, July 24, Hood River, Oregon

I've eaten quite a few pancakes. Fueling a long bicycle trip amounts to shoveling in calories at remarkably high volume in remarkably brief intervals, and one thing this means for me is breakfast, a meal I generally dispatch with a mouthful of something—a banana, say, or a piece of toast with peanut butter—as I head out the door to the office. I don't ordinarily wake up hungry, especially if I eat a big dinner the night before, and I have been vacuuming in enormous meals every night.

That said, you wouldn't believe what I'm scarfing down every morning: eggs, toast, bacon, and stacks of light, cakey pancakes the size of Frisbees with warm syrup and scoops of soft, sweet butter. I would like to compliment Oregon's pancakes; the quality—at Riley's Restaurant & Lounge in Seaside (skip the frozen strawberries), at the American Café in Lafayette, at the Cazadero Inn in Estacada—has been uniformly high.

I've had a number of good dinners, too. I don't know if Oregon has a higher regard for cooking than other states, or if restaurant food in out-of-the-way places has vastly improved over the past eighteen years, but one thing I recall from cycling cross-country in 1993 is that when I stopped randomly for a meal I was rarely gratified, to put it kindly. Every town seemed to have two restaurants, a fast-food franchise and Mom's.

Mom's, I learned, was generally the wrong choice.

Maybe I've just been lucky, but without trying I've run across places where they obviously care about, well, taste. In Tillamook, directly across the road from a run-of-the-mill motel, was Kendra's Kitchen, where I had a creamy pepper soup and oysters in a broth of chilies and lime—not exactly run-of-the-mill cycling fuel, or run-of-the mill four-lane-highway food, either.

Last night in Troutdale, a suburb to the east of Portland where the road up the Columbia River gorge begins, I ordered egg rolls and pork and shrimp with vegetables delivered to my motel from a restaurant unpromisingly called Unique Buffet. I was delighted. Hey, I'm no food critic, but I've had bad Chinese food before, and this wasn't it. I'm not forgetting those margaritas and fajitas in McMinnville. And this afternoon along the gorge road, instead of stopping for lunch I bought a pound sack of Rainier cherries from a girl at a makeshift farm stand that was set up in a parking lot; they were superb.

I know, I know. I'm expending so much energy, working so hard all day that anything would taste great. Maybe so. On the other hand, food is comfort.

I've been a little disheartened because I've been struggling so much going up hills. Yesterday, leaving Estacada in the morning, my legs felt rubbery and weak and I rode for only half a day before stopping in Troutdale, early enough to catch Jan before she went to sleep. We've figured out a plan. I send her an email, ordinarily when I wake up, and she calls me. She has a phone plan—must be an expensive one—that includes unlimited overseas dialing. It helped to talk to her.

Then I wrote to Andrew Crooks at NYC Velo for advice. He said I could replace my rear cassette, substituting a larger sprocket with more teeth that would lower my lowest gears and give me some relief on stiffer climbs. It was 53.2 miles from Troutdale to Hood River, a lovely, winding route through gladed woods that climbs above the Columbia, affording a cyclist—and parades of picnic-bound tourists in SUVs— views of pristine waterfalls and striking vistas to the east and north of the wide river and the state of Washington on the other side. It was a rewarding day, though a little too much hard work for the distance I covered, so I decided to take Andrew's advice; in the morning I have an appointment at the local bike shop to install a rear cassette with a more accommodating gear ratio.

Tonight I ate upscale, at an haute fish place with a porch and umbrellas and a view over the Columbia where, at dusk, the windsurfers who gather hereabouts were still gyrating in spectacular orbits, the angled sun glancing off the flashing colors of their sails. The whole thing was as pretty as a music video.

Monday, July 25, Biggs Junction, Oregon

The world wasn't built for bicyclists. The hazards for us are both natural (hills, headwinds) and man-made (bridges, speeding truckers hauling double trailers, fishtailing RVs). On a long-distance ride, a bite of anxiety accompanies every turn onto a new road. What awaits?

Still, forces tend to align favorably just about every day, at least for a while. At one particularly frustrating moment on Day 3 of the trip, after I'd gotten lost climbing around in the hills southeast of Portland, I was trying to find my way to the town of Estacada and my GPS stopped getting a signal. I pretty much picked a road at random, followed it around a corner, and found myself staring at a postcard view of snowcapped Mount Hood. That was more than enough to keep my spirits up.

Anyway, every day it's a bit of a dance, a bargaining session with the universe: your legs are jelly and your will is wavering and suddenly there's a gorgeous mountain to look at; then you find an hour's great ride and pay for it with a dizzying climb, a rough road, or heavy traffic.

As it happens, I had a generally delightful ride up the Columbia River gorge, a stretch of seventy-five miles or so, climbing, dipping, and winding through the woods and high over the water between Troutdale and The Dalles, Oregon.

It's an oddly jury-rigged path, much of it well traveled by sightseers in cars, some of it along paved trails that are off-limits to motorized traffic (I love that!). And then there's the hell to pay: the bike route, much of which follows the Historic Columbia River Highway, runs parallel to the I-84, but it sadly peters out for about ten miles, just west of Hood River, and the cyclist is forced onto the interstate. It's legal to ride on the interstate in Oregon, though I'm not sure it should be; the road gets congested with high-speed traffic. For me, on the debris-strewn shoulder, that was a tense, teeth-clenching ten miles.

Still, I'd have to say it was worth it. Today I continued upriver, and the twenty-five miles or so between Hood River and The Dalles were the most joyous of my journey so far. It began in the late morning, after Eric Anderson, Ben Ketler, and Mike Scott, the skillful bike doctors at Mountain View Cycles, performed rear-cassette replacement surgery on my bicycle, giving me a sprocket with thirty-four rather than twenty-eight cogs and a whole other dimension of low gears in which to climb. I felt the difference immediately. The change wasn't a panacea; it didn't absolve me of the sin of not training enough for the trip. But though the road out of Hood River curved immediately uphill and became a long, twisty ascent, I was able to find the pedaling rhythm that had eluded me on previous climbs, one that propelled me with sufficient progress to be satisfying psychologically, that allowed me to hum along to the downbeat of my left pedal stroke—the soundtrack in my mind was from Copland's "Appalachian Spring" (a.k.a. "Simple Gifts," a Shaker song)—without anguish in my thighs or lungs.

At the top, I reached a lovely bike path, deliciously, smoothly paved, that travels for several miles high above the river, passes through twin tunnels (relics from an abandoned section of highway), and descends into the tiny town of Mosier. From there the route climbs again through woods and dramatic hillsides, up over Rowena Crest, where the views upriver are spectacular, and then snakes down to The Dalles in thrilling fashion, a cyclist's version of a roller-coaster descent. All in all, the best three hours of the ride so far.

The cycling route up the gorge more or less ends there, and had I not felt energized by my new gear configuration I might have stayed the night in The Dalles, but I rode on. Determined to avoid another stint on the interstate, I followed instructions from my GPS, which led me into remote ranchland along a gravel road. By then it was a steamy late afternoon, but I felt surprisingly fresh, and I relished the solitude and quiet as I rode slowly through wheat fields and cattle ranges. The light was amber, beautiful. For a time, my bike performed admirably on the gravel, but the road grew worse, and after several miles I was creeping along, hardly making progress and having to ride with high caution downhill. At one point when the road turned rather sharply near the bottom of an especially steep pitch, I squeezed both brakes, my back wheel slid off to the right and I couldn't click out of my left pedal in time. I went down in what felt like slow motion. It was painful and a little embarrassing, though there was no one for miles around to witness it, but not serious. There's a knot on my left elbow and a bruise on the meat of my palm. The bike is fine. No real harm done.

Still, there was seven miles of undulating road treacherous with sand and gravel yet to negotiate, it was getting toward evening, and I didn't know whether Biggs Junction, the next town, was actually a town or just a crossroads. Perhaps this was one of those bad-bargain-with-the-universe days. Perhaps such optimism as I assumed after the bike surgery was uncalled for; perhaps I'd had too much fun on the snaky downhill ride to The Dalles.

Fate, however, was kind. Jim Markman, who works in financial services for a firm that provides loans and insurance for farmers, lives up in those hills, and he was on his way home for the evening when I flagged him down, and he stopped and let me throw my bike in the back of his station wagon. We chatted amiably as he ferried me over the worst stretch of road and set me on my way here to Biggs, which turned out to be, yes, more or less a crossroads, but also an I-84 truck stop town, where I found a bed for the night and the first truly bad meal of my journey. (For the record, it was an open-faced turkey sandwich, with that pale, gluey gravy we all know so well from our high school cafeterias.)

The town, such as it is—I couldn't make out much more than gas stations, motels, and a restaurant—lies on a plateau just above the Columbia, but the only route upriver from here on the Oregon side is the interstate. There's a bridge to Washington here—I can see it from my motel—and I'll be crossing it in the morning. It's a little scary-looking, and I don't know what Highway 14 on the Washington side is like; I've heard it's rideable but has truck traffic. I'm facing a long day. There are no places to stay for a hundred miles or so, and I'll have to cross back over the river again late tomorrow to find a bed.

After dinner tonight, I found a note in my email from a reader in Walla Walla, Washington, where (fingers crossed) I should be landing in a couple of days. He has invited me to his home for dinner with him and his wife, and I'm thinking this would be a good time to try a little face-to-face reader interaction. It won't get any more convenient than this; after all, I'll be riding pretty much past their front door. (How big can Walla Walla be?)

On the other hand, I also heard from Thus Spake the Dancing Scorpion again. Here's what he wrote:

"In the words of Lin Yutang, 'Besides the noble art of getting things done, there is the noble art of leaving things undone.' Why was it necessary, Webber"—jeez, pal, can you get my name right?—"to repeat an experience, once done, one more time? Was it merely boredom? Lack of imagination to go forward? You, an experienced writer and chronicler of deaths, should know more than most that the wisdom of life consists in the elimination of nonessentials. And this bicycle junket is most certainly nonessential. It's something best left undone. Clinical shrinks have unpleasant things to say about sentimentality. Finally, I find it more than curious that of the thousands of readers of the *New York Times*, only my postings have been a critical voice regarding your ill-advised behavior. The only critical remarks have been about the amount of money you paid for a nice shiny bike in Manhattan. Reader interest seems to be only for their own vicarious ego-centered interests. Get off the road and go back to work writing obituaries. The sooner the better."

Now, I like the idea that leaving things undone can be as noble as doing things. (It's sort of obvious, though, isn't it?) I had to look up Lin Yutang, and it surprised me that in spite of the Confucian tone of the quotation, he was actually a twentieth-century Chinese intellectual. Anyway, Mr. Scorpion—as I will refer to him from now on—has successfully achieved an undertone of doom in his writing voice. Let's forget the dangling modifier and the pronoun-antecedent mismatch (okay, and the loopy conviction that I'm better serving myself and mankind by writing obituaries than riding a bike); as a writer he has something going. I admire the consistent sound of the bell tolling for me in his prose. And I have to say, somehow he seems to have a clear sense of the unease that's keeping me awake tonight: this betting-with-the-universe business is anxiety making. You have to lose one, eventually, right? Something bad has to happen.

3

Billy "Salad" Joseph

Wednesday, July 27, Walla Walla, Washington

*B*illy died yesterday. The funeral is Sunday, and I have to decide whether to interrupt my ride and fly to Los Angeles. I'm inclined not to. I was with him less than a month ago, and I said good-bye then.

That was a dark weekend. I went to visit with my friend Bobby Ball—we met almost forty years ago, when he was Billy's college roommate. We found him weak and distracted, in seemingly permanent discomfort and occasionally delirious. His stomach was bloated, his eyes vacant, his voice small and far away. His midsection was riddled with cancer, and he bellowed in agony at regular intervals. He slept only fitfully, with the help of drugs, and drama accrued to that as well. Often deluded and hallucinating, Bill had a prescription for morphine tablets, but persuading him to take them was an exercise in black absurdity. We'd put a pill in his palm and he'd stare it.

"This isn't a pill," he'd say, pointing at the pill. "This isn't a pill."

"What is it, Bill?"

"I don't know," he'd say.

"Take the pill, Bill. You'll feel better."

"No. No. This isn't a pill."

This happened half a dozen times. It would go on for ten minutes before he would swallow a pill, which allowed him to sleep for a while.

Bill was angrily divorced two years ago, but his ex-wife, Sophia, had invited him back home in his illness, and she was exhausted by the caretaking and the emotional strain. Their two children, Andrew, who is fourteen, and Sharon, twelve, were pretending to live their normal lives, though the specter of their father stalking the halls in his bathrobe, clearly in pain, was nowhere near normal.

He'd had a nightmarish few years, had lost his job at Canon, a company he'd started working for in the 1970s, had seen his marriage disintegrate, had moved out of his house and into an apartment in a complex more suited to college students than a middle-aged businessman. At least his kids enjoyed the place; they liked visiting, swimming in the pool, and playing in the game room. That was cheering for him.

Diagnosed a year ago, he had an operation last fall to remove his bladder; the initial tests afterward were promising, but then he stopped going to the doctor, even after he started experiencing pain in his gut in the early spring. He thought he had hemorrhoids; that was his unlikely story, at any rate.

Billy's sister, Margie, called me with the news this afternoon. I'd just made it here after a brisk fifty-five-mile ride from Umatilla, Oregon, following the Columbia until it turned north and, somewhat ruefully, waving it good-bye and continuing east into the dusty onion fields of Washington State toward Walla Walla.

Brisk? Ha! It was hot, and my ass hurt—I'm beginning to worry that I'm riding the wrong saddle—but the route was not especially challenging, the wind was well behaved, and my legs are slowly growing

from the sun. At one point I looked up and in the distance the colors of the boxcars of a long freight train were melting together in the bright light.

Finally, I reached the crossroads where Highway 14 intersects with Interstate 82, which leads back across the river to Umatilla. I'd been told there was a bike and hiking path attached to the bridge along the interstate, but I didn't find it. The roadway over the bridge had no bike lane, so I hitched a ride into Umatilla with a pickup truck. The driver dropped me off at a gas station, where the attendant gawked at me as if I were either a movie star he recognized or an alien.

All in all, it was a trying but fine ride, though maybe not an especially interesting or dramatic one that would demand I write about it in such detail. But it's how I spent the day my oldest friend died.

Saturday, July 30, Los Angeles

Forgive the immodesty, but I seem to have a gift for writing about the recently dead. I'm speaking mostly about obituaries, of course, for which the idea is to muster whatever you find out about your subjects into a form that will persuade readers that you know all about them. You want to sound both knowledgeable and subjective. Unless you're writing about a villain of some kind—in the pages of the *Times*, I've sent off corrupt pols, famous racists, and violent criminals—this usually involves a kind of flattery, making the person sound not only accomplished but singular. If you're lucky you can suggest an intimacy with the subject that you never had and with a sentence or two or a paragraph give loved ones the comfort of a eulogy.

But a eulogy motivated by deep feeling rather than news value is something else again. Billy's sisters have asked me to speak at the funeral, something I'm feeling as a terrible obligation but one that I'm gratified to have on my shoulders. I've written only two others. Here is the first, from ten years ago:

Once when I was a teenager I came downstairs for breakfast in torn jeans with frayed bell-bottoms and a steel gray work shirt that my mother hated because, she said correctly, it was something a garbage man would wear.

I remember the occasion the way you remember a movie scene, as though I were watching the two of us, and I can recall my mother's expression perfectly, the absolute revulsion in it at the slouching, sullen, alienated know-it-all with long unkempt hair and ratty sneakers that she was sending off to school as a representative of her family. She was already in a wheelchair by then, and she rolled it up close to me, her mouth contorted into a grimace. Without referring at all to the shirt—the foreshadowing had already been accomplished—she said, hurtfully but again accurately: "Get out of here, you look like you just rolled out of a garbage can yourself."

Now the reason I tell that story, the reason I love that story, the reason I've remembered it for more than thirty years is that it was, of course, anomalous. This was a mean little scene, and my mother, as all of you know, was deeply, thoroughly, profoundly not mean. "Sweet" is a word I've heard often applied to her. "Kind" is another. So is "lovely." My friend Rick said to me the other day that he thought my mother was the most sentimental person he's ever known.

These are the qualities her disease couldn't hide, and everyone in my family is grateful that the multiple sclerosis that robbed her of so much never touched the part of her that treated other people with respect and affection and a joy in their company. She loved everyone here. I say that even though you all know it because she made it perfectly evident.

But as a way of honoring her, and her courage, I want to speak about what wasn't so evident. Because of her illness, it was easy to miss a great deal of what my mother was, and I don't mean to suggest that she wasn't sweet or kind or sentimental, just that those things ended up so defining her that it feels to me almost diminishing to remember her only that way.

That's why I relish that moment of anger from thirty years ago; she had it in her to be convincingly brutal. That she wasn't that way often was a great strength, but that she showed me it was there was one of the many reminders I had that she was deeper, more complicated, and more present than she was always able to show.

My mother had some really interesting foibles. For someone so considerate, she was a terrible tipper; I think I learned my first lessons about the virtues of generosity chasing the pizza delivery man back to his car with an extra couple of bucks after my mother had stiffed him.

She held long grudges—against Richard Nixon, for example, and against the move to Tucson, a place she didn't like from the moment she got there, but also against people she knew and whom, after her illness, she felt dismissed by. I could name names. The fury she could muster at low volume was impressive.

In her tiny voice, she could be profane at surprising, inopportune moments; she took pleasure in cursing though she deployed that part of her vocabulary prudently—so you'd remember it. The last thing she said to me before I went off to college was a dirty aphorism about sex (this was before I'd ever had any), a caution to employ my good judgment instead of my, well, you know.

She could be stubborn to the point of lunacy; ask my father, who hated to shop with her, for clothes, for furniture, for anything—the last instance I know about was a lighting fixture for the new house in Atlanta—because she would never accede to the purchase unless it matched perfectly the aesthetic vision she had in her head.

And she could be tenacious—ridiculously, foolhardily, hopefully tenacious. She never accepted her disease, not even after forty years, and dealt with it by fighting it. She preferred always to help herself rather than be helped, preferred to spend the day struggling to take a shower instead of cultivating a hobby. It made me crazy that in the basket of her electric wheelchair she would carry the same book for months. She didn't have time to read; she was too busy trying to put on her shoes by herself.

For years, against all good sense, she insisted on driving lessons, and my father dutifully, or perhaps to escape the pestering, had hand controls installed on the old Dodge. But she was incapable, it was clear. Her instructor in Teaneck, a nice guy who really liked her, told me he was always a little nervous in the car with her. But even years later, in Tucson, she believed that if she could only get behind the wheel she would somehow be free of the entrapment she felt.

I found this a particularly painful quality to observe in her; I think it cost her a great deal, in terms of her ability to extract enjoyment out of the life her illness left her. But that's me, and maybe it's a self- ish sentiment. Because I also understand that that unyieldingness was also a kind of optimism that kept her going. In the end, when she was bedridden and truly helpless, she apologized for putting us all out, not to me but to Pearl Kinnard, the wonderful woman who was her last home caretaker. And when Pearl told me that, I recalled what may be the most vivid memory I have of my mother.

It was in the early eighties, not long before my parents left New Jersey. I was living in the city, and my father had to leave town on business so I went home on a Friday afternoon to spend the weekend. There had been a blizzard the day before, and when I got off the bus at Queen Anne Road, it was snowing again, and I looked down Van Buren Avenue, past our house, and saw something I couldn't believe.

At the end of the block, maybe two hundred yards beyond our driveway, the Dodge was embedded, front end first, in a snowbank. I knew the engine was still running because exhaust was coming out of the exhaust pipe. I tore down the block and found my mother in the driver's seat. She was perfectly calm, listening to the radio, waiting patiently, and rather cheerfully, to be rescued.

She'd woken up that morning and decided to go to the supermarket. She asked the woman who was working for us then—someone not too bright, evidently—to help her into the car and to put the wheelchair into the trunk. Then she'd just backed out of the driveway (no mean feat, actually, if you recall our driveway) and took off. How she was going to get out of the car once she got there, how she was going to get the wheelchair out of the trunk, or shop, for that matter, or come home—she just trusted those things would somehow get taken care of. When I found her and expressed, um, dismay, she said she was disappointed she hadn't gotten any farther. Still, I think she considered the outing a success; it was not something she apologized for.

My mother endured more indignities than I want to recall, enough so that I often felt she was suffering for me and for our whole family, and enough so that I stopped believing in God, though now that she's gone I'm beginning to rethink that, believing He has a great deal to answer to her for and hoping that He knows it.

She was sick for so long that I remember her only as ill. That's partially my fault, but mostly I blame the disease, which not only crippled her physically but kept the healthy part of her buried. It restricted her access to the world of information, it created gaps in her memory, it weakened her voice, and toward the end it undermined her intellectual capacity and ability to speak clearly. She was robbed of the tools of social engagement that most of us take for granted, and this, I think, was the source of her greatest suffering. She rarely complained—to me, anyway—about her physical problems. She did say often that she had a hard time making friends.

I've been thinking of how lonely she must have felt, living vibrantly inside the crypt of disease; it's unfathomable to me that so much of what was going on inside of her never came out. Two or three days before she died, in a sudden moment of recollection, she spoke of Elvis Presley, someone no one in our family could remember ever hearing her mention. I miss her now terribly, not least because I'm heartbro-

ken at what I missed while she was alive. And I'm simply in awe of her survivor's will and the courage it took for her to endure.

There's no question it took patience to be with her, really with her. This was true for me as a son—I didn't always have that patience, I'm sorry to say—but I want to add a word about my family and how proud I am of their endurance as well.

My brother and I complained together about Mom and Dad, siblings do that, but I've always admired Robert's open affection for them both, and his ability to talk to my mother at length and to encourage her participation in family conversation; he had the unflagging instinct never to leave her out. My brother's wife, Lynne, has become someone I adore, in part because of how easily, naturally, and lovingly she accepted my mother beyond her limitations. My mother's sister, Claire, often confessed to me her anguish at her little sister's troubles, but around my mother she was never anything other than upbeat, honest, and intimately bonded in a way that only sisters—I'm guessing here—can know; she buoyed my mother enormously with the joy of their complicity.

As for my father, he has spent far too much time regretting the times he lost patience with Mom; she not only forgave him for it, she understood. She knew to her bones that what he gave her—more than fifty years of companionship, partnership, caretaking, and love—was the greatest gift of her life. Maybe she didn't tell him—she told me— that she knew how lucky she was. She was grateful to him beyond expression, as am I.

In her last few days, my mother talked a great deal, though not much of it was audible or intelligible, and as I watched her try to get her final thoughts into the world I took the effort as a message in itself, a metaphor; this was her life. And I'm delighted to report the final words I did hear her say. They were ridiculous, tenacious, hopeful.

She said: "I feel pretty good."

My aunt Claire used to say all the time, "Your mother is a pip." Her name was Eileen.

"Just remember: A stiff prick has no conscience." That's what she said to me before I went off to college.

For two nights before her funeral I stayed up until dawn writing and rewriting the eulogy. I was forty-seven, and I'd never written anything with a greater sense of urgency. That's one reason I decided, after all, to come to Billy's funeral. I guess I was never not going to. In fact, before I left New York, I packed a suit, a white shirt, and black shoes and socks, and gave them to Bobby Ball just in case, so he could bring them to L.A. for me.

I flew here yesterday and since then I've been holed up in a shitty motel on the Pacific Coast Highway—where, at the moment, cops are questioning one of my fellow guests in the parking lot—working on what I want to say at the funeral tomorrow. I've been having trouble, though in a phone conversation a friend of mine just pointed out that Billy died on Mick Jagger's birthday, and that strikes me as a promising idea to begin with.

I've been thinking about my mother for a number of reasons, some of them obvious, but mainly because her death begat a short train of emotionally bruising events that have colored my life since then. The day we buried my mother was the last time I saw my former girlfriend, Catherine, and it was the day before my father and I nearly came to blows in a raging argument about whether or not he'd been attentive enough to his children—not to his children, to *me*—while my mother was alive.

Of course, at the time I was feeling acutely that I hadn't been attentive enough to *her* while she was alive; the guilt and remorse vibrates like a bass note through the eulogy. Doesn't it?

As it happens it wasn't the first time I'd written about death, or even the first time I'd written about the death of someone I knew. Michael Maggio, a theater director in Chicago who was also a friend, had died the previous summer, and I'd written his obituary. That was long before I started writing obits every day, and at the time it seemed to me a strange but welcome way to make work—journalistic work—more personal than it usually is.

Mike had a wild life story. He had been close to death from cystic fibrosis when a double lung transplant in 1991 gave him his vigor back, turning him from a barely breathing, walking corpse into a robust, ruddy-looking man with a soccer player's bounce in his step. Shortly after his recovery, he came to New York to direct a show at the Public Theater, and we met when I wrote a story about him. Later, after I moved to Chicago for the *Times*, one of the first social occasions of my time there was Mike's wedding. That was three years before he died of complications resulting from all the drugs he had to take to keep his body from rejecting his new lungs.

Out of friendship, out of a sense that I could do justice to Mike's talent and his courage, out of wanting to be of service to Mike's friends and family, I volunteered to write the obit. Ordinarily, a reporter will recuse himself from writing about someone he knows, but that's when the person is alive. The rules change a bit after death, I decided. Mike's résumé and his medical story together made him a suitable obit subject, but I thought I'd write about him with more sympathy and intimacy than someone else might, and it's true, I did. Still, I have to admit that what I wrote was probably a little more eulogy than obit. I know now there's a line there that can be hard to see.

Anyway, that was the first time as a writer that I seriously thought about death, probably because it was also the first time I thought about it seriously as a mortal human being. I'd been lucky up to then. My grandparents had all died when I was young, too young to feel myself anything but indestructible. I'd had no experience with death as an adult, and so I'd had no occasion to mull over what the living owe to the dead or how we best acknowledge them, serve them, honor them, remember them, and go on living without them.

Mike's dying, even though we all knew it was coming—after his operation, he'd been warned that he would be living on borrowed time—was, for me, the leak in that dike. From then on I knew people close to me were going to start dying more often and that the more time went on the more experience I was going to have with loss and grief. I think everybody must have a moment like that, the moment you feel your mortality acutely for the first time. The humility it creates in you, not to mention the anguish and the fear, is made only more haunting by the knowledge that you are not extraordinary in this regard at all.

My mother died five months later, on January 12, 2001, at home in the suburbs of Atlanta. Her body was shipped north to be buried in Westchester, north of New York City, near where my parents had lived for a time after they sold the house in New Jersey where I grew up. I chain-smoked Camels as I composed the eulogy—three months later I quit cigarettes for good—and felt absolutely desperate the whole time, as if I could, somehow, reclaim her life for her, change it in retrospect, make it better than it was. If only I could write about her well enough.

So early Thursday morning I called Jan in Paris and told her the news about Billy and said I didn't know what to do. I was just beginning my trip, I said, just finding my legs. I saw Billy just a few weeks ago, I said; I feel like I already told him good-bye. And oh man, do you know how much it's going to cost to fly from Walla Walla to L.A. on a day's notice?

She let me talk and then said if I didn't go I was going to be very sorry very soon and for a long time afterward. Just as she was saying that I understood that I'd been thinking only of the Billy I last saw, the diseased, diminished version of someone who had taught me, by his example, what independent thinking is, what original humor is, what a singular personality is. It didn't serve either of us, me or him, to keep thinking that way. That afternoon, I made a plane reservation for the next morning. Then I spoke to Tom Scribner, the Walla Walla lawyer who had invited me to his home, and made a dinner plan. He gave me a good route to ride that afternoon around Walla Walla, and I rode it, a sun-seared twenty-five miles through spectacularly golden-white wheat fields under a spotless blue sky. It was a marvelous ride; the landscape was stark and beautiful and somehow both fertile and remote. A southerly wind came up and made me work especially hard on the way back into town, and for two hours, thankfully, I was completely subsumed in the bubble of a bike ride.

I drank two beers in a local roadhouse and dropped my bike off downtown to be stored for the weekend at Allegro Cyclery, where I also bought some shoe inserts I was told would ease the foot-burning problem I'd been having.

Afterward, I met Tom and his wife, Margo, an English professor at a local school, Whitman College, who was about to retire, and we discussed what a relief it would be for her not to have to grade—or even read—student essays anymore. I was hugely sympathetic and pleased for her; in my twenties I taught junior high school and high school English and had nightmares about being smothered by uncorrected papers.

We had dinner on the porch of their home on a leafy street; New Yorkers never lose their amazement at leafy streets. The salad tomatoes and the dessert blueberries came from their garden. Tom said that when I returned from L.A. he'd pick me up at the airport, I'd stay at their house for the night, and we'd take off on our bikes together the next morning. Tom, it turns out, is one of those people, like me, who will use almost any excuse to take a long ride. He had a couple of days to spare, he said, and knew a route into the Palouse, a region of rolling hills and vast wheat fields in eastern Washington and western Idaho, that he wanted to show me. I can't tell you how much I wished we could get started right away.

At dawn the next morning, I got on a plane, and on the first leg of the trip, from Walla Walla to Seattle, I was treated to a view of the snowy peak of Mount Rainier nosing above the clouds as though I were on my way there, having been summoned to Olympus to answer for one thing or another.

Sunday, July 31, Los Angeles

Billy died on Mick Jagger's birthday. Is that fitting? I don't know whether I'd say that, but he did do the greatest Jagger imitation I ever saw—I even borrowed it—and they were both terrific entertainers. In fact, I don't think I've ever known anyone more naturally entertaining than our friend Bill. He wasn't really a storyteller and I can't remem-

*ber him ever telling a joke, but he might have been the funniest guy I
ever knew.*

*He had strange appetites; he was the only person over the age of
eight that I ever saw wash down chocolate cake with Coca-Cola. He
could be sophisticated and adolescent in the same sentence. He had
an eccentric mind that traveled its own singular path, rarely accommodated conventional wisdom, and, among other things, allowed him
to express anger, frustration, or bitterness with a pithy absurdity. A
natural commentator, he was rarely sarcastic but often deadpan. I
remember a phone conversation we had at the beginning of the Gulf
War in 2003, when everyone—my liberal friends, anyway—was in
high dudgeon about the administration's dishonest tactics in persuading Americans that an invasion was justified.*

"I'm supporting Iraq," Billy said.

*He understood wit, verbal nuance, intonation. He knew how to
deliver a zinger or make a comic declaration without landing on it
too hard. A few years ago, I was visiting, and Sharon was in an especially, shall we say, acquisitive phase.*

*"My daughter likes money," he said, in front of her. "That's her
main interest."*

*More recently I was out here, and Andy had a couple of bad games,
especially at the plate, and Billy delivered his judgment: "Andy, I
think it's time for you to give up baseball."*

*I knew Billy for almost fifty years and the image that comes to me
first when I think of him now—actually it's always come to me first—
is Billy playing basketball on the pavement at the Eugene Field School
in Teaneck. He was almost always one of the smallest guys on the
court, and one of the least disciplined, and when you passed him the
ball you didn't get it back. He liked the ball. He liked shooting it. He'd
make a wild, frantic drive toward the hoop, seemingly determined to
find a seam and hit a layup, but at the first sign of trouble, the first
defender in his path, he'd veer suddenly, take a quick step back, and
fire a jump shot like a lightning bolt—bang! with almost no arc at
all—at the basket. Sometimes it went in.*

Not to make too elaborate a metaphor out of this, but this was the Billy I knew for the rest of his life. He was a guy who had incredible optimism. At the moment he got the ball, he thought he could score on anybody.

He had enormous enthusiasms, a huge desire to participate in the world, a fabulous sense of what should be but what was probably not possible, and a gigantic, lovable, hilarious bravado. Before he went to work for Canon, he drove to Hollywood, convinced he would become a movie star. After he went to work for Canon, he became, in his own words, "the world's greatest copier salesman."

He was, in many ways, a lot like the character he played so well onstage in high school and in college, Nathan Detroit. They were both scamps, both dreamers, both pushers against authority. They were both reliable, both had friends who looked up to them. They were both sentimentalists.

People like that, optimists of Nathan's and Billy's magnitude, tend to live roller-coaster lives, with big satisfactions and big disappointments. On the satisfaction side, Billy had a fine career at Canon and, obviously, he had many devoted friends. He had love affairs that, while the relationships ultimately didn't work out, were so meaningful and significant that Sophia, his former wife, stepped back into his life and took extraordinary care of him during the last ten months, and two former girlfriends traveled great distances to be here today in Los Angeles.

And, of course, he had a loving family, his sisters, Margie and Laurie, and his children, Andy and Sharon, who were his greatest satisfaction, his greatest joy. And I want to add a word about his parents, Lenny and Jean, who are no longer alive but who were thrilled by a son whose decency, humor, and sense of responsibility were so apparent to everybody. His father, a world-class grouch, was tough on him, but he instilled in Billy a sense that living in the world was not such an easy thing and that you had to fight for a foothold in it. His mother doted on him and taught him, I think, that looking after other people is not just a duty but a pleasure. I remember when we were teenagers,

*I showed up at Billy's house one night when he hadn't finished din-
ner. His mother was watching him eat, and I was trying to hurry him
up, and she wouldn't let me. It was an occasion that became famous
among our friends.*

*"Don't rush him, he's eating his salad," Mrs. Joseph said in her
Minnie Mouse voice. "Billy loves salad."*

*The way she said it made it a point of pride. She was beaming at
her son.*

*"Billy loves salad so much his middle name should be 'Salad,'" she
said. "They should call him Billy 'Salad' Joseph."*

And so we did.

*His disappointments—well, we know what some of them were.
He had a tough time the last few years of his life. He was divorced.
He lost his job at Canon, and, of course, his health went south. But he
also lived with other disappointments, philosophical ones. Billy was
remarkably tolerant of people's petty foibles. His default mode when
he met someone was to be accepting.*

*But he was infuriated by powerful people who blindly exercised
their power. He loved the Knicks and he hated Isiah Thomas. He
loved the Yankees and he hated George Steinbrenner. He loved this
country and he hated George W. Bush. He loved Israel but hated
its intractability and its reckless military might. He loved news-
papers and the news but thought Rupert Murdoch should burn in
hell.*

*As for that other powerful being, God, in the end it's hard to know
what he thought. He was, I suspect, dubious, but not committed to
any certainty. As he told me the story, after he learned he was dying,
his friend and neighbor, Kenny, a devout Christian, visited him in the
hospital and urged him at his bedside to acknowledge Jesus as his
savior. They were discussing this when the rabbi came to call. Bill
asked Kenny to let them speak in private, but as Kenny was leaving
the room, Billy couldn't resist a bit of mischief. Gesturing at Kenny, he
said to the rabbi, loud enough for Kenny to hear: "He thinks I should
accept Christ in my life."*

Bill was, in other words, not a fearless man, but he feared the right things, the big men in the middle ready to swat away a jump shot, the forces in the world that prevent the best things, the good things, the just things, from happening. Cancer, for him, was the last of those forces. He died way, way too young; his death was not in the least just.

Yesterday I was talking with Andy, and he said that all his father's friends had told him the same thing, that Billy altered the way we consider the world. And that's true for me, too. In big things, like politics, he showed me, by example, that it was not only okay but desirable to think independently and to express yourself honestly. In small things, like how to deliver a straight line or how to intone the word "goodbye" over the phone in a way to get a laugh, he affected me so much that I've adopted many of his mannerisms as my own.

Like everybody here, I'm going to miss him. I'd give a lot for him to be here today, listening to this eulogy, so that he could hear exactly what I thought of him, how much I loved him and why. On the other hand, maybe he wouldn't have wanted to listen.

"Web," he said to me more than once, "I don't really like your writing very much."

I'll be leaving for the funeral to deliver this in a couple of hours. I'm nervous, of course, at the prospect of speaking in front of a crowd, and I hope I manage to convey the naturally ironic manner that made Billy so funny and so dear. The last line is especially worrisome to me. He said it to me half a dozen times, and I always wondered whether he meant it, or at least half meant it, and deep down it always irritated me a little even as it made me laugh.

Which is why it was so touching to me that yesterday afternoon, as I was helping Billy's sisters pack up his apartment, I discovered my baseball book lying by itself on his night table.

4

⌯⊶○⊷⌯

"The Horse Doesn't Think
It's a Real Cow"

Tuesday, August 2, Pomeroy, Washington

W*hew!*
I made it to the end of the day, I'm pleased to report. And I
made it here, too, to Pomeroy, which is one of those small towns—population 1,500—that makes you gasp at the size of this country because
it is so remote. Embedded in the Palouse, a region that specializes in
wheat, barley, and grass-seed farming and cattle and sheep ranching,
it's the seat of Garfield County, the least populous of the thirty-nine
counties in Washington, only 2,400 residents. It's really empty here, in
other words, even in town, which coalesces around a single east–west
thoroughfare, U.S. Highway 12.

There isn't a lot of traffic on 12, though if you follow it east it takes
you through Lewiston, Idaho, and then through the Rockies over the
Lolo Pass into Montana and then into Missoula, a common bike route,
apparently. I'm not going that way.

Much of the thrill of a long-distance ride has to do with the astonishment you often feel about where you've managed to get to on a bike.
Sometimes it's because you can't believe the reward of the view you've

achieved. Sometimes you feel like you're in exotic terrain, as I did most of the time between Hanoi and Saigon, for example. Sometimes you just feel relieved and lucky that you managed to arrive anywhere at all, Pomeroy, Washington, included.

The ride here from Walla Walla was about sixty-five miles, and there was a genial tailwind most of the way. But just at noon, not quite forty miles in, we stopped for lunch at a spot on the map, Starbuck, where horses and mules were corralled at the end of Main Street, and when we emerged refueled from an air-conditioned café about forty-five minutes later, the temperature had leapfrogged at least ten degrees.

For the first time on the trip I wasn't alone. Tom Scribner, my new Walla Walla friend, had designed our mostly back-road route, and he rode blithely ahead as we turned onto U.S. 12 and began the final stretch to Pomeroy, where he had made motel reservations. Before long I crossed an invisible threshold, five hundred miles since I'd left Astoria. But the exhilaration was short-lived. With the temperature north of ninety, I began to fade. Big time.

In bicycling, the term of art is "bonking." To bonk is to hit the wall, to feel the strength drain out of you, to suddenly lose the wherewithal to proceed. Tom, a stronger cyclist (and thankfully a patient one), was fine, but I needed three or four stops, to rest and soak my head from my water bottles on the treeless roadside the last thirteen miles to Pomeroy. I took an awkward fall starting up after one of them, scratching my shoulder on some roadside brambles. When we finally arrived at the motel, I found dried grass in my hair. I napped briefly and, evidently dehydrated, was awakened by cramping in my hands and feet. Simply put, the day was too much for me.

Before I began this ride, people were always asking me if I was in training. How would I handle the physical demands of such a trip— ahem—at my age? Now just about everyone I meet wants to know what I did to prepare for the rigors of riding six, seven, or eight hours a day. It's a reasonable question, I guess, but how do you train for daylong strenuous exercise without spending days strenuously exercising?

In the weeks before I left, I spent an hour or so at the gym most days, stationary bicycling, stretching, doing some modest weight lifting and core strengthening, trying to stay in the kind of shape that would make this trip at least feasible.

Weekends, I took rides of twenty, thirty, or forty miles, mostly on the level roads of Long Island. But I knew that I'd be biking myself into shape as I went along, that the first weeks would be especially grueling, and that (if all went well) I'd be sufficiently trained by the time I hit the Mississippi River. Now, five hundred miles into the journey, I've learned some things and made some adjustments—it was smart of me to ship some clothes and equipment home, and *really* smart to have my rear cassette replaced in Hood River. I obviously have a few more adjustments to make.

For one thing, I'm not yet prepared for sixty-mile rides in blistering heat. For the time being, I'll have to modify my schedule with reduced daily distances in mind. For another, I've been trying to make my morning ritual more efficient. So far it's been clockwork regular: two hours from the time the alarm goes off (usually between 5:00 and 6:00 a.m.) until I get on the bicycle and depart. Partly this is about eating breakfast—you have to eat even if you're not hungry, though I almost always am—and then (a crucial element of preparation that rarely gets mentioned) waiting for your digestion to kick in sufficiently. There's nothing quite as discomforting on a bike as your stomach making threats. It's also true that saddlebags are designed more for easy transporting than for convenient packing and unpacking, and it's pretty much the case that whatever you discover you need at night is at the bottom of the second bag you look in. So every evening my motel room looks like the aftermath of a windstorm, and every morning my bags must be thoroughly repacked.

Finally, there is route planning, which is a lot like shopping for a computer or a camera. You think it's going to be simple, but no model has everything you want for the price you want to pay. I try to plan for the day, and then for a day or two ahead. How far should I travel and in which direction? What will the terrain be like? How much truck traffic will I encounter, and do the roads have adequate shoulders? Am I likely to find a place to stay? Which way will the wind be blowing?

Optimally, one would like an amiably undulating, curvy, deserted, newly paved road through a scintillating landscape with a pleasant tailwind. Never happens. I find the decisions anxiety-making, which is one reason I was happy to throw in my lot with Tom for a couple of days. He handled all the arrangements—what a guy!

Tom, who is sixty-four, is an avid cyclist who made a cross-country ride with his son in 2003, and before that he celebrated turning fifty by riding fifty miles in each of the fifty states.

Our ride, especially early on, was lovely, winding through vast, remote fields of soft white wheat (the kind used for noodles rather than bread, I was told). To our satisfaction, we were pushed by a modest tailwind. Margo joined us for the first fifteen miles or so, but at the top of a rise where you could watch the blanket of wheat shimmer in the breeze all the way to the horizon, she turned and headed back to town against the wind to begin her day.

Tom and I pressed on to Starbuck and Pomeroy. Along the way we crossed paths with three cyclists going the other way, two young women and, a hundred yards or so behind them, a bearded man wearing a shirt tied around his head like a kaffiyeh. They'd left Portsmouth, New Hampshire, fortysomething days earlier, a remarkably fast trip, by my lights. We had a short conversation with the guy, during which it became clear that he was tired of traveling with the women; he was pissed at them, grumbling in the manner of a put-upon husband (a put-upon bigamist, I guess), that they were stubborn and aligned against him. We commented that they'd chosen to ride east to west, against the wind for the most part. The guy scowled.

"That's a myth," he snapped, with a breeze blowing in his face. This bike trip didn't seem to be making him happy.

During the most rugged part of my afternoon, I sat in the mottled shade of one of the few roadside trees we encountered that day, my head bent over and held between my legs to recover from a bout of dizziness. Not surprisingly, I was having gloomy thoughts about this cross-country enterprise, namely: How the hell am I going to make it?

But I also thought, You can't stay here by the side of the road, deep-breathing with your head between your legs. Now, or in five minutes or ten minutes or an hour, you're going to have to get back on the bike and pedal the final miles into town. And I did, and I recovered. (A couple of milk shakes helped. I'm not sure I ever drank two milk shakes in a day before.) I'll be ready to ride again tomorrow morning.

This is a process—minus the milk shakes—I've gone through before, on this trip and on previous ones, and it's instructive in the same way every time, drumming the basic philosophy of long-distance cycling into my head: Moving forward is the cure for all ills. Keep pedaling.

The more I think about that, the more powerful and human a message I find it to be. Maybe because I'm on this trip I have to think of cycling as a metaphor. Or maybe I'm on the trip because I think of cycling as a metaphor. Or maybe because I write obituaries for a living and just buried my best friend I've been thinking about the inevitable direction that all lives take and that it behooves us to get as far as we can before we can't go any farther. In any case, it's clear to me that something existential, something darkly comic, was coursing through me this afternoon. It shouldn't be a surprise—and it pleases me no end—that Beckett was an avid cyclist.

"The bicycle is a great good," he once wrote. "But it can turn nasty, if ill employed."

And he certainly understood bonking. Remember this, from the end of *The Unnameable*? "You must go on, I can't go on, I'll go on."

Thursday, August 4, Cheney, Washington

It's pronounced CHEE-nee, apparently. The motel clerk was a little unpleasant when I said "CHAY-nee." Must be a pet peeve around here.

A difficult ride through the Palouse has left me leg-weary and sun-roasted, and reminded of how bicycle touring lets you experience the country in intensely felt geographical segments. I made it here, a college town (Eastern Washington University) just south of Spokane, and it feels like a pivot; next I head east, toward Idaho, Montana, and the Rockies.

Two hundred and fifty miles ago I left the Columbia River gorge behind me, and along with it the sense that the world is verdant and damp. I've been in wheat country since then—rolling hills spread with vast blankets of, um, amber waves of grain. Amber actually isn't the right word—the hills are a kind of blanched yellow—though it is harvest time now, and with huge combines raking through the fields the fine grain dust that settles in the air changes the light, especially at dusk, when everything takes on a golden glow.

It's a landscape unlike anything I've ever seen, essentially tree-less, a game board of wheat fields in vast quadrangles of burnt browns and beiges and road names with words like *gulch* and *dead man* in them. With undulating hills, some of them quite steep, that seem to go on forever like the rollers in the middle of the ocean, few outposts of civilization, and temperatures that click up suddenly at noon from tolerable to scalding, it is a challenge for a cyclist, to say the least.

Tom and I left Pomeroy late in the morning—I slept a couple of extra hours—and immediately climbed a fierce hill in heat that made the air wiggle. A photographer from the *Times* was following us, and he captured us just as we crested the hill and a curious dog wandered out into the road for a good sniff.

It was a short day that felt like a long one. The road curved and dived for a while and hit bottom at the Snake River. We crossed at Central Ferry, where harvested wheat was being loaded onto enormous barges. I soaked a hand towel in water and wrapped it around my neck, tucking the ends into the front of my shirt. Then we climbed for seven winding miles, and at the top—I stopped once for a breather—the muscles in my thighs wouldn't stop twitching. I got off my bike and walked back and forth across the highway to get them to feel like my thighs again and emptied an entire water bottle, most of it down my throat, the rest over my head. We'd had very little traffic, but I was so distracted by fatigue that I didn't hear the truck coming up the other side of the hill until it blasted its air horn at me and I jumped, nearly tumbling over the barrier that separated the road from a steeply pitched wheat field. I remember feeling both proud of what I'd accomplished for getting up the hill and entirely ready to take in an air-conditioned movie.

From there, it was twenty miles or so, a good part of it downhill, to Dusty, an aptly named town on the flats, where I stayed overnight in a bunkhouse at the Alkali Creek Ranch. Tom had somehow found the place—it was pretty luxurious for a bunkhouse, with a flat-screen television and a full kitchen—and reserved a spot for me. He, however, had to go back to work. Margo picked him up—she brought us sandwiches and cold beer—and an hour or so before dusk they took off. I immediately felt homesick for two people whom just a few days earlier I had never met.

At the ranch, I met a friendly woman named Kimberley Gustafson, who operates Alkali Creek Performance Horses, training animals she likens to world-class athletes for cutting-horse competitions. These are contests that require horses to start, stop, and turn on a dime as though they were working on a cattle range and having to separate, or cut, one cow away from the herd. I can explain this to you now because she explained it to me yesterday.

The sun was going down when Kimberley arrived with a trailer and led three strapping three-year-olds onto the ranch grounds. There, in spite of having been through all-day training at another site, they joined several other horses and ran joyously about, whinnying, rearing, sprinting so their hooves kicked up thunder and dust, and finally pretending to charge at Kimberley and me before pulling up with sudden casualness and snorting mischievously. I was made nervous by this; she was not.

Then we went into the barn, where the company's trainer, Tim Johnson, demonstrated cutting technique, riding a six-year-old named Roofie—short for Raise the Roof. Tim used a common teaching tool in cutting, something called a pro-cutter or a string cow. It's a fake cow, a bovine Halloween costume—a mask with horns mounted on a pulley whose movements can be remotely controlled by the rider in order to give his horse something tangible to react to.

"The horse doesn't think it's a real cow," Kimberley said, a little defensively, I thought. I hadn't made an accusation. "He knows it's practice."

Tim put Roofie through his paces in the darkening barn, and the horse, running, shifting, and changing direction like an enormous point guard playing defense, worked up a good sweat.

After cycling the Palouse, I knew how he felt. Kimberley led Roofie outside, gave him a good soapy lathering and hosed him down. He was clearly delighted with his shower, and I got the hint. I excused myself and took one of my own.

This morning, fortified by an enormous ranch breakfast—fabulous bacon!—I got started before eight, in the beautiful bronze light of the early sun over the wheat fields. It wasn't hot yet, but you could tell it was going to be. Between Dusty and Cheney were more than sixty miles, and as Kimberley had described the ride to me it wasn't going to be easy—hills and heat, hills and heat, precisely the sort of day I'd just realized I should avoid. She'd unnerved me a bit and I'm sure she saw that in my face; she gave me her card and made me promise I'd call if I ran out of steam. It would be no problem to come and get me, she said.

"There isn't much between here and there," she said. "You'd be in trouble if you got stuck."

She didn't know me from Adam. I was genuinely touched.

The ride was as she described. There were two towns on the way, both with a few grain elevators, a café or two, a saloon, and a gas station: Endicott, about twenty miles north of the ranch, and then, another fifteen miles along, Saint John, where I stopped for lunch and a gallon of lemonade, and passed an hour of rest time reading in a local newsletter about the unassailable virtues of Jesus and guns.

From there I began the last thirty miles or so to Cheney in the heat of early afternoon, a bit of a dangerous ride, with long, looping hills that sapped my strength. By the time the road passed through the Turnbull National Wildlife Refuge, just south of here, and I began to remember what trees look like (though where the wildlife was I don't know), I felt assaulted by the sun. My feet were burning and the flesh over my sit bones—my ass, in other words—was aggravatingly tender. When I got to the Holiday Inn here, a couple of miles through town on a long shopping strip, I was really, really tired.

However, I'd learned something from the near-disastrous bonk. I rested frequently, paid more heed than I usually do to hydration (I'd strapped a good amount of water and Gatorade to the back of my bike in Saint John), focused on gearing carefully and pedaling with a steady rhythm, resisting strain when possible, and generally proceeded not with desperation to arrive somewhere but with diligent attention to riding a bicycle as productively as possible. I parceled out my physical and mental resources thoughtfully and efficiently. The result was an exhaustion that left me more satisfied than unnerved.

To celebrate I wanted a good dinner, and the clerk—much nicer to me after I'd showered and pronounced the name of her town correctly—suggested Lenny's, an Italian joint about a mile away, back in the direction I'd come. I walked it, giving my tailbone a rest, had a substantial and tasty lasagna on Lenny's outside porch, and walked back.

On the way I phoned Danny Lubin in Los Angeles, an old friend whom Billy and I had grown up with and whom I'd seen at the funeral. Years ago, when we were all in college, Danny's roommate at Macalester in Saint Paul, Minnesota, had been a guy named Barney Brewton; I'd met him then, and several times afterward, and liked him, but hadn't seen him in decades. Didn't Barney live in Spokane? I asked Danny. He did. He and his wife, Patti, worked in schools in the area.

Back at the Holiday Inn, I sent Barney an email. Within minutes he called me. Spokane is maybe fifteen miles from here, and he invited me to spend the night tomorrow. I can look forward to an easy morning in the saddle, a pleasant evening around a friendly dinner table. I'm beginning to recognize a theme: that a solo journey—this one, anyway—is not so solo after all. That on a trip like this you're never as alone as you think; you're propelled by one helping hand after another.

Friday, August 5, Spokane, Washington

A very short day, less than twenty miles along a flat bike path, mostly wooded, into the city limits of Spokane. This is maybe the country's most isolated city of any size, by all accounts a peaceful, outdoors-oriented, conservative place and an exceedingly pleasant one to visit. Barney picked me up as I emerged from the woods onto an overpass above some railroad tracks and into a parking lot; we loaded my bike into his

SUV and drove to his spacious and comfortable home on another leafy street. He and Patti invited some friends for dinner and we had a heartily amiable evening, characteristic of the kind of weekend in the country I'd have enjoyed this summer from time to time in the Hamptons if I'd stayed home. Tomorrow I'm off into the wilderness again. Well, maybe not the wilderness—Idaho.

I've been putting off recounting the day of the funeral, I know, but naturally I've been thinking about it, and about the long string of events in my memory that has attached itself to that day. Two hundred people showed up, and both of Billy's kids spoke, leaving everybody in emotional tatters.

My eulogy was well received; Billy's sisters, Margie and Laurie, thanked me for it, and Andy, Billy's son, told me it was the most awesome speech he'd ever heard—the most welcome review I'll ever get. I was a pallbearer, an agonizing duty, and at the burial after the service, I was among the first to shovel dirt into the grave. I've had that experience once or twice before; the sound of the clods landing on the coffin is enough to make you wail—or want to, at least.

Happily, it was a warm day. A couple of years ago, we buried my uncle, Jack Skilowitz, Claire's husband, on a bitter, gray February morning in Westchester, and the consignment of the body to the frozen earth was terrifying to me, a commonplace and necessary errand that seemed unimaginably cruel.

When Billy's ceremony was over, Danny and I stopped at a fancy hotel for a stiff drink—I had two, actually—and then we drove back to Billy's family's house, where people had gathered to eat and drink and laugh and remember that the world wasn't yet over for the rest of us. It was a festive wake, lively. Most of it took place outdoors, at the back of the house, and I was standing there near the garage talking to Andy, I think it was, when Catherine, my former girlfriend, whom I'd been with for five strenuously emotional years and hadn't seen in ten, not since the day of my mother's funeral, came walking up the driveway.

Catherine had gotten to know Billy when we were together and had taken to him the way women often did—he was funny, nonthreatening, attentive, and unusually solicitous, if eccentrically so—and after she'd moved to Los Angeles they'd socialized a few times. But when we split, the friends got divided up and Billy was returned to me. Bobby, who had also been friends with Catherine, and I had both written to tell her about Billy's death and the funeral, but neither of us had heard from her so we assumed she wasn't coming.

Then, shortly after the burial, she sent word that, coincidentally, just that afternoon she'd been cleaning out an old email address's inbox and discovered our messages. She'd called the funeral home, she said, and found out about the gathering at home.

"Would it be all right if I came by to pay my respects?" she wrote.

"Of course," I wrote back.

An hour later she was standing in front of me in the driveway. She looked stunning, the way ex-girlfriends always seem to when their ex-boyfriends catch a glimpse of them again after years and years.

"Thank you for the 'Of course,' " she said. "I really didn't know if you would want me here."

Hmmm, what is the appropriate background here? There are a few salient facts. Catherine and I met at a dinner party at Christmastime in 1993, three months or so after I returned from my first cross-country ride. At the end of the trip there had been a picture of me in the paper on the George Washington Bridge, and at the party—or maybe it was on our first date a week or so later—Catherine said she'd seen it, read my last story about the trip, and asked herself why she could never seem to meet a guy like that. She was fetching, flirtatious in the Southern manner—she'd grown up in Louisiana—curious, bright, verbally deft, no pushover. She was an actress, a struggling one at the time; I was covering the theater for the *Times*.

The relationship quickly became serious but somehow never

certain. Our mutual feelings were strong; so were our apprehensions. We fought, sometimes over consequential matters, sometimes over trivialities that fanned our frustrations to a boil, interestingly never about the theater, which we attended together a lot. I never criticized her acting. She was talented, especially fun to watch in a role that called for high dudgeon. I was smart enough to know not to give her notes. Partly I learned this from her because now and then she would make a suggestion about something I was writing, and sometimes I would take it, sometimes not. If I didn't she'd be insulted and we'd end up in a brouhaha. It was the kind of fight we had often no matter what started it—obviously not about whatever it purported to be about.

We chased each other around the country. She went back and forth from New York to L.A. I moved to Chicago for a *Times* job that kept me traveling. And we chased each other around a Mobius strip of emotions: she was in agony for me when I was cool, I couldn't bear to be without her when she was in independent mode. In our separate moments of desperation, each of us proposed marriage and was turned down. That became a bit of a joke between us. "Will you marry me?" one of us would say. "Not today," the other would reply.

But finally none of this was a joking matter. You know how it is: you want it to work, you badly want it to work, but it doesn't. It feels as though your own psyche, your own brain, is working against your own contentment, but the fact is you're not content. We went to therapy together, and we went separately.

Therapy wasn't new for me. I'd been going to a shrink since the late 1980s for periodic bouts of depression, but the extended strain of the relationship was triggering episodes more frequently. The bedroom became an anguishing place more than a consoling one, where things got worse instead of better. There was a tense, awful weekend in New Orleans for the wedding of one of her brothers. Finally, in 1998, as we were getting ready to take a vacation together in Istanbul, I fell apart. Catherine was in L.A. I was in Chicago. I began panicking each time we spoke on the phone, and then for a day or two didn't answer the phone at all. When we finally spoke again, she canceled the trip—out of sympathy and probably weariness, not anger—and that was pretty much the end.

That same year my mother lost a breast to cancer and my father had a heart attack. On each occasion I traveled urgently to Tucson, a place you can't get to from anywhere in less than a day. I thought they were goners then, both of them, one right after the other, but they pulled through, and after they were both recovered and able, they moved to the suburbs of Atlanta, near my brother and his family. They'd been there maybe a year and a half when my father called to tell me my mother's cancer had returned, this time in her liver, and that she would shortly be dead. That was December 30, 2000; on New Year's Day I was on a plane to Atlanta, and for twelve days I, along with the rest of my family, waited for the inevitable.

I hadn't been in contact with Catherine much and I think we'd seen each other only once, for an afternoon in Los Angeles, after the Istanbul trip went down the drain. But I called her every day I was in Atlanta; make of that what you will, but obviously I was unable to face my mother's death without the other important woman in my life. She promised to fly to New York for the funeral, a declaration that staggered me. I hadn't asked her because I had no standing to.

She kept her word. We met for a drink the night before the funeral. I showed her a draft of the eulogy and she said she loved it, and offered one or two changes, which I didn't agree with but made anyway.

Throughout most of the next day she was by my side, holding my hand, and that night we had dinner together, just the two of us. There was a moment at the end of the evening when we stood looking at each other in front of my apartment building and I knew I could have asked her to come upstairs and spend the night, but I didn't. She returned to Los Angeles the next morning; I spoke to her on the phone, and she was just a bit distant. A month later, not long after Valentine's Day, I got the letter that said she was marrying someone else.

*   *   *

After Billy's wake, Catherine and I sat at a restaurant on the beach and watched the sun go down.

"We only see each other at funerals anymore," I said, and we both laughed.

Our conversation, which began with mutual apologies for bad behavior long ago, was startlingly easy and warm, but I was nervous. I joked again and said that from the moment we broke up her life had improved. After all, she'd begun getting regular work in television and the movies; she'd met a man she could love *and* live with, she'd created a home and a family. She showed me pictures of her six-year-old son.

I thanked her for helping me quit smoking. In the weeks after I'd gotten the letter about her engagement, my habit cranked up to more than a pack a day. I was smoking unfiltered Camels in those days, and I developed a cough so persistent that my shrink—my shrink!—to whom I was venting despair about my mother and Catherine twice a week, insisted I go for a chest X-ray. I threw out my cigarettes after that session—March 21, 2001—and haven't had one since, but over the early months, marking the days without a smoke was positive reinforcement for a guy whose self-esteem was pretty shaky. Every minute I spent congratulating myself for not smoking was time I didn't spend in guilt-ridden self-loathing over the two women I had just lost.

It had been quite a while since I'd been actively angry at Catherine, since I'd had the regular, agitating dreams that made me obsess for hours about that moment in front of my apartment building, since I'd anguished over whether Catherine or the years I spent with her was the more unsettling loss. Still, it felt as though I had a score to settle: Why did she fly across the country to be with me at my mother's funeral if she was no longer in love with me?

"I thought we were going to have another chance together," I said to her.

She looked at me very evenly and said that she had thought the same. She'd wanted to be there for me when my mother died, she said, but also, before she went ahead with her marriage to someone else, she wanted to give me one last chance to ask her myself.

But I hadn't done it, she said.

It ached a little bit to hear that, of course, another inner bruise in a day of them.

She drove me back to my crummy motel and we stared at each other in the car, one more potent moment for me to think about over the next twenty or thirty years.

We talked a little bit about not having seen each other in so long and agreed that having to say good-bye again so quickly didn't seem quite fair, even though it was undeniable that both of us are probably happier now than we ever were with each other. We were both thinking the same thing, I think, that if we hadn't missed that connection ten years ago the last ten years would have gone differently.

What would that have meant? That we would be married to each other? That we would be divorced? That we'd have resolved our painful difficulties and been happy? Or that we'd have had ten more years of scratching at our neurotic wounds? At this point would we be bitter and grudge-ridden, unwilling to communicate, incapable of the mutual gratitude and goodwill that had suddenly dawned on us? Or would we somehow have gotten here anyway, to this precise point in our lives and in our relationship, by some convoluted other path? Would she have a child? Would we? Would I have found Jan, or anything approaching the peace I seem to be feeling with her?

The day you bury a great friend who died too young is a reasonable enough occasion to ponder fate, I guess. In the car, Catherine thanked me for letting her know about Billy's funeral, and we said a chaste good night.

As I got into bed, it occurred to me that on top of everything else it was my father's birthday. He would have been eighty-five. The day finally got the best of me and, with some relief, I wept.

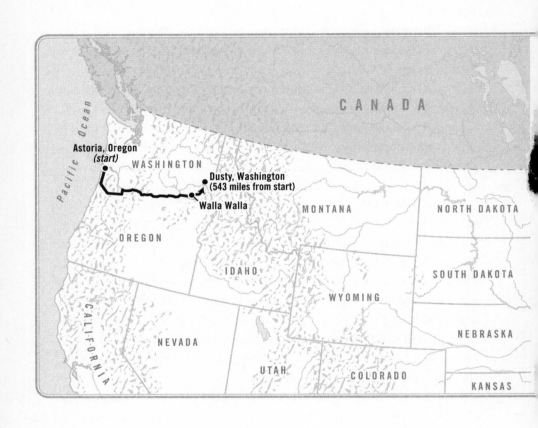

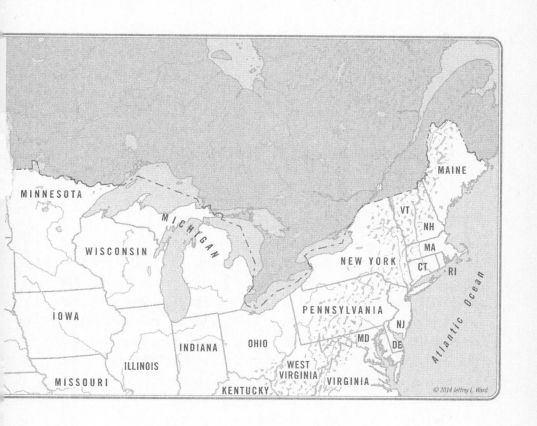

MINNESOTA

WISCONSIN

MICHIGAN

IOWA

ILLINOIS

INDIANA

OHIO

MISSOURI

KENTUCKY

WEST VIRGINIA

VIRGINIA

PENNSYLVANIA

NEW YORK

MAINE

VT

NH

MA

CT

RI

NJ

MD

DE

Atlantic Ocean

© 2014 Jeffrey L. Ward

5

⚘

Pie

Sunday, August 7, Sandpoint, Idaho

*T*o judge from reader comments on my blog, from tweets of those who are following me, emails to my *New York Times* address, and from inquiries of people I've been meeting along the way, the practical aspects of a cross-country bike trip are of real interest. People want solid facts. Not just where did you start and where are you going, but what's your route, how many hours a day do you ride, and when do you think you'll be finished? How do you do your laundry, how many flat tires have you had, what sort of GPS are you carrying? Then there's one I've been asked three or four times recently: What's your favorite thing about the trip so far?

This is Day 19, counting the four days I spent off the road for the funeral. I can answer these questions, some of them anyway, on a first-impression sort of basis. I usually ride six to eight hours a day: 8:00 a.m. to 3:00 p.m. is a perfect schedule, by my lights, though it rarely works out perfectly. (And then there are days like today, when I rode thirty miles in two and half hours, arrived here just after noon, and spent the rest of the day napping on the town beach.) I think I'll be back in my apartment by mid-October, but I could be wrong. As for laundry, now and then I'll find a washing machine in a motel, but more often I simply wear my bike clothes into the shower with me, peel them off, and then hang them to dry on a nearby fence.

I haven't had a flat yet (that can't last, can it?), but I did take the bike in for a tune-up this afternoon—the brake cables were tightened, the wheels trued, the chain cleaned and oiled, the derailleur adjusted. Yes, I'm guilty of using a bike shop to tune my bike. Anything I can do for a bicycle someone who works in a bike shop can do better.

Another confession: a couple of times, faced with unrideable conditions—a gravelly and sandy road, a highway bridge with no bike lane—I've turned my bike upside down on the side of the road as a signal of distress and stuck my thumb out for a pickup truck or a van. I've done this on other trips and it works; the suspicion of people who wouldn't ordinarily pick up a hitchhiker seems to be salved by the sight of a cyclist with his wheels up in a supplicating pose of surrender. I've ridden maybe eight hundred miles by now, and I've been in a car for about five of them. If this offends purists, that's okay with me.

I'm using the GPS on my iPhone. It's a little erratic. When I'm lost, it tends to be out of signal range.

The route question is one that flummoxes me on a daily basis. Sometimes I think ahead two or three days, but I tend to figure out where to go the night before, and often enough—say, if the wind is blowing in an infelicitous direction or the waiter at breakfast gives me a better idea—I change my mind in the morning. What I'm mostly trying to do is avoid mistakes: that is, stay away from danger, ugly places, and more work than is necessary.

After leaving Spokane, I had a tense, unhappy ride north along the Washington-Idaho border on Idaho State Route 41. It was pretty enough; the hills were few and easily conquerable, and though the day was warm it wasn't oppressive. But it was a busy road, with a speed limit of up to sixty miles per hour, and the shoulder was narrow, with an ominously jagged border that dropped off into a sandy ditch. For forty miles, I rode the white line at the right-hand boundary of the highway and felt the wind of passing vehicles behind my ears. Drivers occasionally honked or shouted at me, and for a while I even crossed the highway and rode facing traffic. It was much slower going—I simply pulled onto the shoulder and stopped at intervals to allow oncoming vehicles to go by—but it felt much safer.

About halfway through the afternoon, I took a break at a gas station and was guzzling a root beer when a young man jumped out of a pickup and came over to speak to me.

"Hey, why do you guys ride on the road?" he asked. He was affable, not belligerent at all, and, it seemed, genuinely puzzled. He was concerned, he said; he didn't want vehicular homicide on his driving record. "I was the guy who yelled at you," he added.

I told him about the shoulder problem, pointed out that I had no choice and that I'd just as soon ride more safely. That I hadn't chosen to put myself in danger seemed to amaze him.

"No kidding?" he said. When he turned to go I suggested that he be kind to bicyclists.

"We're defenseless out there," I said, and he cracked up laughing. Was that funny?

As for my favorite things, well, I've been weighing them, and I've come up with two. The first is being able to watch the landscape change. After a long sojourn among wheat fields, the world, in the last few days, has turned green—pines along the road, farmland that looks lush instead of baked, and the Pend Oreille River, which runs wide and purple-black and opens into a bay here at Sandpoint.

The other is drinking, not alcohol necessarily (though beer tastes awfully good after riding in the sun), but anything liquid and cold. Thirst is a dreadful thing, and anyone who travels by bike knows what it is to be plagued by its symptoms—a dry mouth, a sense of depletion, the feeling that you're emanating heat from the inside, as though your very guts were simmering. You're told to hydrate continuously, but that's just to complete the ride. Afterward, you're still thirsty for hours into the night. So that's what I like, the slaking of thirst in the tranquil hours after a ride—I've been swallowing gallons of Gatorade, lemonade, soda pop, cranberry juice, and beer—which is as delicious a physical sensation as I can think of. It's sex for a solitary cyclist.

My packing list: I've got two pairs of bike shorts, four lightweight bike shirts (two long sleeved, two short sleeved), two heavier bike jerseys, a pair of jeans, three T-shirts, four pairs of socks, a pair of gym shorts, two pairs of boxers (I sleep in them), bike shoes, sneakers, a pair of flip-flops, a lightweight sweater, a rain/wind jacket, rain pants, a first-aid kit, a toiletries kit, and, as I mentioned, to make sure I never have to sleep outside, a tent and a sleeping bag. Actually, now that I write it down, I think I'm carrying too much. To the reader who suggested front wheel bags to go with my rear panniers to distribute the weight, I've spoken to a number of cyclists and bike store people about that, and the jury is split. I don't like the burden that front bags place on steering, and though it's true you can get used to it, and it's also true that all the weight on the back makes you wary of fishtailing, after eight hundred miles or so I'm adjusted to it and pretty comfortable riding that way now.

Thanks to all for checking in, even Mr. Scorpion, my most diligent and irritable critic. Here's his latest diatribe. He's getting a little nasty:

> *Weber, listen (if you know how), the country's merrily blowing up, devouring itself, and the only contribution you can think to make at this moment of crisis, as an educated, upper-class American, is to waste time and resources tooling through the wreckage of a nation pursuing private, hedonistic pleasures. Wonderful. How many of the 25 million unemployed have you encountered on your senseless trip, how many people have you encountered who no longer keep a home, how many of the starving among us have you shed a tear [sic]. I bet an $8,000 shiny bike really inspires the vanquished. People are what*

they do. And you do nothing but amuse yourself while a nation suffers
foolish behavior from an entitled class flaunting its greed.

Well, he's jumped the shark a bit, revealing an alarmist nature—
"wreckage of a nation"?—and making a bicycling obituarist the representative of an American entitled class. Maybe hyperbole isn't so
surprising, though, from a guy whose chosen pen name is just a tad
self-elevating; with its biblical verb construction and faux imagery
from Native American mythology, it's pretentious in two cultural idioms simultaneously. But he's prompted a couple of other readers also
to declare that my trip is self-indulgent. Like him, they're pissed about
how much I paid for my bike; it also bugs them that I can afford to stay
in motels.

My first response to this is: Hey, guys, you don't like what's on?
Change the channel. And that has been the leading sentiment of the
many other readers who have come to my defense. Also that if people
are to be blamed for fiddling while Rome burns, maybe others should
be ahead of me on the list.

Of course, by some lights, I *am* fiddling while Rome burns. By riding
across the country I'm going out of my way, after all, to add substance,
heft, accomplishment, satisfaction, eccentricity, individuality, spice—
something—to the narrative of my life. And then I'm writing the narrative down.

Is that self-indulgent? Well, sure. Do I need to apologize for that?

Can't say so. Riding and writing—avocationally and vocationally, it's
what I do.

Still, I admit it: Mr. Scorpion has gotten under my skin a bit. Whether
I ought to be aiming at heroism other than in my own life story—that's
a decent question.

Wednesday, August 10, Eureka, Montana

A sign on the highway outside of my motel room says I'm seven miles
from the Canadian border. The motel is at a crossroads, up a long hill

from a small town and with just about nothing else in sight. Oh, except those mountains to the east and south.

For those of us in the Northern Hemisphere, north is the most dangerous and romantic direction to travel, the direction of the edge of the world. Granted, within the bounds of the U.S. the limits on danger and romance are severe. But even so, here in the upper reaches of Montana the sense of adventure vibrates—and so does the sense of isolation. I like heading toward places like this on a bike, where it takes some effort to arrive and at least as much to get the hell out. On my Vietnam ride in 1995, I headed alone one day into the jungle and passed through villages where I'm sure no one had seen a white man since the end of the war. It was exhilarating and scary.

I felt then the way I feel now, that I'd been lured irresistibly in the direction of a place that could, with reasonable hyperbole, be called nowhere, and that as soon as I arrived I wanted to be somewhere again. Not for the first time, I'm wondering: Am I riding toward something or away from something?

Yes, I'm a little homesick. Is it homesickness? Maybe loneliness? Anxiety? Whatever it is, I've been feeling a little sulky the last few days, less the intrepid traveler and more the kid at camp who's had enough and wants to go home. I'm battling that more than headwinds and hills. The question is why. Okay, I lost a friend to cancer a couple of weeks ago, and I'm sure that's part of it, but this doesn't feel like grief. Rather I'm blaming it on the solo-ness of this adventure and the sense that the fortitude of any relatively sociable person (like me) is at least partly a function of the nearness and support of, well, those we want to be near and supported by. We can get along fine for a while on our own, but without the fuel of a kiss, a scratch behind the ears, a drink and a laugh with our pals, our self-reliance begins to dissipate like the juice in a cell phone.

I choose that metaphor with some irony because in many ways I've never been more connected in my life. The last time I rode across the country, in 1993, whatever phone contact I had with New York was from motels and phone booths. I went for days at a time without being in contact with friends or family or editors. Now, I have a smartphone mounted on my handlebars—having the GPS where I can refer to it is pretty handy—and texts and calls from friends sound the ringtone two or three times a day. This morning, taking a break on a particularly quiet stretch of Montana highway, I fielded a call from Paris. (No finger wagging, please: I don't answer while I'm in motion.) Then, of course, there are the blog readers who have been remarkably voluble with their comments, and those following me on Twitter, many of whom are tweeting back. This is an interactive bike ride, that's for sure. Someone in the office texted me a few days ago to ask how I like having my own reality show, and for a slow-to-arrive-at-social-media type like me that doesn't seem entirely like a joke.

Still, I'm waking up in the middle of the night and having a hard time getting back to sleep. I miss my girlfriend. I miss my neighborhood bar. I miss not having to rise at dawn and push my body to exhaustion. I miss the life I was leading before I left, the one that made me ache to take a trip like this in the first place. I wonder if all this simulated connectivity feeds my hunger for the real thing, making it worse instead of better.

Anyway, one thing has occurred to me; I'm right up against the Rockies now, and the landscape is pretty intimidating, the roads slicing between mountains and climbing and dipping along the shores of rushing rivers and majestic lakes. In such a setting, a lone cyclist feels awfully small—and though that kind of humbling can be a thrill, I admit it can make me feel vulnerable, too, especially in the early morning when the air is crisp and chilly and the silence on the highway is broken by a rumbling double-trailer truck speeding past at seventy miles an hour. It isn't cheering that the Montana roadsides are dotted with white crosses, some wreathed in flowers, denoting highway deaths.

Putting yourself out in that environment at the beginning of each day takes some self-persuasion and some nervously applied self-discipline; it's easier if you have company. I realize this is a kind of conditioning; your will has to get in shape for a venture like this as much as your legs and your lungs.

I'm pretty sure I went through this nagging melancholy the last time, too, but I'd forgotten. My memories of the last trip are mostly from late afternoons, when I was finishing a day's ride in exhausted glory, when the morning trepidation had been banished by hours of good, satisfying exercise and sightseeing and the anticipation of primal appetites being slaked with food, drink, and sleep.

Monday I rode a pretty long day, nearly seventy miles, starting north up the Idaho panhandle from Sandpoint to Bonners Ferry, where a waitress advised me as she set down my French toast that if I were heading into Montana, I should stop at the swinging bridge just before I got to Libby, her hometown.

As a bike route, the Sandpoint to Bonners Ferry leg, where two U.S. highways overlap, is less than ideal, and I was agitated most of the morning, finally crossing the Kootenai River on a wind-whipped bridge and climbing out of town on a four-lane hill noisy with tractor-trailers and motorcycles. At the top, U.S. 95 continues north, and U.S. 2, which I planned to follow, turns east. I stopped at a truck stop for lunch and left my phone and wallet in a toilet stall. Happily—amazingly!—they were still there when I circled back after half a mile and pedaled like crazy to retrieve them.

The rest of the day was better. A few miles in from Bonners Ferry, U.S. 2 bends to the southeast, entering Kootenai National Forest and beginning a meandering path toward and then through the Rockies before it straightens out for hundreds of miles across the plains of Montana and North Dakota. It's a well-traveled road for cyclists, and I was thinking I'd be on it for a couple of weeks, so the thirty-some-odd miles I spent on it Monday were encouraging.

Traffic was light, the hills not especially disheartening (though the mountains were out there waiting), the temperature moderate (though it got warmer in the late afternoon), and the scenery engaging. The landscape was different again, with an enveloping sense of wilderness— deep pine forest with sun dappling the floor; the road runs alongside the Kootenai and at one point crosses a wild tributary, the Yaak. (Great names, right?) As I passed from Idaho into Montana, Pacific Time changed to Mountain Time, a significant psychological boost. Jan and I were now only eight hours apart instead of nine.

Even so, that night I stayed in a hunting cabin in Troy and felt the first tweaks of the unease I'm feeling now. Something about the size and scope of things here, the depth of the forests, the height of the trees, the furious onrush of the rivers, and, of course, the gigantic mountains that are waiting for me in a matter of days. The Columbia River gorge and the wheat fields of the Palouse were daunting in their way, but somehow their magnitude and beauty seemed manageable, and as I trudged through them and put more miles behind me, and my strength improved and I grew more confident in my physical ability, I began to feel larger in relation to my surroundings.

The last few days I've been shrinking again.

The ride yesterday was on the short side, less than fifty miles. I started early, along Route 2, and was shaken a bit by a pair of trucks careening around a downhill corner from behind me. Before the morning chill had lifted I passed a road sign beckoning me to a parking lot at the head of a scenic hiking path: this way to the swinging bridge. I parked my bike and locked it and walked off into the woods.

The trail is about half a mile. You go over railroad tracks on an enclosed path and then descend into deep woods, where with each step the sun seems to recede a bit and the temperature clicks downward. I was wearing my bike shoes with the pegs that clip into the pedals fixed in the center of the soles, so walking was a little unwieldy. But I kept going and finally came upon the bridge, a wood-planked footpath with cable-strung fencing along the sides that was built during the Depression by the Civilian Conservation Corps (it's been reinforced since then) for use by miners. The river is, I don't know, maybe a hundred feet wide there, and the bridge does swing, creaking in the wind even with no one on it, twenty or thirty feet above the water.

It's intensely beautiful, and the view up the Kootenai River gorge includes a thirty-foot falls. I didn't cross, I made it maybe two steps onto the bridge before chickening out. I'm not so great with heights to begin with, and with my fortitude at a low ebb and declining, I decided to marshal whatever I had left for bike riding. The whole scene pleased my literary self if not my actual one; the swinging bridge is a hell of a metaphor, a dangerous, rickety path from one safe haven to another, and you have to overcome your trepidation to make progress, to succeed, to get to the other side. In general, cycling across America, I feel like that's exactly what I'm doing; in particular, this morning, on the literal bridge, I failed.

Three miles outside of Libby I ran into another cyclist, disabled on the side of the road, with his bike turned upside down and a tire tube slung over his shoulder. He was an Australian, a guy on one of those walkabouts that last for a year or two or three, and he was going the other way. He had started in Portland, Maine, and was headed for Seattle, and he seemed pretty cheerful—"Some days are better than others," he said with a shrug—but he was stuck; his tube was shredded, irreparable, and he didn't have another.

Our wheels were different sizes; I couldn't help him. He was going to have to walk back into Libby and hope the sporting goods shop there— there is one, he said—had the right-sized tube. I offered to ride into town and bring the tube back for him but he checked his watch—it was just after nine—and he said the store didn't open for another hour anyway.

"It's just a day," he said. "I've had worse ones on this trip. Haven't you?"

I laughed.

"Yeah," I said. It was a little bit of a lie, but actually he'd made me feel better.

* * *

In the Libby tourist office I was told that Route 2 between there and Kalispell, ninety miles away, often roared with trucks and the shoulders weren't especially good. There weren't going to be many places to stay, either; looping south, it was a road through the wilderness. The agent urged me to turn onto a small state road, head for Eureka, and there pick up U.S. 93, heading south. That would take me to Whitefish, where I would have options for getting over the Continental Divide, either by finding my way back to U.S. 2 or crossing Glacier National Park. It was good advice.

From Libby, state Route 37 rolls quietly north for about 70 miles, following the Kootenai to the Libby Dam. Beyond the dam, as the river widens into Lake Koocanusa, a pristine reservoir that Montana shares with British Columbia, the road rises and falls along its eastern shore, yielding lovely vistas. The name of the lake, by the way, sounds Indian but isn't; it's an amalgam of Kootenai, Canada, and U.S.A.

I stayed overnight in a fishing camp along the lake, where the bar opened early and night fell in spectacularly serene fashion, and the next morning—this morning, that is—I took off just after sunrise.

I still had a lump of anxiety in my throat. I was heading north, north, north, and the light, early-morning breeze had a nip in it, raising goose bumps on the back of my neck. And even though it was gorgeous and even though Jan called from Paris and thrilled me with the sense of our being able to communicate between here and there—"You should see where I'm sitting," I said to her, staring out over the midnight-sky-colored surface of the lake—I felt as though by virtue of arriving here on my own power I'd gotten myself into a terrible fix that was going to take an enormous effort to get myself out of.

This chapter has a sweet coda, however.

Maybe eight or ten miles before I got here, I chugged up a hill and, in front of the entrance to a campground and marina, suddenly encountered Mattie Miller, a woman from nearby Rexford who was selling baked goods and jellies (her specialty is jalapeño-raspberry) on the side of the road. Her two toddler daughters, Erica and Marissa, were underfoot, and she was chatting with a customer, Lesli Frost.

Ms. Frost, who owns a bait company in Kalispell, makes a weekly trip to this spot, where she had just finished "distributing night crawlers and maggots to all the fishermen," as she put it. Two very friendly women.

I admired Ms. Miller's cherry pies and lamented that I was unable to carry one with me, but Ms. Frost, who was with her young sons, Caleb and Cody, offered to ferry a pie for me and drop it off at my motel here in Eureka. She did.

I just wolfed down half of it. It's delicious. Not home, but homemade.

6

Downhill From Here

Saturday, August 13, Saint Mary, Montana

I was almost killed on the way into Whitefish.

U.S. 93, which I rode for most of the fifty-some-odd miles southeast from Eureka, traces a pretty enough route, through woods and ranchland and some exurban home tracts, but the road isn't in great shape, the shoulder doesn't exist for long stretches, and even when it does it's narrow and often chewed up. You have to ride on the edge of the traffic lane, and there is too much traffic, fast-moving traffic, including trucks, ever to get comfortable. There are no alternatives, so 93 is nonetheless a regular route for the long-distance cyclists who decide they want to tackle this part of the country.

Just outside of Whitefish, a regional tourist center with a strange, half-lumberjack, half-hippie air about it—a lot of ponytailed guys with fishing poles—is a stretch, infamous among cyclists, where a couple of blind curves are spiced with an especially crappy road surface and a bed of rocks to land on when a careering truck forces you off the shoulder, which is what nearly happened to me. I managed to stay upright, but the close call sent me into town a little shaky, and when my motel room turned out to be a closet-sized space with a tiny window opening on an alley—I was lucky to find a bed in town, the clerk told me—I had a hard time taking my usual solace in having put fifty rugged miles behind me.

Plus I was coughing badly. My acid reflux problem has begun asserting itself in the past week, I assume because I haven't been watching at all what I've been eating, just shoveling in everything in arm's reach, including all the acidic foods that do the worst work on the stomach: tomato sauce, orange juice, coffee, chocolate, beer.

Acid reflux manifests itself different ways in different people. A lot of my fellow sufferers deal with agonizing heartburn. With me, it's as if occasional drops of the acid that my stomach marshals during the digestive process defy gravity, leaping up my esophagus like salmon eager to spawn and inflaming the back of my throat. At this point, I can count on an uncomfortable fit of coughing after every meal.

I've been plumbing the cash register racks at every pharmacy and convenience store for effective lozenges. My favorites are fiercely minty ones, Halls Ice Blue, but they aren't easy to find. In any case, I've been leaving a voluminous trail of cough drop wrappers behind me. In motel rooms and trash barrels, I mean, not on the side of the road.

Even if I'm going to cough, I have to eat, and I arrived in Whitefish just after midday, so I took my miserable self out to lunch, where I didn't recognize it at the time, but my luck and frame of mind were about to change. Around the corner from the motel was the Buffalo Cafe, a busy joint at lunchtime, renowned locally for its burgers, omelets, and beer choices. I sat down at the counter and the guy next to me was slurping up a bowl of soup that looked good, so I ordered it—beef barley, and yes, delish!—and that started a conversation. He was an ex–New Yorker (I never got his name) who came out here for the fishing several years ago and stayed. A guy about my age, with a graying ponytail, he wanted to know what brought me there, and I told him, and he began asking about how I was going to get through the mountains, and I said I was going to head for Route 2 and go over the Marais Pass, and he just snorted.

"That's ridiculous," he said, and I knew why and I was ashamed. I was being a chicken.

Whitefish is half a day's ride from the western entrance to Glacier, possibly the most arrestingly beautiful of all our national parks, and the most direct route west to east through it, called, famously and aptly, Going-to-the-Sun Road, is one of the more celebrated bike rides in the United States.

Fifty-one miles long, it begins in the town of West Glacier, proceeds pleasantly along the wooded southeastern shore of Lake McDonald, providing intermittent glimpses of soaring peaks, and then, as if a giant had stepped on the end of the road, mistaking it for a seesaw, begins ruthlessly, if gorgeously, climbing to Logan Pass. There, at 6,646 feet, the road crosses the Continental Divide, and makes a thrilling, winding descent that spills you out on the other side of the park.

I had read about it and was simply intimidated. I knew that it had just opened a few weeks earlier for the summer, the pass having been clogged with snow until mid-July. Maybe it was my dark mood working, but I envisioned an endless, impossible grade that would leave me gasping and feeling entirely ineffectual, completely not in control of a venture that, after all, was supposed to be a way for me to seize control of my life story. Plus I knew if I didn't make it to the top by 11:00 a.m. rangers would scoop me up and take me off the mountain because by then the tourist automobile traffic was heavy and made cycling dangerous both for cyclists and drivers. Route 2, which goes around the southern end of the park and over Marais Pass, is a lesser climb and a far less scenic, more mundane ride.

"You've come all this way and you're *not* going to ride Going-to-the-Sun Road?" my lunch companion said.

I couldn't refute his logic. The follow-up question was in my head: What are you doing this for in the first place? Just to get it over with?

He sent me to Glacier Cyclery, a few blocks away, where the owner, Ron Brunk, a tall, slender man who seemed near my age, said the previous weekend he and his wife had had nothing else to do and had ridden up to Logan together on a tandem.

"It's a very doable ride," he assured me.

Doable?

Mr. Brunk advised me to call the lodge at Lake McDonald in the park and reserve a room for the next night, then leave from there at dawn. A couple of days earlier, while I was still making up my mind about my route through the mountains, I'd called the lodge and was told it was full. On Mr. Brunk's suggestion, I tried again, and—lo and behold!—a vacancy.

Fate, I thought. And between fits of coughing, I made the reservation.

Is it corny, or clichéd, or simply predictable for me to say that reaching Logan Pass has been the high point of my cross-country trip in more ways than one?

Of course. But what the hell. There are just so many reasons to feel like the king of the world when you're standing, well, on top of the world, chilled by your drying sweat and waiting for your heart to stop drumming.

Lake McDonald Lodge is ten miles inside Glacier Park, a serene and bucolic ride from the park entrance along the southeast shore of the lake with postcard views of snowy peaks in the distance. It's a cheery resort campus, with a capacious central lodge and a handful of satellite buildings, a cross between a luxury hotel and summer camp. I had dinner sitting at the bar in the lodge restaurant, where a professor of Native American studies at the University of Montana—I wrote his name down and lost it—told me I shouldn't be fearful of stopping in Browning, the first prairie town beyond the park, largely populated by Blackfeet Indians, even though I'd been warned about staying there overnight by several bicyclists who said they'd been hassled or even threatened by local residents. A lot of class resentment, they said, toward college-educated white people on sleek new bicycles with the leisure to ride them.

Yeah, it's a rugged place, my companion told me, but there are two fine museums there: the Blackfeet Heritage Center & Art Gallery and the Museum of the Plains Indian. Worth spending a day, he said.

The next morning, I was on the road in the dimmest gray light. It was technically before sunrise, a little after six. That hour on a long bike ride is fraught with anxiety anyway, the beginning moments of something you know is going to be a test that will seem until it's over like it's never going to end, and as you're reacquainting your legs with pedaling and working out the stiffness of a night's sleep, it's usually a little damp and shivery, too. I'd eaten a couple of oat bars and was coughing a bit, though not too badly; I'd learned that for some reason I didn't cough much while I was on the bike and I knew the impulse would pass in a mile or so, and it did.

It didn't take long for things to begin looking up, so to speak. From the lodge, Going-to-the-Sun runs northeast along the lake and then continues beyond the far end with the accompaniment of McDonald Creek, a waterway of modest volume but unsurpassing loveliness. I kept thinking I'd start climbing around the next turn, but the gentle undulations of the road remained evenly up and down for quite a while: Nature was counseling me to be patient.

After I left the lake behind, instead of looking over the water at the mountains, I could feel them crowding me; I was in them, if not yet *up* in them. The sun began glowing behind the peaks—and then peeking through them. Other than the water rushing quietly by and an occasional whisper of wind, it was silent. I was entirely alone, and even though I was riding on a paved road, to this city dweller it felt like utter wilderness, and I marveled at the thought that the sun came up on this spot and revealed its splendor every day.

I had ridden for not quite an hour at an energy-conserving pace, meaning I'd gone about ten miles, when the ascent began in earnest. From there the road travels northeast for three miles or so, then makes a hairpin turn and heads southeast on the outer edge of a mountain.

I propelled myself with enthusiasm, and without a break, to the turn, surprising myself with my leg strength and easy breathing. The view to the creek side of the road began taking on greater majesty, and I passed some tourists who'd pulled their car off the road to take pictures. They were on the way down, knew what I was heading toward. Eyeing my saddlebags, one of them said to me, clearly aghast: "You're going to the *top*?"

"Gonna give it a shot," I said between short breaths—and left them behind.

The hairpin was a natural rest spot. The park service has widened the road into a parking lot and several tourists were stretching their legs and admiring a wintry-looking vista with snowy peaks hovering in the distance over hillsides covered partly in pine forest, partly in spiny, leafless trees. Perhaps there'd been a fire.

I had a conversation there with two of the strangest cyclists I'd ever met, young women, one in her twenties, I think, the other even younger, who said they were from California and had been on the road for several months. Both were obese. Their bikes were piled high with gear, inexpertly, and sloppily packed. The younger one had a huge pink teddy bear strapped on top of her stuff, and it sat behind her, not quite upright, listing like a small child fallen asleep in a car seat with Mom at the wheel.

Their story—that they had traveled by bike all over the West, had been up and down the coast, and that they intended to cross the country eventually—seemed implausible. On the other hand, they spoke with unflagging cheeriness and here they were in front of me, some four thousand feet above sea level. They were leaving for the summit as I arrived at the hairpin, and I said I'd see them on top.

"Probably before that," the older one said. "We go pretty slow."

Indeed, I rested for about fifteen minutes and passed them within another fifteen. They were moving, but barely. I never saw them again and can't imagine they made it to the pass by the 11:00 a.m. deadline.

*   *   *

All told, from the lodge it was twenty-one miles to Logan Pass, about eleven from the place where the road began climbing, eight from the hairpin, after which it's just up, up, up—endlessly up along a road that traces a precipice, switching back and forth, in and out of the sunlight, in and out of the shadow of the mountain. The views of the river valley below, into which a couple of errant pedal strokes could have sent me tumbling, were gasp-inducing—or maybe that was just because my lungs were heaving in and out with my effort. Across the valley were moss-green mountainsides and a set of stony peaks lined up like the craggy, erratic dentition of a colossal ogre.

The slope was harsh and relentless, and I was watching the clock. It was just about eight thirty when I left the hairpin, meaning I'd have to average between three and four miles per hour in order to reach the pass before eleven. That doesn't sound like a burden, I know, a very brisk walk, but among other things, climbing means plodding. It also means resting, and with a deadline, resting means feeling uneasy while you're supposed to be relaxing.

If you've ever labored up a long hill on a bike, one where you can't see the top from the bottom, and you've tried, on the way, to imagine yourself on top and figure out how long it would be before you got there, then you've had the experience of envisioning defeat. In Oregon, on Day 2 of my trip, I dismounted on the side of the road halfway up a stiff climb and, with my thighs quivering, stared uphill at the quarter mile or more of the slope that I had to continue climbing. I'd been watching my speedometer as I inched uphill, and as I strained to push the pedals, the whole notion of ever completing a cross-country journey seemed ludicrous. I calculated that at four miles per hour and needing intermittent breathers, I'd get to Manhattan the following June. It was a low point. I thought about quitting, just getting somehow to the end of the day and then figuring out a face-saving reason to fly home and take on a new pursuit not quite so taxing on my lungs and quadriceps.

Then I got back in the saddle and pedaled, ever so slowly, to the top, where, of course, my perspective was entirely different. And now here I am, not in Manhattan yet by any stretch, but about eight hundred miles farther down the road.

When you move forward, even slowly, things change; when you stand still, they don't. This is the lesson that bicycling teaches me over and over again, one that is so sensible and obvious you'd think it would be easy to remember, especially when I'm not on a bicycle. But off or on I tend to forget it—along with the corollary I've already mentioned: You can climb only one hill at a time. On a long-distance trip, that one is a worthy mantra: One hill at a time. One hill at a time. *Ommmmmm.*

I did remember it, however, on the way up to Logan, and it informed a strategy: Divide the big hill into a bunch of little ones, take small triumphs on the way to the ultimate one. I rode in bursts of distance—two miles, a mile and a half, a mile, three-quarters—before resting, then in bursts of time. Eight minutes. Six. Five. And the rewards began to come. For one thing, on the way up, as difficult as every pedal stroke was, I became aware with each one of an incremental rise, a change in my elevation. I focused on the fact that my perspective on sea level was broadening, that my general purview was becoming more lordly, so that each time I stopped to rest the natural spectacle before me was wider, deeper, and more glorious.

I hasten to add that as the morning went on and I neared the top of the mountain, I wasn't alone up there. I'd been passed on the way by several riders and passed a few myself. And particularly as I got close to the top, the day had advanced enough that the tourists had woken up, had their breakfasts, and started driving up and over the mountain. It got a little crowded, actually, especially because there were stretches the last few miles of gravelly or chewed-up pavement on the road either being caused by or repaired by construction crews; I couldn't tell which.

But all this gave me an unexpected sense of an audience. Half a mile from the pass, road workers had been halting traffic in one direction, then the other, letting single streams of vehicles go by. I waited with three or four other cyclists as a few cars rolled by us, then we followed behind a tour bus to the summit, riding past a line of cars waiting their turn to go down. Most were full, adults in the front seat and kids in the back, and the windows were open.

They were all cheering for us.

Of course, there was the reward not just of the unexpected applause, not just of reaching the crest, but also of riding down the other side. The eighteen miles to Saint Mary, the tiny town on the east end of Going-to-the-Sun Road, went by quickly—too quickly—though I prolonged them with picture taking and simply by being awed at the landscape I was hurtling through. If you can be thrilled and humbled at once, today I was.

But in truth the downhill simply wasn't as memorable as the climb, which was an experience that revealed me to myself. I can confess it now: the first two weeks I nearly gave up and flew home half a dozen times, thinking I could feign an injury. But I didn't. The stick-to-itiveness I needed to build up the stamina in my legs and my lungs was something I didn't know I still had. As I approached the Rockies, I'd grown sad, disappointed, weary, self-doubting. I was living with the kind of perpetual lump in my throat that I have associated for forty years with the aftermath of a broken teenaged heart.

Today was the turning point. Provoked by a stranger at a lunch counter to put aside my intimidation and do what I'd set out to do—meet the challenge of riding across the country, which of course means climbing over the Rocky Mountains—I did. After all, he was obviously right.

It was a truly difficult ride, a real test. I crept uphill, but, importantly, I kept creeping. For the last three exhausting miles, I found myself turned inward, searching inside myself for the will to keep pedaling. Guts: Where are you? That I actually found them was a tremendous satisfaction.

At the pass, I stood alongside my bicycle, breathing hard, suddenly aware that I was soaked with sweat and feeling a deep chill in the high-altitude breeze. But the relief, the wonder, the thrill of the moment were previously unimaginable. The seventeen-year-old girl I longed for as a seventeen-year-old boy had just kissed me. It was exactly like that.

Sunday, August 14, Cut Bank, Montana

An hour before dusk it's well over eighty degrees here on the prairie, I've been drinking liquids for about four hours, and it seems hard to believe that I was here once before on a journalistic assignment, back in the 1980s on a January day when Cut Bank registered the coldest temperature in the continental United States, twenty-three degrees below zero. No wonder nothing looks familiar.

I'm in the flats of Montana now, and maybe thirty miles back the Rockies finally disappeared behind me. I watched them go as I rode, looking back over my shoulder, stopping now and then and staring as they became smaller and smaller and finally shrank into the horizon. Happily, though, the kick of conquering the Divide, the prolonged effort to reach the Pass, and the breathtaking glide down the other side linger. I didn't describe much of the descent yesterday, but it was exciting: tumbling mountain streams that spilled chutes of water over rock ledges, splendid and towering buttes of gleaming rock, and Saint Mary Lake, deep and violet amid the peaks, majestic as an inland sea. I'm carrying yesterday with me, and the mountains, too; if I can't see them in the distance any longer they're in perfect focus in my mind's eye.

Cut Bank, meanwhile, is a surprise after so many miles of Montana air and space, a legitimate town with banks and hardware stores and restaurants, houses with yards, people with daily schedules and responsibilities, an air of competence, and if not exactly prosperity, then pride and durability. It is, in other words, an island of sorts, a true prairie oasis; when you're in it, you're in it, safely at home. Get to the edge of town and you're surrounded by emptiness; the next thing in sight is the horizon.

The sheer expanse of the continent has never been more evident to me than it has been just about all day today. I woke in Saint Mary, a crossroads town just down the road from the east gate of Glacier. There was a beautiful view back into the park from the parking lot of my shabby motel, and just as the sun came up I said good-bye to the six men I'd met the day before, professional men, all of them longtime friends, from Idaho and Montana, on a weeklong cycling vacation. All were older than I by a decade or more. We'd ridden over the Continental Divide together, or rather, they'd all passed me on the way up and I'd followed them down. We had reservations at the same motel, it turned out, and last night we celebrated our achievement at dinner at a restaurant in a roadside log cabin that has been there, evidently, for more than sixty years. Johnson's Cafe—or as it says on its website, Johnson's World Famous Historic Restaurant—is a family-style place, obviously a local landmark, and we gobbled down huge platters of pork chops, fried chicken, and steak, and the biggest slices of ice cream cake I've ever seen. A meal to match the day—I was stuffed.

This morning my new friends were headed north, into Canada. I was going south and east. Though I'd made it over the Divide, I wasn't done climbing, and from Saint Mary I rode once again up—straight up, it seemed—maybe five miles, through a forest landscape that had been devastated by fire not so long ago. I ascended for well over an hour. The views back toward Glacier were eerie, striking, and I stopped two or three times to appreciate them, the broad and majestic stony peaks rising behind a vast meadow of ruined trees reduced to ash-colored, upright needles. It was a brilliant day. At the top of the climb was a rounded hilltop that seemed strangely empty and lunar—aside from the billboard advertising a restaurant called Two Dog Flats. The road was wide, as if some sort of rush hour were to be expected, but this seemed unlikely, and as I crested the hill and looked east, I saw that the plateau of land I was on ended abruptly and plunged, and the road—it's U.S. 89, by the way—followed it down. There was simply a drop-off, and beyond it in the distance the whole rest of the nation seemed to be spread out before me like a vast table that was waiting for place settings. I was amazed. Really, this must be where someone coined the phrase "It's all downhill from here."

If only. In fact, there were some uncomfortable ups and downs before I finally hit the flats. The road pointed south for several miles, with a number of twists in it, no big help against a stubborn wind from the southwest, but I finally found myself heading due east toward Browning on Starr School Road, a desktop-straight thoroughfare for pickup trucks with little weather shelter, and was able to use the wind a bit to my advantage. It wasn't quite a sailboat ride into town but it was good to feel like the gods were at least a little on my side.

After my conversation at the Lake McDonald Lodge about the Indian museums, I was planning to stop in Browning, for an hour or two at least, overnight maybe. And after my conversation at the Buffalo Cafe, I didn't want to feel accused again—even if only by myself—of passing on a potentially valuable experience for the sake of expediency.

But, at the end of Starr School Road, I turned south into town, and someone riding in a pickup that was pulling out of a nearby gas station tossed a bottle out the back and it smashed on the road about twenty yards away with the sound of a gunshot. I'm not convinced the bottle was aimed at me—I'm not even sure the guy saw me—but yeah, I was spooked. And I was also being persuaded out of Browning by what I saw. The road went along the edge of town and didn't show the place off to much advantage—auto body shops, unattractive housing developments, storage sheds, scrubby fields with litter blowing across them like tumbleweed. Besides, the wind had picked up and the road had turned into it, and I could tell by the map that if I made it beyond town, I'd find the junction of Route 2, heading east, and somewhat easier pedaling.

So I passed on through, though not without difficulty. Just south of town, Browning ends abruptly, and so does civilization, and so does anything resembling a crest of land or a grove of trees. Really it's just two flat planes, the sky and the prairie, meeting at the horizon, with a stripe of road slashing through the blank-scape like the lone brushstroke on a minimalist canvas. I had a lingering flash of terrifying awareness—a sudden bolt of panic, and then a gradual increase on top of it—of just how little protection from the elements is available to a cyclist on the high plains, and just how vulnerable I was going to be for the next *several hundred miles*. The first mile marker I remember passing on Route 2 said 422—meaning it was 422 miles to the North Dakota border.

This may be a good time for a disquisition on wind, which is, naturally, a huge factor on a trip like this, a thrilling friend when it's behind you, a wily foe otherwise, which feels like most of the time. (A rejected title for this book was "The Wind Is My Enemy," rejected not because it is inaccurate or misleading but because the tone was a little too arch and because "Life Is a Wheel" is just a little bit less arch and I like it just a little bit better.)

The psychological battle between a cross-country cyclist and the wind is more complicated than you would think. First of all, the wind isn't a singular force but a plethora of little forces that coalesce into a prevailing notion, though not without a number of contrary opinions. In other words, the wind is a million winds, most of them working more or less in concert but many not, so that no matter which direction is prevalent, you're being buffeted by a battalion of little dervishes: Think of a car being tugged through an automatic car wash with all the spritzing and polishing that goes on in there.

West to east is the direction of the prevailing wind, though all that ostensibly means is it blows that way more often than east to west, and I'm not sure how significant that is, given the number of days I've already had on this trip with winds from the south. It's true that riding east you rarely face a straight-on headwind, but it's also true that it doesn't line up a hundred percent behind you very often either. Rather, most days, it's a question of angles, a steady breeze or a gust coming at you from one side or the other, or hitting one shoulder or another, a slight (or maybe not so slight) deflection from your purposeful path. It's a bit like being nudged by a bully, again and again, frustrating at the least, disheartening at the most. Plus, crosswinds and headwinds are noisy. Passing through the slots in your helmet, rushing past your ears, they become a kind of tinnitus, blotting out birdcalls and insect songs and obscuring the delightful quietude of country roads. They also make cars and trucks coming up from behind you hard to hear. What you hope for—what I hope for, anyway—is semi-stillness, motion in the air but nothing that feels like a force to contend with. You don't want stagnant air that feels stifling and soggy, and a gentle cool breeze is surely a boon to anyone who is exerting himself over an extended period.

This afternoon I had a fairly accommodating wind, though I've discovered that on the prairie rogue gusts are hardly uncommon, coming from anywhere at any time. And when a car, or worse, a truck, goes rumbling by in one direction or another, the whooshing rush of air that comes with it combines unpredictably with whatever nature has going at the moment and can make it seem as though a helicopter is alighting nearby, leaving you desperately gripping your handlebars and envisioning Margaret Hamilton, the Wicked Witch of the West, pedaling through the tornado in *The Wizard of Oz*.

That's the image I conjured up about an hour or so beyond Browning when I encountered a cyclist going the other way. He stopped only briefly to say hello because, he said, he intended to make it to Glacier Park that night, sixty miles or so from where we were, and he was bravely contending with a wind that was clearly more problematic for him than for me. As I watched him pedal off, he seemed to be working much harder than I had been and making slower progress—this was when the musical theme for the wicked witch passed through my head—and I didn't know whether to pity him for the miserable afternoon he was looking at or admire him for having made it this far across the plains already. I didn't know where he had started, but given where we were standing it had to be a long ways away. In any case, I was glad not to be in his toe clips.

From Browning I progressed through the empty landscape for thirty-five or forty miles, accommodating myself to a road I'll be living on, perhaps, for weeks. I know I've described it as a tabletop, and taking it in as a panorama that's the impression you get, but it isn't exactly flat. Rather, like the ocean, over the long haul it's vast and uninterrupted but full of swells, the sorts of gradual inclines and swoops that only cyclists and sailors notice, that don't make you strain but make you work. (Enjoying the seagoing metaphor, I entertained myself—please forgive the self-aggrandizement—by comparing myself to Columbus; even though I'm heading in the opposite direction over dry land and knowing that civilization actually exists out there, it's also true that for who knows how long I'm not going to see anything appreciably different in front of me than I see right now.)

On my 1993 ride, I was farther south—traversing a hillier, more varied part of Montana, between Livingston and Billings and down through Little Big Horn, followed by a dip into northern Wyoming—and never had a stretch like this, facing days on end of prairie riding, chasing an ever-retreating horizon. The closest I came were the two days it took to cross the bleached ranchland of eastern South Dakota, from Pierre to Grand Forks, on the Minnesota border. Tom Scribner had warned me that the landscape of the Montana plains would be maddening, that after not too long, twenty or thirty miles, I'd begin to hunger for something new to look at or a different set of conditions to ride in and to despair that such a thing was so far off. About halfway to Cut Bank I discovered he was right. It isn't boredom, exactly, but a blurring of focus.

The pedaling you do when the terrain changes underneath you is natural as a heartbeat; you do it without thinking. But when the road and roadside go by beneath you and beside you with mile-after-mile uniformity you grow self-conscious, and I began watching my knees pumping up and down and counting my pedal strokes. How far do I get in a hundred revolutions? How many strokes to a mile? How many until I let myself rest and ease the perpetual soreness in my tush? This is a way of passing time, of course, of not being where I am until I'm somewhere else, and that's not how I want to ride. I'll have to figure out something.

Just before Cut Bank there's a brief respite from the sameness as the road plunges into a river gorge and clambers out again, so when you get there it feels as though you've ascended to a hilltop aerie. It was welcome even though I was beat and climbing to end the day isn't what I ever wish for. I rode completely through town and took a motel room on the far eastern end, just where Main Street heads off to rejoin U.S. 2 and spills the refreshed traveler back out onto the endless pancake of prairie.

I ate an early dinner at a nearby steakhouse—my entrée's family probably lived around here—and then took a brief walk past my motel to the highway entrance. The sun was still an hour or so from going down, but the moon was already up, night chasing day, and I had the humbling thought that time itself, passing so quickly, was making fun of my progress. It was quiet and beautiful in a lonely way. I hadn't noticed while I was riding, but standing still I did; the wind actually whistles out here.

years after he had his last cigarette and nineteen months after I convinced him to move to Manhattan.

A Jew, a native New Yorker, he was born and raised in the Bronx and commuted to Manhattan from our home in New Jersey for twenty-five years, but he didn't live there until the end of his life. His name was Sam. He was trained by the U.S. Army to be an electrical engineer, but he ended up in trade journalism. In the 1960s and early 1970s, he was editor in chief of *Electronics* magazine, which made him a big deal in the computer industry just before the computer industry became such a big deal. At his funeral, my brother, Robert, told the story of Dad's coming home from work one day and complaining about a young man he had interviewed—stubborn, insubordinate, sloppily dressed, impatient with his elders, a know-it-all: " 'He reminded me of you, Robert,' " my father said. Of course the young man was Bill Gates.

My relationship with him as I grew up was, for the most part, a loving one. He could do Donald Duck's voice, an imitation that made me laugh from the time I was three until I was in high school. A baseball fan who adopted the Mets after his New York Giants split for California—he had to hold his tongue after Bobby Thomson's famous home run in 1951 because he was working that day among Dodger fans on a ship in the Brooklyn Navy Yard—he taught me to throw (though he had a terrible arm himself) and watched me pitch a Little League no-hitter. He was delighted when I decided to major in mathematics in college (he thought I was aiming at engineering), became incensed when I dropped it (he didn't buy my explanation that somewhere beyond my second year of calculus I got hopelessly lost), and was exceptionally proud that I ended up in publishing, like him. He said to me, many times, with rueful pleasure, that I was a far better writer than he ever was. And I remember his trying to teach me to ride a bicycle, a quixotic enterprise; he never learned to ride one himself.

My father was always a pessimist and a bit of a grouch, though not always an uncharming one. He was able to laugh at himself and now and then appear silly; he was small, about five seven, and soft, but once for a Halloween party he dressed as Superman in snug baby-blue flannel pajamas with a red *S* drawn on the front.

He never outgrew his Depression-era frugality, a nice way of saying he was a skinflint. Once, when he bought a new car, he offered to sell me his old one, a white Mazda from the late 1980s, for $2,000. My mother intervened.

"Just give him the fucking car, Sam," she said.

This part of the portrait is possibly unfair. My father fed me, clothed me, paid for my bar mitzvah, put me through college. We were a middle-class family and I never wanted for what middle-class children had. In the mid-1960s, when I was in junior high school and the Vietnam War was blazing every night on the evening news, I had the first symptoms of depression, riven with terror that within a few years I was going to be drafted and sent overseas to die in the jungle. My father found a psychiatrist specializing in teenagers and sent me on the bus into Manhattan once a week to see him, clutching the $25 check that was the doctor's fee. (Yep, that was a long time ago.)

This went on for a couple of years, and I don't know if the therapy did any good or if I just grew up a little bit (though the fears were certainly rational enough). In any case, I was a reluctant patient; my recollection is the doctor and I spent most of our sessions playing chess. I do know I felt preoccupied with the money.

There were a few blowups—I was a teenager, this was the sixties—but we made it through my high school graduation without too much more than the usual amount of conflict. He hated my long hair, didn't much care for my cheerleader girlfriend, and was suspicious of my friends, whom he was sure smoked pot. (He was right about that.) It was in later years that a kind of chill settled over us. I wasn't home much—not enough, according to him; I didn't call my mother enough. (Years later I learned that my mother's nickname for me was "the Phantom" and that she and her sister, Claire, referred to me that way routinely: "Heard from the Phantom?" Claire would ask. "Not lately," my mom nearly always responded.) I wasn't being enough of a family member. I wasn't, I don't know, loyal. Dad and I weren't enemies, just a little distant.

When my mother died, they had been living in a cookie-cutter house in a subdivision outside of Atlanta for no other reason, really, than to be close to my brother; his wife, Lynne; and Jacob, my parents' only grandchild. After he returned there from the funeral in New York, he was besieged by well-meaning neighbors bringing casseroles and inviting him to attend their Baptist churches and accept Jesus Christ as his savior. That's when I started suggesting he might rather spend his time where he would never have to drive; where he could go to Lincoln Center or Broadway or the Metropolitan Museum or Madison Square Garden on a whim; where he'd find people to whom the name Ralph Branca meant something; where he'd have access to decent pizza, corned beef, and bagels and lox; and, though I didn't say so explicitly, where he and I could settle the hash between us before it got to be too late.

My parents were married for fifty years, and my mother was very sick for forty of them. My father cared for her. It was exalted of him, nearly saintly—I say this without irony—because her illness ruined not just her life but his, and when I say ruined I mean in the sense of poisoned; the burden was so profound that it infused even his moments of pleasure with a sense of anguish and doom. When I was nineteen, my uncle Jack, Claire's husband, made a confession to me. If I were your father, he said, I would have up and left. That was almost thirty years before my mother died.

I was astonished, of course, even more so because he said this in front of his wife. Claire and I have spoken about it in mutual amazement more than once since Jack died. But even at nineteen I understood that what he was saying was not entirely ignoble; he was letting me know that my parents had been dealt terrible, terrible cards and that I was sitting at the same table with a hand in the game. It seems interesting, and maybe even meaningful, to me now that this conversation took place in San Francisco, where they were vacationing and I had just happened to arrive, hitchhiking, after my first trip across the country.

In the decade before my mother died, as she grew more and more feeble, the strain finally began to overwhelm my father, and especially in the last few years of her life he became impossible company. Bitter, impatient, short-tempered, blustery, occasionally irrational, he expected deference from everyone, gave none, lectured me and my brother and Jake, his grandson, not yet six years old, on our insufficiently respectful attitudes, and generally sucked the air out of every room he entered. My sister-in-law, ordinarily an avatar of gentility, told my brother that if Sam were not his father he wouldn't be welcome in their home. I didn't blame her. He was behaving like an aggrieved old man shaking his fist at the universe, and however understandable his feelings or even justified, he was a boor. And a bore.

Still, on the day of my mother's funeral, my father was dignified and distraught. Perhaps the most sorrowful few minutes I ever spent took place before the service that day as I watched him address her lying in her coffin, kissing her forehead, calling her "sweetheart" and "my darling," and apologizing for not having done better, for not rescuing her from her suffering.

The next morning, just before he returned to Atlanta, my father visited me at my apartment and we argued. He arrived looking sad but unmistakably relieved. I was feeling acutely lonesome. My mother had died and Catherine was on her way back to Los Angeles.

"So let me ask you something," my father said after we'd sat down with coffee. "Did your mother's illness affect you?"

I was flabbergasted.

"When your mother first got sick I made a vow to myself that I would give you and your brother a normal life," he said.

"I know, Dad," I said. "You've told me that a million times."

"So?"

I lost my temper and a host of resentments came pouring out of me. It was a dreadful tirade, really, sardonic and mean, fueled by long-term frustration and momentary unhappiness, having been incited probably by a therapist who had pointed out to me over and over that my mother's illness robbed me of a just childhood, had made her the focus of the household and not my brother and me.

Did he think it hadn't occurred to me, I asked my father, that I took as much care of my mother when I was a child as she was able to take care of me?

Did he think I hadn't noticed that my friends never gathered at our house? Why do you think that was, Dad? Because it was a household focused on coping with a disease, that's why, and not raising children. Tell me, Dad, do you think it's a normal thing for a fifteen-year-old boy to lift his mother out of a wheelchair and put her to bed? Or to pick his naked mother up off the floor after she's fallen off the toilet and is lying sprawled and helpless in the bathroom? You think that might have an effect?

Why did he think I was almost fifty years old and hadn't been able to sustain a relationship? Guess what? The example in front of me was that if you fall in love and commit yourself, you end up drowning in responsibility, burdened by pain and obligation. Why did he think I'd been in therapy for fifteen years? Why did he think I'd been treated for depression, including a handful of episodes that were legitimately debilitating? Or maybe he thought that was a normal life.

I had kept my depression from him for years, reasoning that he had enough on his plate with my mom, and letting him know only after my shrink told me I had to. He's your father, she said; you should let him have the opportunity to act like one.

"Do you remember when I told you I'd been depressed and had been taking medication?" I shouted at him. "Do you remember what you said? You said 'Well, I hope you're feeling better now.'"

"I don't remember that," he said.

"I'm not surprised," I said, with a sneer I regret to this day. "I fucking remember it."

You won't be shocked to learn that he reacted with something less than equanimity to all this. You're blaming me, he said. You think I was a lousy father. You think I failed. And you're telling me this the day after we buried your mother? He snorted.

"Your brother turned out all right," he said.

"Yeah, well, congratulations," I said. "But check with him before you take it to the bank."

This went on for a while, bile and vitriol spit back and forth. I don't remember all the words we said, just the fierce resentment at how we'd had to spend the previous forty years that we were now, with nowhere else to direct it, aiming at each other. That morning I was the son, a chip off the old block, of the unbearable man my father had lately been. It was an appalling, hugely distressing couple of hours, and we were both wounded. It ended finally in a truce, part mutual understanding, part exhaustion, part unwillingness to stay angry.

"I think you did the best you could, Dad," I said finally. "And I admired you for everything you did and tried to do. I'm a healthy, functioning adult, Robert is a healthy, functioning adult, and you can take credit for that. I don't blame you for anything. But you missed a lot. You had a lot on your plate, and you missed a lot."

"I guess I understand that," he said.

I think that's pretty close to what I said and what he said. It's a decent summary, anyway. I went on: I can't believe you would think I would be untouched by all this. I grew up in the house, remember. I was a witness. I saw my mother unable to do anything other mothers could do. I saw her walk first with a cane, then with an aluminum walker; then when she couldn't walk at all, we posted wheelchairs upstairs and downstairs and mounted a chair glide on the staircase so she could get from one to the other. I remember when we had a ramp installed in front of the house so the wheelchair could get down the stairs from the porch to the sidewalk. And it wasn't only her mobility; it was her mind that contracted, too, until her connection with the world was tenuous, so tenuous. She asked me once who Michael Jackson was. She spent hours of each day at a table in the kitchenette taking pills, remember? Her pillbox had more pills in it than I've seen in one place before or since. And for years there was a parade of strange women, some of them young and good-looking, from England and Latin America and Maine, living in the tiny guest room, cooking for us, doing the laundry, and making the beds; how weird do you think that was for a kid going through the horniest years of adolescence?

My father was quiet for a while. He had an indignant expression on his face, but after a few moments the indignation drained away and he just looked forlorn.

"Okay," he said. "I get it. I haven't listened. I'm listening now."

* * *

I've never been a father, but maybe here's one reason I've been thinking about all this. A couple of evenings ago, strolling the half dozen or so streets of Chester (where I had stopped for the night in Judy's M X Motel), I spotted a loaded-down bicycle parked outside Spud's Cafe. Inside, I found its owner, Sean McDermott, a younger version of myself (although fitter and better-looking than I ever was), finishing dinner and putting off setting up his tent in the city park by reading a Salman

Rushdie novel. Sean is twenty-two. He graduated as an English major in the spring from the University of Wisconsin, and he was riding from his home in Minneapolis to the West Coast. I never was much of a Rushdie fan, but I did study English at the University of Michigan, another Big Ten school.

He was glad for the company when I sat down with him, and he amused me by saying he couldn't wait to get to the West, as though he weren't already right in the middle of it. He meant mountains and the ocean. He asked me to tell him about Glacier with the hungry optimism of Dorothy putting her faith in Oz.

Sean said he had been averaging seventy-five or eighty miles a day on his trip—remarkable in my opinion, given the wind about which I've spoken at such length. I've been averaging about fifty going more often with its help. He spoke cheerily and thoughtfully about his adventures but seemed a trifle worn and was in a confessional mode: That day the wind had tired him out and he'd taken a ride from a farmer in a pickup the last twenty miles or so into Chester. He sounded as if he were guilty of something, as if he were trying to talk himself out of the feeling that he had cheated. I assured him he hadn't, that safety is paramount on a trip like this and exhaustion can be dangerous. When I offered to let him sleep on the floor of my motel room rather than in the city park, he accepted.

Sean talked for a bit about the rugged time he'd had getting through North Dakota, from Minot to Williston, where the oil and construction boom has made motel rooms and even campsites scarce and has rendered the roads dangerous with truck traffic.

"There were literally rows and rows of trucks," he said. "The traffic was giving me a tailwind. I was pretty scared."

I'd heard versions of this report from others, and I took his warning under serious advisement; I'm actively looking for routes to circumvent that part of North Dakota—and if I can't find an adequate one, I'm prepared to follow my own advice and accept a ride through the trouble spot.

Sean and I said our farewells after breakfast at Spud's the next morning. He said he'd text me when he got to Glacier and told me to take care of my cough.

"I'm not usually such a freeloader," he said. "But it was kind of like running into a parent."

Then we pedaled off in opposite directions, and I was sorry we couldn't travel together.

8

Lost in the West

Saturday, August 20, Wolf Point, Montana

I've been traveling by bicycle for twenty-five years or so, since the mid-1980s when I bought a bike at the suggestion of a doctor. I'd had two operations on my right knee by then, the first in 1977 just as I was finishing an MA in English at Columbia, to clean out cartilage that I'd shredded in a basketball mishap. Unfortunately, arthroscopic techniques were not yet in wide use for this kind of surgery, so my knee was sawed open and during my recovery I wore a hip-to-ankle cast for several weeks.*

Five years later, I had cartilage surgery again after I wrenched the same knee playing softball. This time, the procedure was arthroscopic and I was on my feet the same afternoon, out of the hospital the following day, and walking to work shortly thereafter. The bad news was

---

*A week after the operation I started my first job out of grad school teaching eighth-grade summer school students, one of whom enjoyed imitating my painful gait in front of the class whenever I was out of the room. The kid grew up to be the television journalist Jon Frankel, and I grew up to work for his father, Max Frankel, now the former executive editor of the *New York Times*.

that during the operation the surgeon had discovered, to his surprise, that not only was every bit of my knee cartilage ground into sand, but also that the anterior cruciate ligament was torn. Judging by the state of the tear—the once-frayed ends had congealed, he said—that injury had occurred a few years earlier. In other words, I'd torn it that day on the basketball court in the Columbia gym, and my initial surgeon had missed it completely.

Not terribly eager to have a third, considerably more serious operation to knit the ligament back together, I asked what my options were. He told me to say good-bye to basketball and softball and take up bicycling.

This seemed rather alarming to someone who was about to turn thirty, had played team sports all his life and wasn't aching to give them up prematurely.

Well, the doctor said, among other benefits, bicycling would strengthen the muscles around the knee and increase its stability, giving me a better shot at continuing to play the games I still wanted to play.

Eventually, I listened to him, but it took a while. Living in Manhattan long before the era of bike lanes, I didn't really see the prospect of riding around the city as inviting, and anyway I'd never been a bicycle devotee, even as a kid.

There exists a photo of me—I can't have been older than three—astride a four-wheeled contraption that looks like a bare-bones automobile chassis and grinning as though I'm having a great old time. But growing up I was the last in my neighborhood to seize the alchemy of pedaling and steering that keeps you upright on a bicycle. I was somewhat famous for my failure, in fact, and can recall vividly the summer evening when, already nine years old, I was suddenly blessed with the necessary physical revelation and found myself finally wobbling down Van Buren Avenue on a squat green Huffy. Up and down the block and around two corners, onto Palmer Avenue and then Herrick Avenue, neighbors saw me and cheered. In the chamber of my mind where I've sealed away my most embarrassing memories, the adolescent whine of my then best pal, Bobby Cerone, someone I haven't seen or heard about in forty-five years, still echoes if I let it: "Hey!" he cried when I passed his house that night. "Brucie's riding!"

That I was not a natural cyclist, that I was initially an indifferent and incompetent one, strikes me now as one of the great, serendipitous ironies in my experience.* Obviously, I've been thinking about my life as a narrative lately, and it tickles me that the way things are has evolved from the way things were. I'm titillated by the idea that I'm living some sort of a story, that my earlier cycling self and my current one are intimately related, that one has naturally followed the other in spite of how surprised I am by what has happened, and that like the events in a good novel, the outcome was impossible to predict looking forward but was inevitable looking back.

---

*Another is that after nearly flunking Introduction to Drama my sophomore year in college—I received a D and deserved it—I became a theater reporter and critic for the *New York Times*.

*   *   *

So I didn't take my surgeon's suggestion right away, though I did go out and get a stationary bike and for a couple of years worked up a daily sweat pedaling in the direction of the television set. Eventually I went to work for a magazine that was supposed to celebrate the active lifestyle—you've never heard of it, it didn't last long—and one of the articles we ran was about a new kind of bicycle, known as the city bike, that was designed with wide tires and straight-across handlebars for riding in an urban setting. A cousin of the mountain bike, which was just being developed at the time, it was an antecedent to the so-called hybrids—crosses between road and off-road bikes—that are all over the place now, as well as the bike I'm riding across the country. Figuring it was about time I took my doctor's advice, especially if I could be on the cutting edge of recreation at the same time, I bought one, for about $300, pretty expensive in 1984. It was so unusual-looking in the time and place that I remember often being stopped for a traffic light and being stared at or asked about it, as if I were wearing a fashion by a bold new designer.

Oddly enough, in the end I didn't ride it in the city very much, but for a couple of summers I took it with me to the Hamptons, where I shared a house with several friends—including Jan and her then-husband—and it quickly became my habit to eschew afternoons at the beach and ride twenty or thirty or forty miles, exploring the largely untraveled back roads between Hampton Bays and Montauk. By today's lights the bike was a tank, but it was during that time that the eureka moment occurred: you could actually get somewhere on a bicycle. When you took your bike out for a ride, you didn't necessarily have to turn around at some point and go home; you could just keep going until you ended up someplace else. In 1987, I took my first multiday ride, from Sag Harbor on Long Island to Martha's Vineyard in Massachusetts. (Yes, there were a couple of ferries involved.) And then I began searching for other suitable trips and bought a more suitable bicycle, my first drop-bar road bike.

Discovering I could take it with me on a train, I rode from Savannah, Georgia, to the Outer Banks of North Carolina; from Philadelphia to New York; from Boston to New York; from Montreal to New York; from Bangor, Maine, to Middletown, Connecticut; from Jackson, Mississippi, where my brother got married, to New Orleans; from my apartment in Manhattan across the George Washington Bridge and down the length of New Jersey to Cape May. Great fun, but small-potatoes rides, really. Then in the summer of 1993, the year I turned forty, I decided it was a now-or-never moment and set off across the United States.

The editor of my baseball book said something to me once that I didn't pay much attention to at the time. This was a while ago, when I first had the idea for a cycling semi-memoir and I was trying to convince him it would be worth publishing. I had told him about a couple of my solo rides since the first cross-country trip: from Santa Fe over the mountains to Tucson, where my parents were living, after I'd just had a big blowup with Catherine; to Tucson again, this time from Phoenix, where for some reason I felt it was worth it to schlep my bike on the plane from New York just to have a day's ride before coping with my folks.

My editor said that in the book I'd have to consider why I do this, why long-distance cycling is my outlet of choice.

"Duh," I said.

He ignored me. It sounded to him, he said, as if I ride out of defiance.

What am I defying? I asked him.

You tell me, he said. Time passing? The demands of the women in your life? Whatever guilt you feel about your parents? The constraints of your job?

I wish I could claim defiance as an attribute, but I'm not an especially defiant fellow. Stubborn occasionally, sure. Moody, okay. Brooding, maybe resentful from time to time. But both overall and moment to moment I like things to go smoothly. I've got a conciliatory streak that mitigates against real defiance.

Nonetheless, this afternoon, after I arrived in Wolf Point—a cowboy outpost and the last significant town along U.S. 2 in Montana before the North Dakota line, eighty miles or so from here—I reread what I've written in this journal so far and a thought similar to my editor's seized me: that for me riding a bicycle isn't mere leisure or recreation but a response to things, a proactive answer to events that unfold without my input or comprehension. That isn't quite the same thing as defiance, I know, but I do think that my impulse to ride has its source in disaffection. Traveling by bicycle is, actually, my personal antidote to a good deal of life's irreconcilable vexatiousness. It is, after all, a simple thing to succeed at—not simple in the sense of easy (it's not) but simple in the sense of uncomplicated. However far you go, your achievement is measurable and unequivocal. You make an enormous effort, you worry about all sorts of things, you strain and sweat, you self-examine, self-aggrandize, and self-loathe, you exult, you despair, you exult again and despair again, but at the end of the day, at the end of the journey, you've arrived at a destination or you haven't. What a relief from life's more common challenges—family, work, love—and their irreducible ambiguities. There's an hour or so at the end of each day, when I swing my leg out of the saddle in front of a motel, check in, peel off my gear, collapse naked on the bed, and begin envisioning pleasant things—a shower, clean clothes, a beer, dinner, a ball game on TV, an uninterrupted, rejuvenating sleep—during which I feel indisputably worthy as a human being, someone who has spent the day profitably and deserves happiness. (Clearly, Mr. Scorpion would take issue with this, but fuck him.)

Any minute I'm expecting the arrival of another *Times* photographer, who is supposed to accompany me—in his car—for the next couple of days. It says something about where I am on the map that he was the closest guy the photo editor could find and he's driving ten hours to get here.

Fearful of the highway mayhem and the shortage of potential shelter amid the North Dakota oil fields that other cyclists have been bruiting about, I've decided to turn south here. The next town in that direction, a speck of civilization called Circle, is fifty miles away, and according to my web search it has one motel. I just called the number there and got a recording, so I phoned the photographer in his car and suggested he stop on the way and reserve a couple of rooms for us for tomorrow night. After that, in a day or two, I should at last be across the state line, and though I'm hopeful of circumventing the oil chaos, it looks as though I'll have to ride a bit on the interstate or else go considerably farther out of my way. Still, any of that seems preferable to going through Williston.

My mood has improved since Havre. I've made good progress, more than two hundred miles in the past three days, and the landscape, though still vast and isolating, has grown increasingly, subtly warmer. The fields and ranchlands have seemed more fertile, with deeper colors, and the light is starting to change, gradually hinting at autumn. Yesterday I left Malta in the early morning, and the sun, risen but mostly hidden behind dark, fast-moving clouds, suddenly pierced through them as though with an awl and sent a cone of rays down on the prairie in the distance. In the movies, it would have been the herald of a spaceship landing.

Another uplifting event: I've sighted—had an inkling of, anyway—a colleague in the neighborhood, a fellow writer. Just west of Malta on the south side of U.S. 2, the state has carved out a historical site commemorating a region where, evidently, the west was once especially wild. Early in the twentieth century, Butch Cassidy and the Sundance Kid operated around there. At any rate, at an otherwise unextraordinary roadside location, a small parking area looks out over the prairie and a wooden plaque has been erected marking the spot. It reads unlike any official prose I've ever seen, and I can only assume that a former MFA student, unable (thankfully) to land a teaching job, had been hired by the state department of public works. "Early Day Outlaws" is the title, and the inscription begins like this:

The old West produced some tolerably lurid gunslingers.

Their hole card was a single-action frontier model .45 Colt, and their long suit was fanning it a split second quicker than similarly inclined gents. This talent sometimes postponed their obsequies quite a while, providing they weren't pushed into taking up rope spinning from the loop end of a lariat by a wearied public. Through choice or force of circumstances these parties sometimes threw in with the "wild bunch"—rough-riding, shooting hombres, prone to disregard the customary respect accorded other people's cattle brands.

I've been trying to imagine the conversation between what must have been the very young person who wrote this and (in my mind) the veteran state employee who approved it.

"'Tolerably lurid'?"

"Yes, sir. It's tongue-in-cheek language, you know, mimicking the idiom of the time and place."

"I reckon. What's it supposed to mean?"

"Well, it means very colorful."

"Why didn't you say that, then?"

"I think people might get a kick out of this, sir."

"You think so?"

"Yes, sir. Most of these signs are written pretty uncreatively. No imagi-nation."

"Yeah, well, I don't disagree. Why do you think that is?"

"I don't know, sir. Seems like a wasted opportunity."

"Opportunity for what?"

"A little flair, sir, and maybe to get people to think about language."

"I hope they're carrying dictionaries in the glove compartment. What the hell are obsequies?"

"Funerals, sir."

"Oh, jeez."

This has been as helpful as a tailwind. I've been amusing myself with it for two days now.

Sunday, August 21, Circle, Montana

Rich Addicks, the photographer sent to join me on the road for a couple of days, showed me a picture he took a few hours ago. I'm in it, riding away from the camera, wearing the iridescent vest that keeps me visible to drivers, but not much more than a yellow dot on a completely empty stretch of highway. The ribbon of road, cutting through a beautifully grassy swath of prairie, is maybe a mile long in the picture, which was taken from the top of a hill and looks way out in the distance toward the top of another hill, placing me in the valley between them. It's a striking image of solitude.

Photo by Rich Addicks

Of course, I've had an occasional bit of company on this trip, and when I get past the Mississippi River and closer to places where I actually know people, I'm likely to have more. But even when you're with someone else—a photographer in a car, say—when you're working to put a stretch of road behind you, especially on a day like today when the heat, the hills, and the headwinds are a malign cohort, you're on your own. The lungs that are heaving are yours alone, the legs that are pumping yours, and the will that threatens to give out and give up is something only you can fortify.

Today was brutal, in other words, a challenge not just toward the end of the ride after I'd run out of steam but almost from the beginning. I'd gotten used to U.S. 2, skimming over the oceanic plain of the Hi-Line, but State Route 13 south from Wolf Point is a sine curve, a tormentingly repetitive series of camel humps that goes on for more than fifty miles. It was a wind-is-my-enemy day, too, a steady, push-in-the-face breeze blowing forcefully enough from the south that I had to push the pedals on the downhills; it was almost a relief to reach the bottom, start to ascend, and ride behind the shield of an uphill slope. There were no services at all, just fields and ranchland, and not even a place to sit on the side of the highway—not a bench, a bus stop, an abandoned car, or a flat rock. My ass was killing me; halfway to Circle I vowed, at last, to replace my saddle at the next opportunity. And it was ninety degrees by 10:00 a.m.

Having Rich along, cruising up and down Route 13 and stopping at odd points to achieve different vantages for his pictures, added a strange element to the ride. Overall through Montana traffic has been light—his passing me a dozen times going one way or another probably doubled the flow today—and with the exception of the occasional farmer repairing a fence or hewing wheat in a combine, actual people on the road have been few. Periodically, lazily grazing horses have been noting my progress, but mostly my company has been entomological. The region had a very wet spring, and insects are everywhere. For the last three hundred miles, grasshoppers have been leaping from the roadside and bouncing off my ankles, pinging off my spokes. Blackflies (I think they're blackflies) and mosquitoes have lain in wait for me to stop for a swig of Gatorade. Moths and butterflies flutter in the weeds. The sound of millions of what?—crickets?—has been following me everywhere, a lighthearted white noise that sounds almost like jingling bells.

I'm stronger than I was back in Oregon, but even so this was the toughest riding day of the trip, which is now slightly more than a month old and slightly less than fifteen hundred miles long; the last

142 ○ *LIFE IS A WHEEL*

few miles today the road flattened out and the terrain grew more forbidding, dry and rocky, a suggestion of the region of badlands that I'll be riding through soon. I could see the town of Circle in the distance and watched it crawl toward me, as if it, too, were facing a headwind. Slow motion. Slower. Arrrrgh.

I took my displeasure out on Rich, I'm afraid. I probably should have welcomed the company; I think that's what he expected. But as we checked in at the Circle motel I was pissy enough that he left me alone for a couple of hours to go off and photograph the town on his own.

The good news is that I'm getting in shape; it's a day's ride I doubt I'd have finished four weeks ago.

This chunk of eastern Montana is as foreign a puzzle piece of the American jigsaw as a New Yorker can imagine. Let's put aside the fact of the eerie emptiness; I've been riding through vacant landscapes for almost two weeks now but I haven't felt quite this odd. And even in this fragmented and hostile political season, let's put aside politics; Montana is clearly a red state and New York City is the brightest blue, but I haven't made or heard a single impromptu comment about the president or the Republican candidates prepping for next year's primaries. For all I know, I've been flamed online by every person I've met out here, but face-to-face I've met with nothing as much as inquisitiveness ("You're doing what?") and kindness. In truth when you're traveling like this, the subject of conversation with local people has to do with food and shelter and directions and weather and safety, and in those circumstances, as the saying goes, we're all Americans.

Still, specific flavors in the culture hereabouts make a Greenwich Village homeboy feel like a space alien, a stranger in a strange land, a sensation at once spooky and titillating. Part of this is simply a New Yorker's provincialism, an astonishment at being so isolated and a sense of exposure and vulnerability to forces of nature like the glaring sun and the wind. Funny, but I never feel that walking through Washington Square Park.

Last night Rich and I ate a dreadful meal at a diner in Wolf Point—a reasonable traveler's axiom is, The more remote the town, the worse the restaurant food—and then we drove twenty miles down U.S. 2 to Poplar, a poor community on the Fort Peck Indian Reservation, home to Assiniboine and Sioux tribes. I've been to reservations before, but on this night a powwow was taking place. The weekend-long event, a celebration of tradition that amounted to a rather wild yet rather wholesome dance party—no drugs or alcohol permitted—attracted hundreds of people, many from hours away. The surrounding grounds had become a temporary tent city.

The dances were propulsive and ritualistic. The dancers, most clad in startlingly colorful costumes featuring beaded leather and gorgeously feathered headdresses, many wearing bells around their ankles, ranged from preschoolers to tribal elders. They were accompanied by several men seated around a single drum, furiously beating out a rhythm and singing, in the Cree language, a mesmerizing, warblelike call to the dance.

I'd never seen—or heard—anything like it. Throughout the evening I had to ask what everything meant. Even though people were genial and happy to explain their cultural idiom to a newcomer, I felt foolish and naïve, embarrassed at being so uninformed in my own country.

Now I'm here in Circle, which is even more remote and seems even further removed from my city-centric idea of contemporary life. What's here? A rickety motel at a crossroads, a crummy diner, a ramshackle downtown that was deserted on a Sunday except for a convenience store at a gas station, a dozen streets with compact but surprisingly nice-looking houses and well-tended yards, and a sturdy school with tidy grounds.

The leading landmark is a life-sized, realistic if friendly-looking sculpture of a brontosaurus. I say life-sized—this one's about ten feet high and maybe twenty-five from nose to tail—but I'm actually not so sure how big brontosauruses actually were. It stands watch over a little picnic area that is next door to my motel and peers out in the direction of the highway and beyond it to the wide prairie.

This part of the country is a paleontological wonderland, it turns out; carcasses, skulls, bones, and fossil remains of prehistoric creatures—triceratops, stegosaurus, and many of their cousins—have been unearthed all over the region. The first T. rex ever discovered (in 1902) was found near Jordan, about an hour (by car) west of here—and many small towns boast museums (though Circle doesn't). Something called the Dinosaur Trail, a network of fourteen Montana museums, parks, and other attractions with exhibits of these things, was created as a draw for tourists in 2005. Riding a bicycle through here suddenly feels especially anachronistic.

Speaking of dinosaurs, I'm a print reporter, which is why one last thing about Circle drew my attention. The local paper, *The Circle Banner*, has an office downtown. The sign over the door reads: TODAY'S NEWS—NEXT THURSDAY. This is evidently the place where journalists go to relax.

Wednesday, August 24, Medora, North Dakota

You can't make a trip like this without taking excited note of markers. When you cross a state line, enter a new time zone, register a number on your odometer ending in 00—or better, 000—the impulse to celebrate, or at least to self-congratulate, is powerful. So yesterday when I finally passed into North Dakota from Montana, after fifteen days and seven hundred plus miles in the same bloody state, I felt as though I'd conquered the West. The Central Time zone is now within a couple days' ride, I've gone beyond fifteen hundred miles on my odometer, and on the map I can see a solid third—more than a third—of the nation behind me. Google Maps tells me I'm within eighteen hundred miles of my apartment. Almost home. Ha!

Still, the West, as opposed to the Midwest (to which I'd consigned the whole of North Dakota in my mind), isn't quite through with me. The very sign welcoming travelers from Montana tried to tell me so, if a little hazily. NORTH DAKOTA, it reads. WELCOME TO THE WEST REGION.

I assume this means that the western part of North Dakota leans more toward Montana, topography-wise and culture-wise, than toward Minnesota, about three hundred and fifty miles east of here. I'm presently in Medora, my motel about a quarter mile from the entrance to Theodore Roosevelt National Park. Today was supposed to be a rest day, a day for sleeping and writing, but at the keyboard this morning I was stuck, the narrative path east out of Montana entirely murky. Nothing drives me out of the house and onto a bicycle seat faster than writer's block.

So, taking a busman's holiday, I rode the park's loop road, a thirty-four-mile excursion through hilly badlands, a river valley dotted with cottonwoods and grassy fields pocked with the mounds of prairie dogs, dozens of which were cheeping and racing around like cartoon characters. For some reason, I found the DO NOT FEED THE PRAIRIE DOGS signs amusing.

You climb to get into the park, and the first hills yield an eagle's-eye view of I-94, the road I'd ridden to get here, and the proximity of civilization to wilderness is striking. (Cycling on interstate highways in this part of the country is, if not entirely desirable, legal and reasonably safe, with sparse traffic and wide shoulders.) As I rode the loop, the sense of a remote West deepened. The scenery—dramatic rock formations and valleys between them—would have suited a John Ford film; you could almost see cavalrymen lining up on a distant butte for a battle, or Indian warriors gathering before swooping down on a wagon train.

I crested a hill to a high meadow, where a herd of wild horses huddled together, haloed by a bright, early-morning sun, and shortly afterward I rounded a bend and startled a bison grazing in the shadow of a boulder. He seemed to lose his footing momentarily as he acknowledged my tires hissing by on the road surface, then turned and glared at me before going back to his meal. I watched him from a respectful distance for a bit, but he paid me no mind. Did he yawn? I think he yawned. Eventually he lumbered out onto the pavement and ambled downhill and out of sight, taking up road space like a vehicle with an oversize load. Heavy traffic.

The bison wasn't the only Western representative I've come across serendipitously. Yesterday, on the service road along I-94 on my way east out of Glendive, Montana, I stopped to ask directions from a man out for his morning run. I was hoping he could tell me whether the road continued or if I'd have to retreat and go back to the highway entrance and ride the shoulder. He didn't know. Wasn't from there. He was just staying with some friends nearby. This was a part of town where some expensive homes had been built in the woods.

He turned out to be Senator Max Baucus. I'm not kidding. I wouldn't have recognized him but he introduced himself.

"Max Baucus," he said, extending a hand.

"The congressman?" I said.

"The senator," he said. I apologized. He thought it was funny, too, that he'd run into me, a *New York Times* reporter, in that spot under these circumstances. He asked after a couple of my colleagues that he knew from Washington.

When I asked what brought him to this far corner of his state, he said he got to Glendive, which has about five thousand people in it and is a pretty big city by Montana's standards, a few times a year to see constituents and supporters, by which I assume he meant campaign contributors.

A note on Glendive. It's a genuine hub for the ranchers and farmers in eastern Montana, the kind of place with a compact, nineteenth-century-looking downtown with two- and three-story office buildings and a whole other, much more contemporary commercial life—motels and restaurants and outlet stores and gas stations and such—out by the interstate interchange. Just beyond the town limits is Makoshika State Park, a series of gorgeously stratified hills, a kind of badlands environment that has been a font of dinosaur fossils and that looks like a science-fiction movie set—the original *Planet of the Apes*, maybe. The town has two museums—alas, both closed on Mondays, the day I arrived from Circle at about noon, though I did walk through the

Makoshika visitor center, which has a small but instructive display of fossils, including the impressive and angry-looking skull of a triceratops, a three-horned beast from something like sixty-five million years ago.

The name Makoshika, by the way, is a variation on a Lakota phrase that means "Land of Bad Spirits" (i.e., Badlands). The park itself is strange and beautiful, with vistas that let you look out over the hills, imagine prehistory, and still see the town. In fact, the entrance to the park is just beyond a Glendive neighborhood; you drive out of a school zone and into the Cretaceous period.

Anyway, Senator Baucus and I talked a bit about the president's new health-care law, and I said I worried that congressional Republicans could muster the votes to repeal it; he said he didn't think so, though he was worried about the challenges to its constitutionality that seem headed for the Supreme Court.* He wished me luck and said if he were me he'd continue down the service road, and if it came to an end, I could always toss my bike and my gear over the separator fence and get on the highway that way (which is exactly what I ended up doing).

I'd done that before, I told him.

"It's probably against the law," he said, smiling as we shook hands.

One more word about markers. When I entered North Dakota yesterday it was for the first time, and in so doing I accomplished a creditable feat: I've now set foot in every state in the union. *Creditable* is a good word for that, right? It isn't quite *remarkable*, and it's not special enough to be *singular*; *amazing* is way overstating it. *Estimable* isn't bad, but *creditable* is better, more modest, a deserved but unostentatious pat on my own back, self-satisfied without being smug.

---

*The Supreme Court upheld the health-care law, formally known as the Patient Protection and Affordable Care Act and less formally as Obamacare, by a 5–4 vote in June 2012. Several months later, Senator Baucus announced he would not seek reelection in 2014. In early 2014, he was nominated by President Obama to be the American ambassador to China.

*   *   *

At the WELCOME TO NORTH DAKOTA sign on I-94, I stopped for a minute and did a little celebratory dance. Then I peered up the road toward the horizon and the Midwest. Where does the Midwest begin, after all? Minnesota? Wisconsin? Or on the east side of Bismarck? Wherever, it is undoubtedly in my future—my near future, I hope. I'm looking forward to cycling through a part of the country where the dots on the road map are a little closer together.

But the long distances of the West, these huge states, especially gigantic Montana, with its perpetual wind and the extra-large dimensions of its hills, valleys, and wildlife, have toughened me up. I've been feeling different lately. The moment when the alarm goes off in the morning and I realize the necessity of abandoning the warmth and safety of a motel room for the uncertainty and risk of a day on the road is no longer accompanied by a clutch of anxiety.

This time through the West, I've realized some things about who I am now as a cyclist. On my last trip I slept later, stayed longer in the saddle, and vacuumed up great distances each day, between seventy and eighty miles on an average. It took me a while to readjust my appetite this time to feel satisfied that fifty or fifty-five miles is a good day's work.

I've learned to get on the road at daybreak and to cover my miles early so when the wind and the temperature rise, which they seem to do like clockwork at noon, most of my work will be done. I've discovered the most efficient way of fueling my body is to eat a substantial meal early in the evening, at five or six—I've become a blue-plate-special guy!—and to subsist on my dinner calories and a small early-morning snack (cereal, maybe, or a muffin) for the first ten or fifteen miles of the day, and then stop for a big breakfast.

My hill climbing, honed in the Palouse and in the Rockies, is much improved. It's a mental thing as much as a physical one. My legs still hurt on a tough climb, but I'm inured enough to the sensation that I can keep pedaling.

Most important, I've grown hugely more confident on my bicycle—more skillful in steering around road obstacles and on narrow shoulders; more in control of the back end of the bike, loaded down as it is with my saddlebags; more adept at shifting gears to maximize pedaling efficiency on flat roads and to maintain momentum going up and down hills.

Altogether it means that I've at last begun to believe I'm going to finish the journey. I've traveled far enough to be able not just to look up the road and see the Midwest on the approaching horizon but to envision the day that I'll cross the George Washington Bridge.

The story of the trip is beginning to write itself, in other words, with incidents accruing into chapters, and my pedal-pushing feet, like fingers on a keyboard, recording experience as it hurtles by. The cyclist-as-novelist thing keeps coming up in my head. For the longest time you can't see very far in front of you, but you keep pedaling blindly, just as you go on composing sentences on faith. Eventually, you can make out the end, or imagine it, but until then you're just a wandering New Yorker, lost in the West.

9

◦◦◦

Nowhere Is Nowhere

Saturday, August 27, Bismarck, North Dakota

Google Maps tells me I'm maybe fifteen hundred miles from Pittsburgh, which means if I don't wander in too many loop-de-loops and nothing too dreadful happens, I can get there by October 6, which is the day before Jan will be in New Orleans for the wedding of one of her oldest friends' sons. Here's the current plan: I'll fly from Pittsburgh to New Orleans to meet her, and then we'll return to Pittsburgh together and she'll ride with me for a few days. To where we don't know. We also haven't quite figured out yet what to do about getting her a bicycle in Pittsburgh; how, from wherever we end up, she's going to get to an airport for a flight back to Paris, or how I'm going to get appropriate wedding clothes to New Orleans.

Meanwhile, here I am for the very first time in North Dakota, where people are relatively scarce but all seem happy to see me. The population is under seven hundred thousand—only Vermont and Wyoming have fewer residents, though I wasn't surprised to learn that though Montana has more people it's actually less crowded—and it has felt to me not only as if everyone knows everyone else but that they've made it their collective business to see that I have a good experience here.

For about two hundred miles, from my encounter with Max Baucus outside of Glendive, Montana, through Bismarck, halfway through the state, I've been on and off I-94, riding when I can along service roads and an old highway that served as the main thoroughfare before the interstate was built and now runs parallel to it, largely unused and unattended to, like some unkempt family member being kept away from the neighbors in the attic. The bicycling has often been rewarding; you go for miles through golden ranchland in the company only of handsome black steers grazing in meadows or cooling off in shallow ponds. However, there are stretches where the pavement goes to gravel and dust or disappears altogether, and the highway has been my only choice—that is, if I want to keep pressing east. While it's legal to ride on the interstate, it's not especially enjoyable, and I've considered heading south to get away from it. But the map tells me that available roads would consign me to a zigzag path through small towns unlikely to afford places to stay, and I'm letting that influence me.

I find it an interesting, slightly troubling dilemma, philosophical almost, and part of me is disappointed that I've opted for straight-ahead progress rather than a more exploratory meander through a region in which I'm a virgin. I made the opposite sort of choice once in Vietnam, venturing off alone into the jungle, and I had the most exciting, perturbing, challenging, threatening, and finally rewarding adventure of my life.

This isn't the same thing, I know; the risk–reward ratio is of a whole other order of magnitude. They speak English in North Dakota, after all, they don't arrest bicyclists for bicycling, and there would be little likelihood of my being stranded without water on an unrideable path through the mountains. Still, something—some need, some momentary weakness, or perhaps some subconscious insight—is dictating my pace here, making me choose briskness ahead of uncertainty. Perhaps it's just that my age is showing, but once again I find myself thinking of the purpose of the journey—the purpose of any journey, maybe, literary included—and I'm struck by the conflicting needs of a traveler: to soak up as much as you can and eventually to get where you're going.

In North Dakota, I got off I-94 as soon as I could, exit 1, at a town called Beach at the state visitor's information bureau. (How does such a landlocked place get such a name? Turns out it was named for an army officer who led a surveying expedition through the region in the late nineteenth century.) The attendant, a woman named Jan (sigh), not only set me onto the parallel road I've been using—old Highway 10—but also suggested a local barbecue place for lunch and offered me cough drops. I've been hacking a bit, though not as badly as a week ago.

Medora and Theodore Roosevelt Park were about twenty-five miles away, and I asked if there were any services on Route 10 between Beach and the park. She said there was just one, a tiny little burg about seven miles down the road called Sentinel Butte. The gas station there is a hangout, she said, where people stop in and shoot the breeze.

"It'll be a good stop for you," she said.

And so it was. A lot of dot-on-the-map towns I've ridden through are pretty desolate and rundown, but Sentinel Butte is an attractive little place that you come upon suddenly after passing through acres and acres of sun-bleached pastures and wheat fields. The midsummer lawns are green and the homes are neatly kept and the whole of it—you can take it in with one sweep of the eyes—gives off an unlikely whiff of prosperity. The eponymous butte is off on the southern horizon.

The gas station, small and weather-beaten, with a couple of pumps and a soda machine under a peaked roof out front and a sign over the door declaring it to be a Greyhound bus stop, sits smack in the center of town. It *is* the center of town, actually. As it turned out, no one was hanging out there when I stopped in—except the owner, Rick Olson, who is also the mayor. We sat at a card table inside, enjoying the air-conditioning on a hot day. A voluble fellow (maybe you'd be, too, if you lived there) with pink cheeks and a not-quite-walrus mustache who looked to be in his late forties or early fifties, he explained that the town was flush even though its total collected property taxes amounted to less than $2,000 a year—"Not even enough to pay the electric bill," he said—because it sells water to the oil companies that are exploring much of western North Dakota these days. Right on cue, two huge tankers rolled past the station, full, on their way out of town.

Mr. Olson had grown up in Sentinel Butte. He remembered when it was a bigger town—more than two hundred inhabitants back in the 1960s, he said—and he was hoping it would grow to be that size again. The population is fifty-five, at last count, down from ninety-four in 2000.

"That's the official census," he said. "We may have a few more now."

Later that day, I met Jennifer and Loren Morlock, the owners of Dakota Cyclery in Medora. I stopped in there to solicit some route advice, to shop, at last, for a new saddle, and to have my chain replaced—it had slipped off a couple of times the previous week and I suspected, correctly, it had stretched a bit—and while I was there I asked them to rotate my tires. With the weight of my saddlebags on the back end of the bike, the tread on the rear one was wearing down. I thought about buying a new set. However, the store didn't carry the Schwalbes I'm riding on. I didn't want to switch, and they didn't blame me: I've ridden more than sixteen hundred miles without a flat.

I asked the Morlocks if they had a noseless saddle. They didn't, but they suggested I try one of their test models—that is, a new design given to them by one of their suppliers but not yet for sale, a status so denoted by a pattern of garish yellow stripes on it. It wasn't hugely different from my old one—a hair narrower and with a slightly shorter nose than the one that has had my ass and a variety of other nether parts in more or less permanent distress—but I took it out for a spin around town and noticed the difference immediately, just one more reminder of the precise physics of bike riding. There are so many measurements within your relationship to a bike whose alterations affect your ride that it always seems possible to increase your comfort or efficiency, if not both. Anyway, it didn't ease the soreness on my sit bones—that's going to be around for a while—but the pressure on my perineum was appreciably eased, and I no longer felt a tiny stab of pain in a region I can accurately refer to as "down there" with each pedal thrust. Plus, the yellow stripes are so incongruous they're cool.

"It's a test saddle so we'll give it to you for half price," Jennifer said. "Just let us know how you like it."

"Sold," I said.

The Morlocks told me they used to own a bike shop in Bismarck, but they became tired of what Jennifer called the big city. They're both former bike racers, both native North Dakotans. Jennifer owns the distinction of having once been pictured on the front flap of the official North Dakota state map. In Medora, a perky tourist town that exists to serve the park, there is almost no place to live, she said, "so we moved to the suburbs."

That would be Sentinel Butte.

I told her I'd been there and met Rick Olson.

"You talked to Rick?" she said.

"At some length," I said.

"That would be Rick," she said.

The next morning I climbed for a solid two miles out of Medora and headed east on I-94. The sun was just getting above the hills—the same ones I'd ridden the day before in Roosevelt Park—and if an interstate highway can be said to be beautiful, this one, in the early light and quiet, was. It was fifteen miles or so before I could exit—an uneventful stretch, happily—and then another fifteen or twenty on the lumpy pavement of Highway 10 to Dickinson. One notable sight: a field of sunflowers, acres of them, a bright yellow smear as far as I could see across the table-flat landscape, spreading out from the road to the southern horizon, their faces knit together and waving lightly in the breeze like a gigantic silk scarf.

It was dazzling, awe-inspiring, and as I stood there I found myself imagining the work it had taken, weeks or months ago, to seed a blank brown field, and I wondered if, as he did the planting, the farmer had in his mind's eye what he was engaged in creating, the lovely expanse I was looking at—the farmer as artist.

Of course, it had never before crossed my mind that sunflowers might be a crop. I mean, aside from the ballplayers who chew the seeds and spit the shells out on the dugout floor, where's the demand? Turns out most of the seeds are crushed for oil. Only a small portion are harvested for snacks; they're also used for bird feed. This is information that perhaps no New Yorker carries around but every North Dakotan does. No wonder: North Dakota has been the leading sunflower-producing state in the nation at least since statistics started being kept in 1977.* I looked it up.

The next day—this morning, actually—I rode past two other sunflower fields, equally vast, and I stopped to marvel at them each time. It occurs to me now that I've seen more sunflowers in the past thirty-six hours than I saw in the previous fifty-seven years—tens of thousands of them, maybe a million—and more than I'm likely to see again.

This is what this trip is for. Right?

Dickinson is a small city, and it was bustling when I passed through, with cars streaming on and off the interstate, long lines at traffic lights, and pickup trucks loaded with building supplies parading along the

---

* Actually, in 2011, more rain than usual (not while I was there, happily) caused a drastic tumble in sunflower production in the state, and North Dakota's annual production dipped slightly below South Dakota's for the first time.

main drag. After a solitary morning on a country road, I felt like an ant returning to the anthill.

It was about noon, and it was hot, and I stopped at a Hardee's for a hamburger and a tureen or two of lemonade. I'm pretty noticeable in a place like that, wearing bike shorts and bike shoes, sweating through my shirt and sitting among working people taking their lunch hour. I took a table in the window so I could keep an eye on my bicycle, and I ended up in conversation with three genial young guys from Bismarck who work for an aluminum siding company. I asked them about the sunflowers, and they laughed.

"Where are you from?" one of them asked, meaning, "Where the hell?"

They were curious about the trip and the bike and what I was carrying with me—and were astonished that the newspaper was sponsoring the trip, that this was my job for the summer. I've had a number of conversations like this, on the nice-work-if-you-can-get-it theme.

Then they asked where I was staying that night, knowing that because of the oil exploration motel rooms are notoriously hard to come by in western North Dakota. They'd heard, they said, there weren't any rooms even in Dickinson, where a lot of construction was going on and workers from around the state were being accommodated. I told them that I hadn't been able to find a vacancy in the hundred miles or so between Dickinson and Bismarck; I'd called ahead to all of the listed motels. All three of them. Finally, though, a clerk in the last one I called suggested I phone the Assumption Abbey in Richardton: "I think the monks there take in strays," he said, and it was true. I spoke to one of them, Brother Odo, and he said yes, there'd be a bed for me when I arrived.

One of the young men—I never did get their names—brightened. He said he'd been there many times, that I'd be impressed by the abbey and the church, St. Mary's, that houses it.

He was right. More than a hundred years old, with dual towers soaring above Richardton, an isolated prairie town of five hundred, it's an astonishing structure to come across. It was a scalding afternoon, the sunlight white. I'd ridden the twenty-five miles from Dickinson slowly, and, desperate at one point for shade, had lain down the bike in the front yard of a lonely farmhouse and napped briefly under a tree so isolated it seemed lost. The flats of North Dakota, unlike those in Montana, are really, genuinely flat, a vast floor, and as I approached Richardton I could see the town huddling on the prairie a long ways away, the brick spires of the church beckoning like the beam of a lighthouse.

The monks (they're Benedictines) took me in, gave me a simple, pleasant room, fed me, and invited me to Vespers. Brother Odo, an amiable, earnest man in his seventies, was my host, and as we walked the grounds together he told me the remarkable fact that he had grown up in Richardton.

"One day when I was twenty, I walked down the street to the monastery and I've been here ever since," he said.

He was surprised when I said I worked for the *New York Times*; as it happened, the paper had sent a reporter and photographer to Richardton just a couple of weeks earlier. During my ride, I haven't exactly been keeping up with the news and my newspaper the way I normally do, but my colleague Erik Eckholm had written an article about the cattle ranch that the abbey has run for more than fifty years and is now in the midst of closing down.

"A cattle ranch?" I said. "You're kidding."

Brother Odo took me out back to look out over the ranchland. Rather startlingly, the flat plateau I'd ridden in on came to an abrupt end and we had a fine vantage point to appreciate the nineteen hundred rambling acres of the ranch. We walked downhill and around a corral where the air was rich with fecund smells and cows were bellowing. Benedictines and bovines: just another summer evening in Richardton, North Dakota.

Afterward, we shared dinner with Brother Placid, the last of the monastery's cowboy monks. He had worked the ranch for half a century, he said, but at seventy-six could no longer contend with the rigors of the job and there was no one to take his place. The abbey houses twenty-eight monks right now, but younger monks haven't exactly been flocking here—the last to enter the Assumption monastery came in 2002, and nine members of the order have died since then. The ones that do live here aren't all that interested in ranching, Brother Placid said. He put it more quotably to Erik: "They're not cattlemen," he said. "They're more interested in the intellectual stuff."

That wasn't the only surprise of my visit. Richardton, like Sentinel Butte, is the sort of place that a New Yorker like me would describe as the middle of nowhere, and even the residents might agree, as Brother Odo did. But if there's one thing I continue to learn on this trip across America, it's that nowhere is nowhere. Just before dinner, the switchboard took a phone message for me and passed it to Brother Odo. A television reporter for an NBC affiliate in Bismarck had gotten a tip that I was staying at the abbey, and she wanted to know if she could meet me the next day for an interview.

I phoned her back. We arranged to meet the next afternoon at a location on the outskirts of Mandan, which is just to the west of Bismarck and across the Missouri River, sort of a twin city. When I got there, it was the end of a long day for me, seventy-five miles in the heat—I left at dawn, witnessing a spectacular prairie sunrise—and as I approached our meeting place on a suburban two-lane thoroughfare with middling traffic but an accommodating shoulder, I hit an unexpected obstacle. I had ignored the signs declaring that all traffic had to exit—generally directives like that don't include bicycles, or at least I choose to think they don't—but presently I was entirely by myself, and after a mile or so the road came to an abrupt end in a construction site.

I had to dismount, an achy, unpleasant thing to do when you're not at the end of a ride but merely near the end. My knees felt stiff, and with my feet on solid ground my ankles felt wobbly. In any case, there was no obvious place for me to go. Directly in front of me, fifty yards of pavement was being replaced, and at the moment there simply was none, just a smoothed-out dirt underlay packed into the shape of a two-lane highway. Workers were smoothing a plastic sheet on top of it in preparation for a layer of steaming asphalt. I couldn't walk across the plastic, and the side of the planned road dropped off three or four feet before leveling out onto a dirt lot where several construction vehicles were parked.

Still, if I could help it, I wasn't about to turn around and loop into Mandan, adding miles of pedaling for my already weary legs. Besides, I could see a TV truck parked a few hundred yards beyond the roadblock and my reporter date waiting for me.

I shouldered my bike, saddlebags and all, and edged down the precipitous roadside onto the dirt lot. Happily, I didn't collapse; my knees didn't buckle, my ankles didn't fold. From a hundred yards away, a guy in a white T-shirt and a yellow hard hat—a foreman of some sort, I think, and maybe the only uncongenial person in all of North Dakota—was waving his hands above his head, warning me not to keep going, but I did anyway and started walking across the site. He caught up with me just as I arrived at the far end and said he would have me arrested.

In the ensuing, brief dispute he failed to follow up on his threat, but merely wagged his finger at me (really!) and said he expected not to see me there again. I was happy to promise him that.

When I reached the reporter, a pleasant if slightly harried young woman named Retha Colclasure who had driven frantically from another story to meet me in time, she was setting up a camera on the side of the road, her own camerawoman, and we joked that if I'd been carted away in a police van she'd have had a better story. We did a short interview.*

I was flattered, of course, but also amazed: How did she know about me? And how did she know where to find me last night?

It was the guys from Hardee's. After lunch, they had called the station.

---

*The interview was broadcast on KFYR-TV on September 1, 2011.

Thursday, September 1, Hillsboro, North Dakota

A word or two about perseverance, which is an essential—maybe *the* essential—carry-on for a cross-country cyclist. If I didn't have it, it would be worth trading my rain gear for it, and I say this having ridden much of the past two days in the rain. The secret truth is that just about anyone can make a trip like this—you don't have to be in great shape or own a top-flight bike—as long as you're willing to keep pedaling. If you can't muster the desire to keep your legs going day after day, your physical condition won't matter, and whatever you pack in your saddlebags won't, either.

It seems to me that everyone climbs on a bicycle with the same idea: a cruise in temperate weather, pleasure masquerading as exercise. That's certainly what I have in mind each morning when I load up my bike and take off for yet another strange motel fifty or sixty miles down the road. There is always, of course, something waiting for me mere moments into the day's ride to disabuse me of that vision. Maybe it's fog, as it was yesterday, so that even though the two-lane backcountry highway doesn't carry much traffic, I was worried about visibility, especially because the shoulder was narrow. At one point I slowed for a rest and hit a small oil slick; my rear wheel slid out to the right and I tumbled onto the roadbed. It was empty and quiet out there, fortunately, and I merely bruised a knee and few knuckles.

Or maybe the humidity is high and the wind has a chill in it—also yesterday, so that each time I stopped to rest, I froze.

Or maybe it's rain; it's raining now, in the morning, which is why I'm writing instead of riding. It's sixty miles to my next stop—Minnesota ho!—and the wind is strong from the west. The weather report is for clearing at noon, and I'm ready to roll as soon as it does. You have to ride in the rain on a trip like this, but if you can avoid it, you do.

Two mornings ago, as I rode not quite fifty miles from Carrington to Cooperstown, on straight-as-a-string, flat-as-a-pancake State Highway 200, the fog condensed into a steady shower, and I had my first drenching since Day 2 of the trip. At the Coachman Inn in Coopers-town, a highfalutin name for a behind-the-local-bar motel, I spent the afternoon wringing out various items of clothing, stuffing my cycle shoes with newspaper, watching *Seinfeld* reruns, and thinking about my curious experience in North Dakota, which I'm on the verge of leaving behind.

The state has given me a lesson in perseverance. I've had beautiful rides daily, but with one irksome problem after another. Okay, it hasn't been so terrible, and I'm not complaining so much as remarking on what life is like on a bicycle (yes, yes, and everywhere else).

To wit: four days ago, I was finally able to leave I-94 behind for good—and I hope that's it for the interstate highway system for the rest of the journey. But I had to pay. I missed a crucial turnoff and was three or four miles beyond it before I realized I was stuck on the highway for the next twenty or twenty-five miles unless I wanted to turn around and go back, which I couldn't get myself to do. So I plunged ahead toward exit 230 for Medina, where, before heading east into Minnesota, I planned to go north into a region of the state that is very sparsely populated and dotted with lakes. Straight ahead on the interstate was Fargo, so I'd have to miss it, which was too bad—a couple of readers from there had invited me to stop by, and I'd wanted to go there anyway because of the spiky Coen brothers movie—but by this time I was itchy to ride without truck traffic and rumble strips.

I was maybe six or seven miles from the exit when I ran into road construction that had closed down the westbound lanes and reduced what was usually a four-lane divided highway to two undivided lanes on the eastbound side—my side—and slimmed the shoulder as well. Alongside me the road was busy, fast-moving, noisy, and threatening.

I had no choice but to dismount, wait for a break in the traffic, sprint across the highway, and push my bike over the grassy center strip to ride on the unused westbound lanes. Luckily, it was a Sunday and the construction crews weren't working. It was a few miles to the end of the construction zone—a bit of an eerie ride, actually, going the wrong way on an empty highway with dozens of cars and their cranky drivers clotting up the lanes next to me—but then I found myself suddenly facing oncoming traffic, so I had to recross the highway again. Scary. But I took pleasure in my perseverance.

Eastern North Dakota isn't what I expected. Its long stretches of flat plains are interrupted by rolling hills and, partly because of a brutal flood season earlier this summer, decorated by a network of ponds and lakes that adds some striking blues and greens to the scenery spectrum. It's the kind of terrain that, with a tailwind, makes you feel as if you owned the world and could gobble up miles without strain. The wind has been peculiar this week, however, some variation on southerly and easterly—an unusual condition I blame on the distant disruption of Hurricane Irene on the East Coast—so instead of riding the wind, I've been negotiating it. I kept calculating in my head: "If I'm going twelve miles per hour in a crosswind, I'd be going sixteen or seventeen with a tailwind."

And "If this wind were behind me, I'd be ten miles down the road already" and "If I'd passed through here on another day, I'd be having much more fun."

The floods unleashed by Irene, by the way, were spoken of with grave sympathy for Northeasterners by every North Dakotan I met. The waters that leveled farmers' fields here in June and July are still receding, and as I headed north from I-94, through a countryside where small lakes that once were meadows now exist between larger lakes, I waded through a couple of stretches of road that were still underwater. Ducks swam within inches of the pavement and skittered fearfully away from me along the water's surface as I approached. Frogs hopped out of my path. It was exciting, actually.

And that's also the point of perseverance. As any cyclist knows, you keep pedaling because you don't know what's next. Uncertainty is not a hindrance but a spur, so you pedal toward it. Conditions change often. Things can get worse, yes, but just as often they get better. A pitted road gives way to a newly repaved one. At the top of the seemingly endless hill is a break in the sky and a perfectly articulated rainbow. Unexpectedly, the wind shifts, or the rain stops, or a herd of dark, handsome cattle comes into view grazing amid a field of dandelions, or a flock of geese settles with noisy grace on a flat pond that perhaps didn't exist a week ago.

There are degrees of risk and reward, of course, but this is how you have adventures.

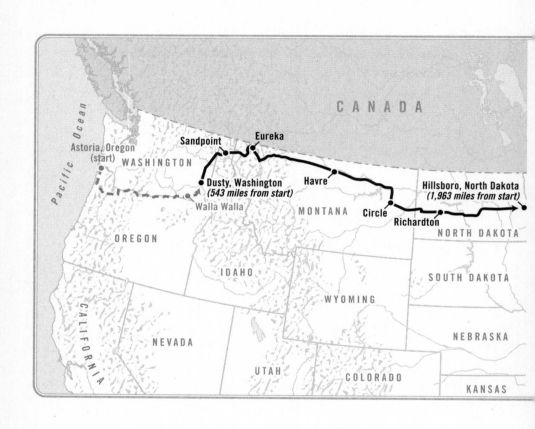

CANADA

Pacific Ocean

Astoria, Oregon
(start)

WASHINGTON

Sandpoint

Eureka

Dusty, Washington
(543 miles from start)

Walla Walla

Havre

Hillsboro, North Dakota
(1,963 miles from start)

MONTANA

Circle

Richardton

NORTH DAKOTA

OREGON

IDAHO

WYOMING

SOUTH DAKOTA

CALIFORNIA

NEVADA

UTAH

COLORADO

NEBRASKA

KANSAS

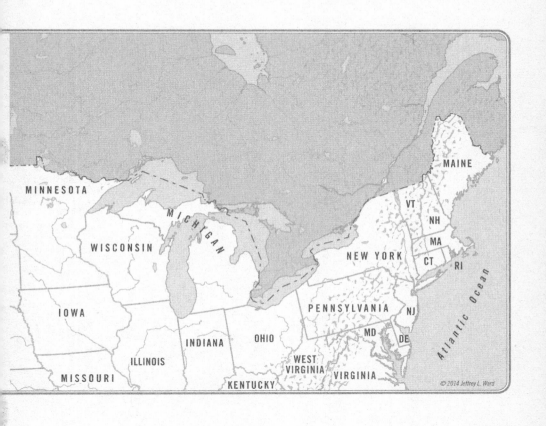

© 2014 Jeffrey L. Ward

PART TWO

American Gulliver

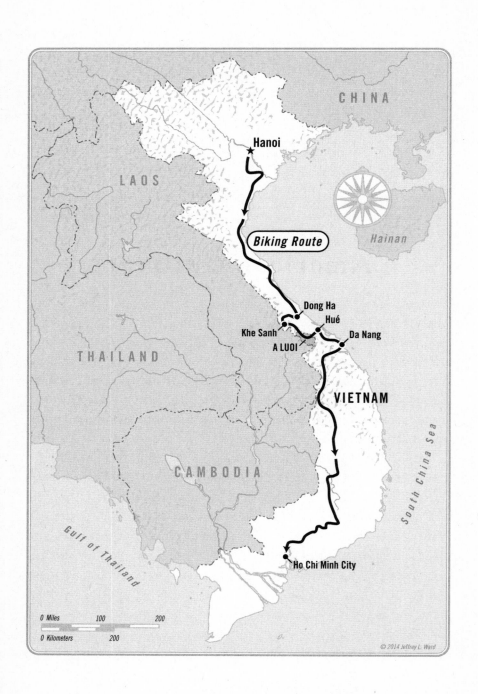

CHINA

Hanoi

LAOS

Biking Route

Hainan

Dong Ha

Hué

Khe Sanh

Da Nang

A LUOI

THAILAND

VIETNAM

South China Sea

CAMBODIA

Gulf of Thailand

Ho Chi Minh City

0 Miles   100   200

0 Kilometers   200

© 2014 Jeffrey L. Ward

10

⌒∽◦∾⌒

My War: Bike Pirates
and an Armadillo

T he trip to Vietnam came about in the fall of 1994 when a small
    tour company based in Portland, Oregon, placed an advertisement
in the *New York Times Magazine* with the headline "Cycle the Ho Chi
Minh Trail."

I was working on the *Times*'s metro desk at the time; it was a year or
so after I'd returned from my first ride across the U.S. I was bored with
my assignments, and I think the paper's executive editor, Joe Lelyveld,
knew it. One afternoon he came by my desk and dropped a copy of the
magazine on it, folded to one of the back pages where he'd circled the
advertisement in black pencil.

"Interested?" he said.

The trip took place in January 1995, just a few months shy of twenty
years after the fall of Saigon and ten weeks or so before President Clinton announced the resumption of diplomatic relations between the
United States and Vietnam.

The itinerary was ambitious, three weeks and twelve hundred miles
from Hanoi in the north to Ho Chi Minh City, as Saigon was renamed
by the Communists after the war, in the south, with stops in some of
the war's memorable sites—Hué, Da Nang, the tunnels at Vinh Moc
where hundreds of people had lived underground for years at a time—
and side trips possible to Khe Sanh, where the famous bloody siege

took place during the Vietcong's Tet Offensive launched at the end of January 1968, and along the Ho Chi Minh Trail, the network of tracks through the jungle used by the North Vietnamese to ferry supplies to its guerrilla troops.

We were not the first American tourists in Vietnam after the war; President Clinton had lifted the American trade embargo the previous year, and Vietnamtourism, the government-subsidized tourist agency that supervised our trip, said that between eight thousand and ten thousand Americans had visited since then, though most were on cruises and didn't venture far from the seacoast. We weren't even the first bicycle tourists—the organizers of our tour had made the trip the previous year. But for virtually all of the Vietnamese we encountered in our three weeks there, we were likely the first Americans—maybe the first white people—they had seen since the evacuation of American troops on April 30, 1975.

There were about sixty of us all told, with varying abilities as cyclists, ranging in age from twenty-three to seventy-four, nearly all Americans, about a third women, and surprisingly (or maybe not) ten or twelve returning veterans of the war. It was way too large a group for such a wacky enterprise; our daily mileage was generally between eighty and a hundred miles and by late afternoon our caravan might stretch for thirty miles or more. The tour organizers, who were well-meaning and competent, were nonetheless overwhelmed by the logistics of feeding, housing, and keeping track of so many people in a third-world country with a stultifying bureaucracy and a nascent service economy, where almost no one spoke English and the local language might just as well have been gibberish. It was a wild three weeks.

Among the journey's dozens of surreal, eye-opening, completely unforeseeable episodes was the kidnapping of my bicycle by bike pirates. It occurred early in the trip, four or five days along, maybe three hundred miles south of Hanoi as we rode the country's main thoroughfare, a not entirely paved road called Highway 1. This was in an especially rural area, with many miles between small villages, where the road was narrow and often muddy and sometimes didn't include the luxury of a bridge across a stream. You took your shoes off and carried your bike.

It had been a long ride that day, beginning in early morning—the distance from hotel to hotel more than a hundred miles—and late in the afternoon, with maybe twenty-five miles to go and sunlight waning, the tour group's support bus came up behind me and a few others and scooped us up to take us the rest of the way. I got on grudgingly; I never like to miss out on the end of a ride, but I had dawdled that day, was close to bringing up the rear of the caravan, and it was late.

The bus was about the size of a regular city bus, but it had luggage racks on top and back doors that opened like a van's, which were used to load bikes into a space where several rows of seats used to be. Up front it still had seats for maybe thirty people. A dozen or so were already on board when I got on, and we started chatting amiably about the day's ride. Out the window, the road dipped down along a hillside and at one point crossed a stream through the streambed. In trying, later on, to figure out what the hell had happened, I recalled the bus slowing down to go through the water and the rear end of the chassis bumping the bank as the bus climbed out. At the time I took no notice.

A few miles later, however, we were rattling along, and I looked out the window and saw two motor scooters had pulled up alongside the bus. One of the riders was holding something in one hand and waving it, gesturing with it. It was a bicycle pump, and after a moment I realized, to my amazement, that it was *my* bicycle pump. I ran to the back of the bus to check that my pump wasn't, in fact, still on my bicycle and, of course, my bicycle was gone.

Now how these guys had crept up on the bus, opened the back doors, made off with my bicycle, and closed the back doors again without any of us noticing remains a mystery to this day. It must have happened when we crossed the stream, but I still don't get it.

In any case, the bus driver stopped the bus, and the two Vietnamese guides—one with Vietnamtourism, one with us—got out with me to negotiate. The kidnappers were small men and my opening ploy was to threaten to beat the shit out of them. The Vietnamtourism guide—we called him Wally, if I recall—was a timid sort, but our guy, Dienh (Dean, we called him),* wasn't. He told me, in so many words, to shut up and talked to the two guys, then explained to me that they said they hadn't stolen the bicycle but had found it—"Uh-huh," I said, and Dean winked—and that they would be happy to give it back to me for a finder's fee. (I can't remember the word Dean really used; it wasn't *finder's fee*. Maybe it was *reward*.) He had bargained them down from $10 to $5, he said.

"How do we know they'll bring the bike back?" I said.

"I'm going with them," Dean said.

So I gave him the five, and he got on the back of one of the scooters and they took off. We waited around for half an hour; the local children came to see what all the fuss was about and we let them pull the hair on our arms. Young Vietnamese were fascinated by our body hair; they don't have any.

Finally, the two scooters came back, Dean on the back of one, holding my bicycle on his shoulder with one arm and holding on to the driver with the other. Through Dean, the kidnappers asked for another five dollars, and I told them no. They said okay, got on their scooters, and waved as they drove away.

The article I wrote for the *New York Times* about the trip appeared on March 1, 1995, under the headline "Vietnam Bike Tour Challenges Hearts and Minds." The accompanying photograph shows me cycling in a remote region on a muddy road that was once part of the Ho Chi

---

*Dienh Huynh, who was born in Vietnam and was evacuated from Saigon in 1975, lives in New York City with his wife and a couple of kids whose Little League teams he coaches. I know this because two years after we met I walked into a bar in Chelsea and there he was: the bartender. I still see him; he now works at Café Loup, a well-known bar and restaurant in Greenwich Village, and pours a good, heavy shot of whiskey, if you're ever in the neighborhood.

Minh Trail and gave me the distinction of being the only *New York Times* reporter ever to have his picture on the front page with a water buffalo.

Here's a section of the article, lightly edited:

The man lying in the hammock remembered the supply trucks rumbling past his house at night.

"Yes," he said, through an interpreter, gesturing at the road in front of him, "this was the Ho Chi Minh Trail."

We got back on our bicycles and continued south.

This was in Giang, a river village some 500 miles north of Saigon, in the Central Highlands. The road is known as Highway 14, but that's a joke. Though it has been widened since the Vietnam War ended, it is still a precipitous and tortuous route that negotiates densely overgrown hillsides, the roadbed in places a red-dirt path that often turns to mud in the jungle dampness, in others an obstacle course of jagged stones.

The Ho Chi Minh Trail was constructed largely in Laos and Cambodia, of course, out of the way of American bombers, but it didn't take much to imagine Highway 14 as part of the network of roads used by the Communists to haul supplies and reinforcements from north of the demilitarized zone to Dak To, Pleiku, Kontum, Ban Me Thuot and the other southern battlefronts.

What was tough to imagine was this as a bike route, and indeed for the next several days it was slow, even dangerous going, a rattling endurance test for both bike and body.

Eleven of us navigated Highway 14—we'd left a larger group in the coastal city of Da Nang—and nearly all of us took nasty spills and were forced into roadside repairs. And more than once we had to cut short the riding day and board our support vans because we hadn't a prayer of completing the mileage to our scheduled stopping place before dark.

Still, in many ways this was the most rewarding stretch of our three-week journey from Hanoi to Ho Chi Minh City; this was the landscape we had come all this way to see, the deep green jungles, the lush riverbank villages, the Vietnam terrain that still looks like a war zone, familiar from newsreels and movies. Hanoi, once the battered enemy capital, is, amazingly, a friendly city. At Khe Sanh, the American garrison that was the object of the miserable siege in 1968 is gone. But beyond Giang, in the seemingly impenetrable wilderness between the village of Phuoc Son and the city of Dak To, the war's terrors lingered.

There, on a thick-misted morning, Morris Erickson, now a 48-year-old real estate lawyer in Bloomington, Ind., dismounted his bicycle on a small cement bridge over a creek and remembered patrolling as an infantry platoon leader in 1970.

His men would go out in similarly forbidding terrain for two weeks at a time, Mr. Erickson said; they'd move through the jungle a few hundred yards a day, eating dry rations, sleeping in their ponchos, ever alert for trip-wires that might set off a mine or a booby trap, or for guerrilla machine-gun nests camouflaged in the hills.

"It's not bothering me at all to be back," Mr. Erickson had said in Hanoi. But standing on that bridge, reliving that time, he looked like a younger, less confident version of himself. He hugged his shoulders, and as he continued the story his grip tightened noticeably.

"I'll tell you one thing," he said. "You'd never, ever stand out in the open on a bridge like this."

*   *   *

Our trip had begun with a brisk ride out of Hanoi, passing through the bleakly beautiful landscapes of the north—the humped mountains looming in the mist beyond vast rice paddies—and the energetic but uninspiring cities: Ninh Binh, Thanh Hoa and Ky Anh. Still, by the time we reached the former demilitarized zone, it had already been eye-opening, exhilarating even, with a reception from the Vietnamese that we could not have anticipated. Entire villages came to the road-side to greet us as we passed through. And from people so far away we could barely see them, hundreds of yards away knee-deep in the rice fields, calls of "Hello!" echoed at our backs.

There were some discomforting incidents—Vietnamese threw stones at our group a few times and one young woman made a threat-ening gesture at me with a machete—but even those of us most unset-tled by the occasional shows of hostility admit that the overwhelming reaction of the Vietnamese in the North was one of unqualified wel-come.

"It's weird," said Wilson Hubbell, 49, who was a helicopter crewman in the war. "I've gotten a better reception as an American returning to Vietnam than I did as a Vietnam veteran returning to America."

I'd been old enough to serve in Vietnam—the prospect had scared me silly from the time I was fourteen—but I avoided being drafted because of a high lottery number, and it's likely I didn't need even that bit of good fortune. My missing fingers might have done the trick; so might have my eyesight, and I remember wishing I could lend out a deferment or two to friends who didn't have one.

That was the way a lot of us thought back then. We were watching the war on television every night, the country was horribly split over it, and the street protests, the angry politics, and the bloody images in our living rooms made the war in Vietnam seem both monstrous and close by. For a trepidatious teenager like me the idea of flying seven thousand miles to spend two years in the middle of it was unthinkable.

I didn't know how to feel about the boys my age who went. Admire them? Sympathize with them? Disapprove of them? I felt all of those from time to time.

Of course, serving their country for good or ill, fifty-eight thousand of them died, and as I grew older the tragedy of that sank in and felt more and more profound. I heard many veterans speak about the grievous experience of having fought in Vietnam; I read Michael Herr and Tim O'Brien, whose works struck me as especially intimate and vivid accounts of what the war was like on the ground in the jungle and how terror-riven it is possible for a young conscript to be. And it came to me eventually that, like having sex for the first time or becoming a father (not that I would know), soldiering is something to be understood only by those who have soldiered. My parents' generation knew this without having it arrive as a revelation; during World War II the national sacrifice was entered into willingly and diligently and it was shared. Boys like my father were drafted and they went.

But that isn't the way it was for us. Vietnam divided my generation of men into those who went and those who didn't, and no matter how awful it had been and how terrified I had been of it, I went into my twenties, my thirties, my forties—I was forty-one when I biked in Vietnam—knowing I'd missed the signature experience of young manhood in my time. That's something I've thought about a lot, with a complicated feeling that borders on regret.

It was strange to be in Hanoi, the very seat of the evil empire of my childhood. It has probably changed a lot since then, but it was strange and thrilling, beautiful and run-down, a maze of wide boulevards and shack-lined alleys, mad with bicycles and mopeds, alive with human voices and pungent with the smells from cooking fires—the most exotic place I'd ever been.

We stayed three days in Hanoi. One morning, I rode with Wilson Hubbell to see the Bach Mai Hospital, rebuilt by then but nearly destroyed during a Christmas week bombing in 1972; a bas-relief memorial to the dead filled a courtyard wall. We stood there astride our bikes looking at the engraved words we didn't understand, both of us thinking that the people who died there died by American hands, and after a few minutes we looked up and we were surrounded. It was a little intimidating. A couple of dozen people milled around us, looking at us quizzically, uncertainly. It seemed possible we'd committed an offense, that being Americans at this memorial—maybe a hallowed spot, we didn't know—was an affront to the local people, many of whom likely had friends and relatives among the casualties. It turned out, though, that wasn't it. No one spoke English, but one man gestured at our city map. They thought we might be lost. Did we need directions? They were curious about the strangers. They wanted to help.

From there we rode to the site of Hoa Lo Prison, the so-called Hanoi Hilton, which for decades housed revolutionaries and political enemies of the state and during the 1960s and '70s American pilots, including, famously, Senator John McCain, and Pete Peterson, the first postwar U.S. ambassador to Vietnam.

Part of the prison was then being torn down to make room for an apartment and office complex. I picked up a brick from the rubble to bring home as a souvenir and was immediately surrounded again, this time by several men who fixed me with severe expressions of reprimand. It was a few seconds before one of them spoke.

"One dollar," he said.

This was actually Wilson Hubbell's second return to Vietnam. Normally an amiable and loquacious man, he had come to the country a year earlier, on the first trip sponsored by our tour group, but when he landed in Hanoi, he said, a crippling anxiety overtook him at the airport, and he returned home to Southern California, where he worked as a transportation official.

"I had put the war behind me years and years ago, I thought," he told me in Hanoi. "But the very first thing that happens when you get off the plane and you go through customs, you see the guy there in the uniform. A North Vietnamese Army soldier. If I had seen a guy dressed like that twenty-five years ago, I'd have shot him on sight and he'd have shot me on sight. So suddenly here I am standing face-to-face with this guy, and I can feel the hair on the back of my neck starting to crawl up.

"Where I had been in Vietnam, especially in the Central Highlands, you couldn't trust little kids. You couldn't trust mama-sans. There were a lot of different ways you could die. It was totally irrational, but what's going on in my head is that any one of these people might kill me at any given moment.

"And then I had nightmares. People I was here in Vietnam with would appear and say: 'You came here on a bicycle ride? Don't you remember how we all suffered in this place? You came here to have fun?' "

Months of counseling and talking to other veterans prepared him better for a second confrontation with his demons, Hubbell said.

"I met a lot of guys who, when they found out what I was going to do, said, 'While you're going down the road, when you get to this place or that place, will you take a picture for me?'" he said. "Guys gave me their shoulder patches and said, 'Nail this to a tree for me.' So this time I've got a purpose."

I wrote about Wilson Hubbell in my article for the *Times*; he was an agreeable interview subject, and I used him as a representative for the guys on the other side of the divide, the guys who went, someone who could speak for an experience that I hadn't shared. I thought it was terrifically brave of him to face down his fears and return, not once but twice, and I kept comparing his experience of the war, actually being in it, actually living it, with mine, fearing it from a great distance. But it didn't occur to me then—in fact, it's only occurring to me now—that Hubbell was using a bicycle trip to take stock of himself, to measure how far he'd come since he'd finished the most consequential experience of his life.

Toward the end of our trip, Hubbell rode his bike through Qui Nhon, a coastal town some two hundred and fifty miles north of Ho Chi Minh City, where he had been stationed in 1968 during the Tet Offensive. There was a Vietnamese Army base on the site of the old American base, and Hubbell went to see it. While he was there he was introduced to a former North Vietnamese soldier, a man about his age, and soon the two men were exchanging recollections. They were astounded to discover that they might well have shot at each other during Tet. The man invited Hubbell into his home. They had tea.

Hubbell recalled their conversation for me later, in a hotel bar in Ho Chi Minh City.

"Finally," he said, "I feel like the war is over."

Inspired, I suppose, by Wilson Hubbell and Morry Erickson—or maybe shamed?—I decided to take off on my own, away from the group, for a few days.

We were taking a rest stop in Dong Ha, a river city near the coast, just south of the former demilitarized zone that had divided North and South Vietnam; at that latitude, the country, which has the profile of a snake tucked against the Pacific, is especially slender, maybe fifty miles from the sea to the Laotian border, and I wanted to cross it, to visit Khe Sanh and from there to make a day trip into Laos. I'd come all this way as a reporter and hadn't left the safety of the group; this was my opportunity to be intrepid. Another cyclist, an older guy from L.A. whom I'll call Albert—retired—decided he wanted to go with me.

In Dong Ha, Wally scurried around to arrange the appropriate papers that would let us leave the country, and Albert and I arranged to rejoin our fellow cyclists in Hué—it's pronounced sort of like "whey," as in "curds and whey," but with a breathy "h" at the front—about fifty miles south. We packed a little food, a change of clothes, and took off for what turned out to be the most vivid, event-filled four days I've ever had.

Albert and I rode to Khe Sanh on a serene road through woods and misty hills. A gregarious fellow—a loudmouth, actually—game for anything but not always capable, he was an enthusiastic cyclist but not a strong one, and it was slow going, though not unpleasant. We passed a kind of quarry, piles of white stones alongside the road where children played and women in cone hats were pounding the stones into gravel with sledgehammers. At midday, we climbed up to a ridge and came upon a village, a handful of lonely shacks looking over a lush valley. One of the shacks was a café of sorts—two rickety wooden tables, dirt floor, a roof of matted reeds—so we stopped. And as happened just about everywhere we went and every time we dismounted, the local residents flocked to us, smiling, eager to touch our arms, to be photographed. I've never seen more stunningly beautiful children anywhere than I did in three weeks in Vietnam.

The proprietor of the café was a shy, attractive woman probably in her thirties, wearing dark slacks and a man's light-colored shirt with a white frill sewn onto it. (My memory is so specific because I have a picture of her in front of me.)

We tried to speak with her, and with the older woman who, I thought I understood, was the chef's mother, and with the various neighbors who dropped by to look at the white strangers, but communication was limited. We did, however, enjoy a delicious lunch—I have a picture of that, too—the spicy vegetable soup known as *pho*, a deep-dish omelet, and a platter of grilled chicken.

Afterward, before we said our good-byes, the older woman approached us and with unmistakable gestures offered either Albert or me—or both of us—the opportunity to spend the afternoon in bed with her daughter, the chef.

We looked over at her and she blushed. We declined politely, and as we got back on our bicycles, I gave the proprietor my baseball hat—dark green, with the insignia of the La Jolla Playhouse on it—which she put on immediately and with a thrilled grin wore as she waved at us, continuing to wave, I saw as I looked back, until we were just about out of sight.

The hilly battlefield at Khe Sanh was an empty jungle by then, the kind of place where a movie director would imagine a dissolve, an establishing shot of a peaceful, lush, yet vaguely threatening landscape that becomes a noisy, sepia-colored, angry scene out of the past. We didn't spend much time there, instead pressing on into the town itself, arriving in the late afternoon and finding the government-owned guest house, which struck me as a cross between a dormitory and a prison, with small rooms with stone walls and stone beds.

The town itself was shabby and poor, but we found our way to the marketplace, which was bustling and lively, rows of stalls filled with bushels of tomatoes, onions, beans, sacks of rice, slaughtered chickens hanging from beams, and live chickens awaiting their fate in covered baskets. Other stalls were selling colored silks, knitted shoulder bags, cloth hats.

Albert and I attracted a lot of attention. Curious kids followed us around as we pretended to shop, and I was amused by Albert, who chatted amiably and volubly with the women in each stall, though no one understood anything anyone else was saying. Eventually, we walked back out onto the main street, and by that time, news of strangers in town had spread and like a pair of Pied Pipers we had a trail of people behind us, laughing, pointing, and indisputably enjoying themselves.

There wasn't much to see on the street—a few lots, a few ramshackle huts. After a couple hundred yards, we passed a house, an actual house, one story, with three or four men sitting on the porch drinking, and see-ing the parade, they waved and motioned us over. We were immediately given teacups of rice wine, and two men vacated their chairs, squat-ting on their haunches—a posture everyone in the country seemed to find comfortable—so that we might sit. As we drank, the crowd on the street stood by watching, as if at a fascinating television program, as if the sight of two Americans drinking rice wine with a handful of Viet-namese men was both delightful and difficult to believe.

After a time the crowd faded away and the men invited us inside to share dinner. It was a small, neatly kept home, but it was unclear who lived there, maybe all of the men we were drinking with, who ranged from their thirties to their fifties; it's possible they were broth-ers or otherwise related. Two young women—wives? sisters? daugh-ters? I could never figure it out—had prepared the meal, noodles and *pho*, which was laid out on a carpet on the floor, and a couple of small children were crawling around, maybe ten people in the room all told. It was a gathering full of warmth, fueled by the rice wine, which was powerful—I have a photo of myself being hugged by one of our hosts, both of us looking more than a little boozy—even though any sort of informed communication was more or less futile. Once again I found Albert's gregariousness noteworthy; it didn't seem to matter to him that no one understood a word he was saying, but it didn't seem to matter to our hosts, either. They were engaged by his evident good cheer.

Finally, well after dark, Albert and I stumbled back to the guest house, fell asleep, and were woken up at 5:30 a.m. by blasts of military music and exhortatory announcements from loudspeakers mounted throughout the town. In Khe Sanh, the government got you out of bed in the morning.

By midmorning, our hangovers not yet banished, we had reached the Laotian border, expecting to flash our papers and pass on through. That

of the bus was open, the driver was standing outside, and a few passengers were getting off.

Suddenly, from out of nowhere, it seemed, a small man, agile as a monkey, scampered up on top of the bus, where he unfastened a few ragged suitcases and wicker baskets from a roof rack and tossed them down to the driver. He spotted me with my bicycle and stayed up there, gesturing; the driver took my bike from me—snatched it, actually—and in one motion slung it to the guy on the roof, who tied it down with an expert's ease.

By that time Albert had emerged from the hut, blinking, groggy, and docile, and without a word or, apparently, a thought to his bicycle (which I fetched and gave to the driver), got on the bus. His bike followed mine, and I followed him.

The bus was a scene, crowded and noisy and rank. People were carrying odd baggage on their laps—baskets crammed with I don't know what, pots and pans, battered suitcases with straining seams—and there were several live animals, including a few chickens, a dog, and a goat. (Nary an armadillo.)

There was a brief lull in the cacophony when Albert and I got on as the other passengers registered the presence of aliens. They seemed to have a sense that Albert, a stocky man who probably weighed as much as any two of them, needed his space, and they left a double seat open for him. He immediately sprawled out and closed his eyes. I sat in the seat behind him, next to a quiet man who smiled at me shyly and offered me the window, and we switched places.

The bus jounced and ground along for a solid three hours, partly on exposed mountainside—I tried unsuccessfully to ban bus-plunge thoughts from my head—partly in the jungle where everything seemed just a little wilted and bleached in the heat. It stopped frequently, at every tiny village, where people got off with their suitcases and their chickens, and each time, the monkey man jumped up on the roof and slung down belongings. More than once we crossed a streambed by simply driving through the stream, and once we stopped beside a pond, and several of the passengers waded in to cool off as the driver dunked an empty gas can in the water and then opened the hood of the bus, unscrewed the radiator cap with his hand wrapped in his shirt, waited a bit for the steam to dissipate and refilled the radiator. I walked by to take a look; the ticking engine was incredibly hot.

Every now and then I'd get impatient and walk up the aisle to pester the driver. I'd look over his shoulder and point out the front window: "A Luoi?" I would say—AH-loo-ay—and he would nod, and I'd feel reassured for twenty more minutes. Albert, meanwhile, slept most of the way. When he awoke he said he felt a little better but not great.

Finally, we entered a deep jungle, darker and greener than anything we'd driven through, and suddenly the bus made a left turn through a portal in the trees. About a hundred yards later, we pulled into a large clearing within which was nestled a village. The bus stopped with a finality it hadn't previously evinced, and the passengers, taking the hint, filed out with all their stuff. The monkey man magically unburdened the roof.

"A Luoi?" I said to the bus driver, and he shook his head: no. We got out of the bus, and he pointed back out of the clearing and indicated that to get to A Luoi we'd have to continue along the main road. Our bikes were still on the roof, and it hadn't yet hit me that the bus wasn't going any farther. I don't know what I thought, exactly, maybe that the village—its name turned out to be Ta Rut—was some kind of remote dispatch center, a bus hub for the jungle. In any case, I figured we'd have to wait a bit before we took off again, and I explored the village, which wasn't much more than a dozen huts arranged around the perimeter of the clearing.

Albert, I saw, was talking with the driver and they were looking at the map. He was a blusterer, yes, but he had a gift for bludgeoning people into understanding him and, more impressively, making themselves understood. After a few minutes, he explained the situation to me. This was the terminus of the bus route; from here it would turn around, go back over the Da Krong Bridge, and end up back in Dong Ha, where he and I had begun our ride together.

Our group would still be there; they were scheduled to ride south to Hué the next morning, and Albert said he was going back on the bus to join them. A Luoi, he said, was still twenty or twenty-five miles away, and he wasn't up to the ride; he was done.

It was four in the afternoon or thereabouts, maybe three hours of daylight left—it was January—and obviously the idea of going on alone was nervous-making. The jungle was thick, the region was entirely unknown to me, and our map was only intermittently accurate. It was foolish, perhaps, for me to press ahead, but the remoteness, the uncertainty, and the potential danger of it all were, of course, as much a spur as a caution. I'd come all this way, been intrepid enough to get here to this spot, and I knew I'd never again be in a situation like this, or, as I tried to put it to myself, I'd never again have an opportunity like this.

I can't say I wasn't daunted, but the idea that I'd regret it if I chickened out, that I'd be pissed at myself for years, was equally intimidating. Frightened American soldiers half my age had likely stood on this very spot twenty-five and thirty years earlier, I realized, and at that moment turning back didn't seem like an option. I told Albert I'd see him and the others in Hué.

11

⌘

The President of
the United States

*T*he payoff was immediate, if temporary. Proceeding south from Ta
Rut, for twenty or so miles, I had the ride of a lifetime. The dirt
road, packed solid enough for rapid progress, led me through a rolling
jungle where people in the two or three tiny villages I passed no longer
returned my greetings but stared with incredulity at me—a helmeted,
six-foot-tall white person on a bicycle that must have seemed futuristic.
In one village, where a little girl stood by herself on a narrow path that
led to a hut hidden in the brush, I waved to her, and she burst into tears
and ran away.

After a while, the road turned upward through the undergrowth for
a long ascent over a mountain pass. For nearly an hour I climbed, in
and out of the sunlight as the road switched back and forth against the
mountainside. There were no people up there, no chickens or cows or
dogs, no water buffalo, no pigs; nor, surprisingly, was there any wildlife
in evidence, not even birds. Earlier, I had noticed the ratchety warble
of crickets, but now nothing. The silence was profound. It was a thrilling, terrifying experience of solitude.

Over the pass, the roadbed turned abruptly and shockingly to smooth
pavement and, emerging from the jungle, I plunged into a magnificent
broad valley. The road bent west for a bit, and as the sun began to settle
toward the horizon, I passed through cultivated farmland—they were

growing lettuce, or maybe cabbage—and then a pair of villages, comfortingly larger and more populous than any I'd seen all day. In one, young men were playing a game of volleyball. It was all very lovely and serene, an exhilarating stretch for a cyclist.

I coasted briskly around a bend, turning south again, and was enjoying the sensation of breaking through the cooling air, when suddenly, in front of me, three young men in long-sleeved brown shirts and caps with gold stars pinned to the crowns appeared in the center of the road, holding up their palms to flag me down. I stopped and dismounted and one of the men brusquely confiscated my passport. In retrospect, I shouldn't have given it up so easily.

I say men; they might have been twenty-two. On the side of the road was a ramshackle kiosk, a kind of jerry-built guard house with an open window over a counter that in another setting could have been a snack bar; on the side of it a machine gun was hanging by a strap.

One of the men entered the guard house and perused my passport with great seriousness and a kind of fury, as if the secret of something or other were hidden in it, flipping the pages with a desperate desire to learn something or confirm something, and I flashed on the scene at the end of *The Maltese Falcon*, when Sydney Greenstreet thinks that at last he has his hands on the treasure he's long sought, but as he grows more and more fearful that he's wrong and disappointment sets in, he begins stabbing at the phony falcon with a penknife. The Vietnamese officer was less than half Greenstreet's age and maybe a third his size, but he was acting with the same sort of anxiety-driven greed. I don't know what he was looking for, but he didn't find it.

Still, I was at their mercy; they had my passport and at least one gun. The man with my passport, who was probably the oldest of the three, pulled a bicycle out from behind the guard shack and gestured for me to remount and follow him, and we headed back out onto the road. He left the gun hanging where it was.

The ride took nearly an hour in dwindling light. It was eerie; I was still going in the same direction, but now as if on a leash. My escort was quiet—we couldn't understand each other anyway—and I was left to wonder, like a pet dog on his way to the vet, where the hell I was being taken and why I was being taken there. Is this serious? I thought. How much trouble am I in? The guy was a cop of some sort, I understood that, but being arrested by bicycle and taken on a long and rather appealing jaunt through the equatorial countryside at pink dusk didn't make me feel entirely like a criminal. The enterprise took on a whole other degree of loopiness after we passed what looked like a school and three teenaged girls decided to ride along with us.

This wasn't entirely surprising. I'd seen this behavior before. All along Highway 1, Vietnamese cyclists, mostly men, spotting a parade of American riders, would infiltrate our ranks for a close-up look at us, and often they would attempt a conversation, every one of which began the same way:

"Hello! What you do?"

It didn't take long to realize that the answer meant little to them, so I'd taken to explaining to each new inquirer that I was the president of the United States, and what generally happened was that my new friend found this a satisfactory answer and we would ride together in convivial silence for a while until he peeled away.

These girls, however, were different. They were pretty and curious and silly, pedaling away alongside me as I pedaled just behind the cop, pointing at me but never really giving me more than a glance, giggling and chattering away among one another but never saying anything directly to me. I tried saying hello—or "Hello!"—but didn't get much of a response.

My police escort never altered his bland and serious expression, never registered the presence of the girls, even as they arranged themselves on either side of me and took turns reaching out to stroke my forearms as we rode along. It was bizarrely erotic—for me, I mean. I don't know what the titillation factor was for them, but they were interested enough to keep up their flirtation for ten, maybe fifteen, minutes, and then they simply stopped, suddenly and irrevocably bored the way teenagers everywhere become with adults, and they turned onto another road and disappeared.

*   *   *

It was nearly full dark when my escort turned off the road into a compound of barracks surrounding a courtyard. Parking our bikes, we climbed the porch of one of the barracks, where several young men were sitting at a picnic table, and entered into a small room where a slender man with a thin mustache and a Vietnamese flag insignia—a yellow star against a red background—sewn on the crown of his brown military cap was sitting at a desk beneath a bare lightbulb hanging from the ceiling. He gave me a wan smile, and I couldn't help thinking of an evil Chinese Communist from central casting, perfect for a James Bond movie. My escort gave him my passport and he shooed us out of his office, and we went back on the porch, where news of my arrival had evidently spread because the crowd around the picnic table had grown to a dozen or so.

No one said anything; they were all very young, maybe a little wary, more likely a little bored. I, of course, was nervous, and I grew more so as minutes ticked by. Every so often I'd look in on the officer with my passport—he was wearing a brown uniform shirt and was clearly the boss—and, like the guy on the side of the road, he was examining it closely, flipping the pages, seemingly mystified and frustrated.

Eventually, he came out on the porch and tried to speak with me, pointing at the passport and asking me questions in Vietnamese, but of course it was hopeless, so he tucked my passport in his shirt pocket, where my eyes followed it, and he gave out some instructions to the young men around the picnic table.

It was the separation from my passport that made me the most uneasy about my situation, as if having it would allow me to go merrily on my way, even though it was pitch-black outside and I had no idea where I was. I'd been entirely cooperative and even docile up to that point, but not understanding why I was being held, maddened by the inability to communicate, and fending off stress—How much trouble am I in here? How much danger?—I decided to borrow a stratagem from Albert and began to yell: "Why am I here? Give me my passport! What the hell did I do, goddammit?"

At one point I snatched at the officer's shirt pocket. He instantly turned angry, pointing to the star on his hat as if to say, "Don't you know who I am?" Then he aimed an imaginary machine gun at me and feigned shooting it. That shut me up.

He pointed at my bicycle, then at a barracks house with an open door about thirty yards away, and as I wheeled my bike over there, followed by a parade of young Vietnamese cops, I had a conversation with myself in which I very coolly laid out my options: *Okay, you can freak out, which would be entirely understandable, but would mean you'd immediately begin having a really unpleasant, anxiety-laden time of it. Or you can go with this, see what happens, remain calm and amused rather than querulous. This is, after all, far and away the most interesting thing that has ever happened to you, and unless something goes really, awfully wrong, you'll have a great story to tell when it's over.*

Now, I do realize that panic and anxiety aren't voluntary, but at that moment it struck me as possible to make a choice and the choice seemed not only easy but absolutely right. I actually shrugged, a gesture to myself—*Okay, let's go with it*—and whatever nascent fear I was feeling drained away. I wheeled my bike through the open door into an empty barracks house with several wooden bunk beds built into it. The young cops followed me in.

They seemed like children to me, none of them older than twenty or twenty-one; one of them was wearing a T-shirt with NEW YORK in block letters across the chest. Some of them milled around my bicycle, touching the brakes, the shifters, the bar ends, the pump mounted on the frame. When I removed the water bottle from its cage and squeezed it, and a stream squirted from the mouth, the boys jumped back, startled and amazed, and they started to laugh. Then they all wanted to try it themselves, and at that moment I had a revelation: *I'm Gulliver.*

We were suddenly having a cordial time, passing the water bottle around, playing with the gadgets on the bicycle; for a few minutes I traded my helmet for one of their hats. The goodwill was abundant, and after a few minutes one of the young men—the smallest of them, and I'd realize later, the oldest—took me by the arm and led me out the door, where I first saw that he was exceptionally tiny, under five feet tall and thin as a stick. He couldn't have weighed ninety pounds.

He showed me to a small room in another building where a cot was made up with a blanket, pillow, and sheets, and next to it a tiny night table with a lamp on it. He made a gesture: *This is my room; you sleep here.*

Then he placed both hands on his chest with the fingers knitted together and said a word that sounded like *Dah-lot.*

"Dah-lot?" I said.

And he nodded, though I'm sure I got it wrong, and tapped his chest again. Dah-lot or something, he said. One of those words I'd never manage to hear or say properly. His name.

"Bruce," I said.

"Roo," he said with a smile, revealing bad teeth and a wear and tear in his face I hadn't noticed before. He was probably thirty. "What you do?"

"I'm president of the United States," I said.

Dah-lot nodded and went on to the next subject, gesturing as though lifting a fork to his mouth.

"Eat?" he said.

It turned out that Dah-lot knew maybe a dozen words of English, and so had been designated as my host. It also turned out that he was hungry. His plan to feed me was to walk me into town—I had, in fact, made it to A Luoi—which was about a half mile beyond the compound and to visit a restaurant he knew. He wanted to know if I had money.

There was a dim streetlight or two along the road, but more prominent was the glow from television sets in the huts we passed. Dah-lot asked me, in a complicated, half hand signal, half verbal sort of way, if I wanted to watch TV, letting me know (I think) that it would be perfectly all right if we just walked up to someone's house and invited ourselves inside, though I was beginning to get the idea that he was using me as an excuse to do what he wanted to do himself.

The restaurant, which wasn't much more than a couple of tables in the back room of a hut, someone's home, was empty, but the woman who lived there let us in and grumpily fixed a meal. We had a bowl of *pho* and boiled cabbage, and I drank beer. Dah-lot asked shyly if he might have a beer of his own—this is when I understood I'd be paying the bill for both of us—and of course I said sure, and when the woman brought a rice pastry for dessert he asked again if he might have one of his own. He'd found himself a meal ticket, and I liked filling the role.

I tried to pump him for information. When would I be allowed to leave? He said tomorrow. I asked him several times to make sure. "I can leave tomorrow?"

"Tomorrow," he said.

After dinner we walked back to the compound, past the houses with the glowing TVs, and Dah-lot suggested again that we go in and watch, but I demurred. I went directly to his room, went to sleep in his bed. When we said good night, I was struck again by his littleness, his sweet temperament, and his plight, which was one of wanting. I don't know where Dah-lot spent the night.

I slept surprisingly well.

When I woke the next morning Dah-lot was waiting to walk me into town again for breakfast.

"Eat?" he asked.

We repeated the ritual from the night before, trudging the half mile to town, being served (*pho* and boiled eggs and rice and tea) at a small table in back of the grumpy woman's dirt-floor home and trudging back again.

Our conversations had evolved a tortuous but semi-effective style involving elaborate hand signals and words repeated over and over again, and while we were eating Dah-lot nervously explained to me I would not be released that day because it was Sunday. From what I could gather that was significant because no one was available to authorize my release.

I'd begun to recognize that when I raised my voice Dah-lot grew fearful—perhaps because I towered over him, perhaps because he was used to a life in which he had no authority whatsoever—and on the way back I kicked up the decibel level, stabbed my finger at him with extra vehemence, and made it clear that I *had* to leave, that there would be no gainsaying that, that many people in Hué were waiting for me.

I'd inadvertently said the magic words. When Dah-lot realized what I was saying about people expecting me his eyes widened for a moment, and as soon as we arrived at the compound he hurried away. I saw him enter the office where the evil Communist officer sat; I followed him there and began making the point, once again at significant volume, that a crowd of Americans, very important Americans, would be waiting for me in Hué, and who knows what would happen if I didn't arrive on time.

Through the whole business, I had kept my identity as a reporter to myself, thinking that to reveal it might be inflammatory or unhelpfully flummoxing, but in the years since I've often wondered whether that was a mistake. My captors—maybe I should say hosts—were probably more easily intimidated by me than I realized at the time. In retrospect, I understood they didn't see me as a threat so much as a problem, or a puzzle. My presence in their midst was a situation not covered in the rule book. And if they were moved to action by the mere idea that other people were waiting for me, perhaps learning their guest was a journalist would have given getting me out of there even more urgency. Hard to know.

In any case, before long there was a flurry of activity. The Evil Communist—I don't know what else to call him—emerged from his office and dispatched Dah-lot on an errand and he hustled off. He returned shortly with a fellow cop (who was closer to my size), and all three men entered a small cottage in the corner of the compound. I tried to follow them, but the Evil Communist shot me a look, and Dah-lot, looking a tad frightened, made a plaintive gesture: *Please stay outside.*

I watched from the doorway as Dah-lot and the other man knelt beside a device I couldn't immediately identify and began taking turns churning a crank; it was a generator, and they were supplying the power for a telephone. The Evil Communist was holding the receiver.

I don't know how many different phone calls were involved, or how many bureaucratic levels they traveled among, but the three men were ensconced in the hut for a full hour. I wandered impatiently around the compound, taking pictures, but every few minutes I'd stop back in the doorway of the hut and the Evil Communist would be speaking into the mouthpiece of the receiver, and either Dah-lot or his friend would be on his knees, cranking away to keep the generator thrumming.

When the three men finally emerged, the Evil Communist confiscated my camera—to this day it irks me that I let him do that—and disappeared into his office. I asked Dah-lot what was happening and he said I had to wait.

Another hour went by. By this time I was impatient but far from frightened. It was a brilliant, bright morning and it wasn't at all unpleasant to be lazily sunning in the courtyard of the compound, but the day was spending itself, and if and when I was released I had a long trip ahead of me. It looked, from the map, to be about sixty miles to Hué, with some mountains between here and there. I was eager, even excited, to get going, partly as a cyclist with pent-up energy and a challenging ride on a beautiful day ahead of him, and partly as a guy with a story to tell who couldn't wait to report to his friends on his adventures.

Eventually, I heard the *putt-putt* of a motor, and a woman wearing a pink dress and a white hat cruised purposefully into the compound on a moped. She and the Evil Communist disappeared into his office for several minutes, and when they came out we all sat at the picnic table on the porch for what turned out to be an interrogation. This was, evidently, an exciting event; Dah-lot, who stood behind me, had spread the word, and I counted fourteen other people standing around us.

The woman was a schoolteacher from a village not far away, I had learned from Dah-lot, and she spoke English. Like him, he said. She was in her 20s, maybe her 30s. With a serious expression fixed on her face, she sat next to me, across the table from the Evil Communist, who was once again obsessively thumbing through my passport. Beside him, a tall, worried-looking lieutenant sat rigidly with a pen and paper, poised to transcribe our conversation. The Evil Communist spoke only to the woman, and she redirected his questions at me.

"When you were captured," she said, "you were traveling lonely. Why?"

"Your passport was issued in New York, but your visa was issued in Mexico City. Why?"*

"Did you go to Mexico City?"

"Why not?"

"Do you have other papers?"

"Why not?"

"What are the names of all of the people you are meeting in Hué?"

This went on for half an hour. In the end, she told me, "You have violated administrative law."†

The Evil Communist whispered something.

"You must be punished," the woman said to me. "You agree?"

I agreed, which meant, as it turned out, a $20 fine. I paid in cash, with a single bill, for which I was given a receipt. I also signed a confession, written out during my interrogation, which included the line, according to the translator: "All he wants is to be free."

---

*At the time, the United States and Vietnam had not yet resumed diplomatic relations. Visas for all of the Americans on our trip were obtained in Mexico by the trip organizers.

†About ten days later, during an interview in Ho Chi Minh City with Dang Van Tin, the general managing director of Vietnamtourism, I told this story and asked for an explanation. Why had I been arrested? Mr. Dang and his marketing manager, Phan Xuan Anh, who was translating, broke into giggles.

"The news of our open society has not yet gotten out to some of the more remote provinces," Mr. Dang finally said.

*   *   *

The Evil Communist returned my passport and my camera, though he removed the film first—we didn't have digital then—and I'm still disappointed that I lost the evidence of that remarkable overnight visit. I snapped a couple of shots of the entrance to the compound on my way out, but not very satisfactory ones.

Dah-lot and I shook hands, and I thanked him for looking after me, though I'm not sure he understood. He seemed sorry I was leaving.

It was about noon when I took off, retracing the path I'd walked into town a couple of times with Dah-lot. By daylight, A Luoi was a drab and run-down place, a single pocked road with dingy huts lined up in the dirt on either side. On Sunday it was quiet, a few kids playing who stopped to stare at me, a woman in a cone hat gardening. I was curious about the guest house that had been my destination before I was rerouted by the police—it was marked on the map I was carrying—but there was no such thing. So perhaps getting arrested was a bit of luck in one regard—I'd had a bed to sleep in.

Having an untrustworthy map in a place so foreign and remote is no comfort. It had never occurred to me that the road I'd planned to follow to Hué, the one on the map marked in relative bold, might be a phantom, but as I passed through A Luoi and didn't find the turnoff, I had a pang of unease. I rode for a couple of miles before my sense-of-direction alarm went off, and I turned around for another look.

This time I located it on the far side of town. There was no sign, of course, just a narrow paved road cutting off at a sharp angle, the entrance partly hidden by a boulder and some trees. I hoped this was the right road, anyway, though it occurred to me that the road to Hué could be elsewhere or might not exist at all; if ever there was a place where "you can't get there from here" could actually obtain, this was it.

I took the turnoff and, despite the uncertainty, for several miles the ride was a pleasure. The scenery was bucolic, the pavement reasonably smooth, the sky a deep, cloudless blue, and thinking back on the previous twenty-four hours, I was pedaling with a sense of relief and self-congratulations at having emerged with aplomb from a sticky situation, forever equipped with a marvelous and funny adventure story to tell.

Naturally, the adventure wasn't quite past. The road wound and climbed, and the views were lovely, if a little forbidding in their revelation that I was heading into wilderness. The only sign of civilization as far as I could see was a telephone wire strung alongside the lonely road like Hansel and Gretel's trail of bread crumbs. Eventually it, too, disappeared, around the other side of a hill, and once again my feeling of solitude was complete. I didn't mind it; it was a little bit thrilling, actually, and I felt confident and purposeful, working hard up hills and coasting happily down, certain that I'd reach my destination later that day in triumph.

I was some hours into the journey when the roadbed began to deteriorate, the pavement giving way to dirt, then pebbly gravel, and finally, abruptly, on a very steep pitch, to a mass of sharp, broken stones, as if a chain gang had just been through with pickaxes to break up a wall of boulders. I had to dismount and walk, maneuvering the bike on foot, up and down hills, on potentially ankle-breaking terrain.

It was midafternoon and, as usual near the equator in late January, the temperature was above ninety degrees. In my haste to get going that morning—foolish, foolish—I hadn't replenished my supplies, and was down to a few gulps of water in a single water bottle and some fig cookies that had begun to spoil. I hadn't been through a village since A Luoi and there was no trace of one in the vista ahead of me. My friends in Hué had no way of knowing where I was. And it occurred to me to be frightened.

But I wasn't. This will sound disingenuous, I know, because it is easy from the perspective of safety to scoff at danger, but I was jazzed. I don't mean excited or happy—I mean, I was *concerned*—but vividly alert, able to think with striking focus and clarity, imbued with whatever inner strength I needed to keep panic at bay. In addition, I felt physically strong; weariness gave way, however temporarily, to vibrancy.

Why this was the case I don't know; if you had laid this situation out to me before it ever happened, I'm sure I would've said something like "Oh shit" and imagined myself in total freakout mode. Yet even as I understood that I didn't have a clue about what I was going to do, I felt, well, competent.

Which is why it doesn't even embarrass me to reveal how I got out of this pickle: after three hours of nothing on the road—no cars, pedestrians, other bicycles, wagons, or mules—a blue bus appeared, its engine grinding, its wheels crawling over the split rocks, and I got on.

Another monkey man clambered up to the roof and strapped down my bike with brisk efficiency, and three hours later, just at dusk—after the road became paved again, after we stopped at a village where men were squatting around a motorcycle with a dead boar tied across the back, after a ferry ride across a river—the bus arrived in Hué.

I don't remember exactly how I found the group hotel. I know I rode on the back of a motorcycle, an unofficial taxi, driven by some guy who was waiting at the bus station on the off chance that someone would need a ride. But how my bicycle came with us, I can't say. It's possible there was a second motorcyclist with a passenger who carried my bike on his shoulders, à la the bike pirates of several days earlier. I just don't recall, though I made it safely and so did my bike.

My helmet, however, didn't; it got lost somehow, and that ended up being the source of lingering embarrassment. There was nowhere in Hué to buy a replacement, but I wasn't about to continue bicycling through Vietnam's rugged terrain without protection, so I went to a hardware store and found a construction worker's helmet—a hard hat. I rode with it for the next ten days. It looked goofy, and it still does: I'm wearing it in the picture with the water buffalo on the front page of the *New York Times*.

At the hotel I climbed up on the porch just as a search party was about to depart. The group leaders had already rented a four-wheel-drive vehicle and a searchlight so they could look for me overnight, back-tracking over the road toward A Luoi.

They were pretty glad to see me. Imagine, we would joke in the days to come, the publicity for their business when it became known that they'd somehow misplaced a reporter for the *Times*. They were good guys, a bit overwhelmed.

Everyone else was welcoming, too; I was the star of the evening, regaling people with my story over drinks and laughs. Only Albert looked a little rueful that I had shown up before the search could get going; maybe he was hoping to recoup some of the excitement he'd missed.

This little episode, a rescue from what I'd perceived to be oblivion, is something I've thought about frequently over the years. In addition to saving my life, or so it seemed at the time, getting on the bus was also a bit of a disappointment. Before the road turned bad I'd had a hell of a ride, and now, of course, I wasn't going to be able to finish the trip on my own.

Still, by then I'd already had one of the great moments of my life, the moment of being an ordinary guy in extraordinary circumstances and not losing my head, the moment of being a hero to myself.

After all, if I'd known in advance that my journey would take me to as remote a place as I'd ever been, but that I'd be stranded there without food or water, I doubt I'd have even started out. As it stands, I can look back with astonishment at where I managed to get to on a bike when I wasn't being prudent or especially smart.

Tonight, sixteen years later, in a motel room somewhere along the border of North Dakota and Minnesota, it's what I remember most from my memorable trip to Vietnam—that measurement of my fortitude.

It doesn't escape me that I learned my lesson in personal bravery in a significant classroom, the distant, almost mythic-seeming land where, twenty and thirty years before, so many Americans—my age or older now, if they even survived, but not much more than kids, really, when they were there—had to plumb their guts for far more courage than I've ever had to do.

Having experienced the war in Vietnam from the New Jersey suburbs, and having felt, even from a distance of eight thousand miles the impact of its radiating terrors, I was grateful for the chance, a generation later, to be more intimately connected to such a powerful chapter of American history. It has been instructive: Character in context is a good thing to get a grip on.

PART THREE

The East, Eventually

12

My Country

Tuesday, September 6, Garrison, Minnesota

And, lo, it is autumn.

This morning when I woke at five thirty, the temperature was thirty-six degrees and it was damply foggy. Even though the sun burned the fog away by midmorning and the mercury eventually rose into the sixties, I pedaled through lunch wearing leggings and long-fingered gloves. This was something I had been looking forward to, riding as the season changed, and the enterprise of traveling all day outdoors changed with it. With the mornings brisk and the afternoons temperate, departing at dawn is no longer ideal. You have to dress carefully, to keep your extremities warm and your body protected from the cold wind, but not so bundled up as to overheat with exertion; when you sweat in the cold, you shiver and stiffen every time you stop. My nose has a tendency to run, too.

Still, if you dress right, cool weather is great for biking, energizing. I had a splendid Labor Day ride yesterday, taking advantage of Minnesota's network of state bike trails and cruising sixty miles untroubled by traffic on a paved, woodsy path through a region sprinkled with Paul Bunyan-iana. In every town center, it seems, there's an oversized sculpture of a bearded, axe-wielding woodsman or a blue ox. I'm heading in the general direction of Minneapolis.

It's remarkable how the nature of my cross-country ride has altered in just a few days. Less than a week ago I was negotiating the Dakota plains in the heat of August, but over the weekend, as though a big clock had gonged, impossible to ignore, summer shifted to fall. The flat plains with distant horizons that give you the feeling of being lost in a vast universe gave way to undulating cornfields and woods that hug you like the walls of a corridor.

Also in the last few days I've had two déjà vu experiences, both harking back to my first transcontinental trip in 1993; and over the weekend I reached the Mississippi River, which I guess means I'm halfway home, symbolically at least.

In any case, in my head I'm in the East now, and everything feels slightly less daunting; there's more familiarity in the air. Most of the people I know in the world are closer to me now—physically, I mean—than they have been in many weeks. I find that comforting.

A few days ago, Thursday, I crossed from North Dakota into Minnesota, and my odometer clicked over two thousand miles. I passed through Ada, a weathered farm community, and stayed the night in the only place I could find, the Shooting Star Casino in Mahnomen, on the Wild Rice River. (*Mahnomen* means wild rice in Chippewa. For lunch in Ada, I had wild rice soup—excellent—at the Wild Rice Diner.)

The casino seemed garish where it was, a several-winged building with a vast parking lot set down in the confines of a town of maybe twelve hundred people that serves mostly as a shopping center in the middle of a region devoted to hunting, fishing, and agriculture. It's the kind of place that books touring performers for one-night stands—country singers, television sitcom actors doing stand-up routines, and the occasional aging rock band like the Guess Who. It's got the big buffet, the windowless gambling caverns open twenty-four hours, the overweight smokers pumping coins into electronic slots, all of it an attenuated facsimile of what made Las Vegas what it is—that is, the glittery promise of instant satisfaction and dream-come-true success.

It was strange to spend the night there, but I wandered around the place. I listened to a dreadful lounge-lizardy singer in one of the bars, though I didn't stay long; the air was rank with stale cigarette smoke. I did eat two meals, dinner and breakfast, at the buffet, complete with gluey desserts that were a boon to my calorie loading, but all in all I was happy to get going again in the morning.

It was a short day, just forty miles, but the destination was a welcome one: Itasca State Park, home of Lake Itasca, the headwaters of the Mississippi River.

I'd always wanted to go there, not for any complicated or even specific reason, but just because the Mississippi is such a vivid American symbol. I've crossed it a number of times before (in a car, mostly), but always in places where its grandeur made an impression. That this mammoth, continent-cutting waterway even *has* a beginning is sort of stupefying, isn't it? Like imagining Paul Bunyan as an infant.

Inside the park, I followed the signs to the headwaters, locked up my bike at the welcome center, and walked a quarter mile or so to the water's edge. It was a little bit cloudy and the breeze carried an autumn chill, and as I waded in the river, traversing its stony bottom barefoot from shore to shore—a journey of ten or twelve feet—I kept my Windbreaker on. It was an absurdly exhilarating experience.

The headwaters are a peculiar attraction, a pretty spot with the water from a reedy lake spilling over a breakwater of rocks but hardly breathtaking. Still, it has the tug of vivid Americana, and so I couldn't help thinking about Mark Twain.

The idea that this unassuming brook becomes the mighty Mississippi is belief-defying, and I kept thinking how incredibly cool it was that I could drop a Ping-Pong ball at my feet and pick it up in a week or two in Louisiana. There were a lot of families around, kids getting wet, parents taking pictures.

As I was sitting on a log over the river, looking in the direction of the Gulf of Mexico, a boy maybe ten years old with unruly blond hair, wearing cutoff shorts and no shirt, came charging upstream, whooping. My own personal Huck Finn.

The next morning, combating a brisk, cold wind in bright sunshine, I rode the park's sixteen-mile loop road: it was a highlight of the whole trip, a swooping jaunt with curvy, smoothly paved downhills through dense forest, past swampy ponds, and along the shores of two broad lakes. When I got back to the cabin where I was staying, I had company.

In 1993, when I made my first cycling journey across the United States, my old college pal Alan Blomquist decided it would be fun to rendezvous somewhere along the way. It wasn't exactly convenient for him. He lived in Los Angeles, but found his way to Pierre, South Dakota, just as I got there on my bike. We rented a motorboat on the Missouri River (and grounded it in the muddy shallows, as I recall). We ate enormous steaks and drank several martinis at a roadhouse, and for a day and a half tossed around familiar stories from our days together at the University of Michigan, where we were both officers of a student movie co-op. It was a great break for me, even though I did have to ride the following day with a hangover.

Al produces movies for a living now, the right profession for someone with a great gift for persuasion and for getting things done. He's a big guy—I mean, like, six four, two fifty—with an expansive personality, admirably un-insecure. Unlike me, he's willing to talk to anyone at any time. Nothing involving conversation ever seems to daunt him—he won over a lot of girls with sheer verbal charm—and it used to piss me off all the time when we were in college when we'd be on the way someplace and run into someone he knew and I'd end up in an agony of impatience waiting for him to conduct some detailed bit of personal business.

Also, he can fix things—I have a hard time driving in a nail—and he is a resourceful problem-solver. For example, he found a way to get hold of me while I was on the road in 1993 in order to arrange our meeting in Pierre. When we were in college, he made money doing carpentry work—he hired me for a roofing job once, out of pity, I think, but ended up firing me, anyway—and for a while we shared a house that had a lot of jury-rigged plumbing and wiring of his design. We made a movie together once; I wrote a pretentious script about an illicit love affair in which the main character was a piano tuner, and Al produced it, talking the owner of an Ann Arbor piano showroom into letting us film there.

Al is a man who respects precedent, and it was his idea that we should repeat our mid-continental meeting. In fact, he wanted to return to Pierre, though I don't think he was too disappointed when I said was a little too far north to get there. Instead, I suggested Lake Itasca.

He had arrived after midnight, having driven three and a half hours

from Minneapolis, where he had flown from L.A., via Phoenix. We'd
barely said hello when he stumbled into the cabin I'd rented, and when
I left for the loop ride he was still asleep. When I got back we began
our reunion in earnest. We rented a motorboat on the lake (and briefly
got tangled in the reeds along the shoreline), hiked a couple of trails
through the woods, swatted some baseballs at the batting cages in a
small, old, touchingly low-tech amusement park, and ate enormous
steaks at a local roadhouse. Passed on the martinis this time, but we did
stop for a drink in Park Rapids at the Royal Bar, where the sign outside
declared it served POSSIBLY THE BEST BURGERS & FRIES IN NORTHERN
MINNESOTA and the waitresses were wearing shirts with the slogan
WARM BEER/ROTTEN FOOD/SEVEN DAYS A WEEK printed on the back.
Then we went across the street to the movies. (*Crazy, Stupid, Love* with
Steve Carell and Marisa Tomei, among others. Mixed reviews. I thought
it was crummy. Al liked it.)

Part of the joy of this kind of day is the culture shock of it, of course,
a reporter from New York and a filmmaker from Hollywood plop-
ping themselves down serendipitously in flyover territory and being
reminded that the America we know on the coasts is a very small slice
of the pie. Just south of Itasca State Park, Park Rapids is a charming,
unpretentious town where an accordionist was playing polkas and Irish
folk tunes on the sidewalk, the A&W root beer stand has drive-in stalls
and carhops, and the old-fashioned confectionery on the main drag is
called the MinneSODA Ice Cream Fountain.

Al was leaving the next morning, and I was going to take an extra
day off to give my saddle-sore rear end a break. We'd pretty much finished chewing over the same old stories and sharing a few new ones,
the kinds of things men our age talk about—retirement plans, new and
old romances, politics, the parts of our bodies that are breaking down.
His second marriage had dissolved not long before. From the first one
he has twin sons, one of whom runs a bike tour company in Barcelona.
I told him about Jan.

I said it was remarkable that he'd come all this way to such an out-of-
the-way place to meet me, and that things didn't seem so different from

when we met in Pierre, even though a lot of summers had become a lot of falls in the interim.

"We'll do it again in another eighteen years," I said.

One thing is different, he said. We'd arranged this weekend with texts and emails and cell phone calls. It was easy.

"How did we do this the last time?" he said. "How did I even find you?"

It gave me a sudden chill to recognize that I'm so accustomed to wireless technology that I can't even remember what it was like without it. One day you're a Flintstone, the next a Jetson. As we grow older, we're always complaining about how fast time goes, but this made me feel as though I'd raced through the last eighteen years without noticing them.

"You did it," I said. "I don't remember how, though."

"Neither do I," he said.

This afternoon I rode through Brainerd, a small city on the Mississippi—the river wiggles as it goes south, and Brainerd is slightly east and south of Itasca—and I realized I'd been there before, on my 1993 trip, though I didn't recognize the place. Back then, it had seemed to me a typical farming center; I stayed in a small motel and spent an evening at a county fair—maybe it was even the state fair—eating corn dogs and watching sheep shearers. I remember a Ferris wheel and a rickety-looking bungee jump concession (I passed on both) and on the midway a set of blond triplets, maybe four years old, all of them stuffing puffs of pink cotton candy in their mouths. They'd be college graduates now.

This afternoon I found a different Brainerd, prosperous and bustling, at least on its outskirts, thronged with traffic and swathed in shopping malls, and I became tangled in a series of busy roads, taking me along one commercial strip after another. I was trying to head south, toward Saint Cloud, but after I found myself on the entrance ramp of Highway 371, gulping with anxiety as I watched traffic zipping along at sixty or seventy miles an hour, I retraced my steps for five or six miles, back into the center of town.

It's funny, but I hadn't once thought about where I might cross paths with my previous trip until today when I did it. And it spurred my memory; all afternoon and evening I've been reviewing that trip in my mind.

In 1993, I came into Brainerd from the southwest and I left heading to the northeast. From here I rode toward Lake Superior, through the cultural landmarks of two generations—Hibbing, Bob Dylan's home-town, and Grand Rapids, Judy Garland's—to Ely, a hunting and fishing outpost amid the boundary waters. That was the northernmost point of the journey, a place where the woods were terrifically dense and beau-tiful—"lovely, dark and deep," I remember thinking, Frost's phrase, though he was writing about winter in New England—the road signs had pictographs of moose and snowmobiles, and at dusk the mosqui-toes arrived in clouds.

Two tiny highlights of that first trip: in Grand Rapids, where Gar-land was born Frances Gumm, I stopped at the Judy Garland Museum on the third floor of a former schoolhouse and discovered that on June 18, 1977, Dylan (né Robert Zimmerman) had been there and signed the guest register. Then I hit the road, coming up behind a friendly jogger going my way, and slowed to talk to him. "I'm heading for Ely tonight," I said, pronouncing it properly: EE-lee.

"If you want to speak to God," he responded, "it's a local call from there."

Backtracking away from Highway 371 turned out well for me. In the center of Brainerd—as in a lot of places, the core of the city was consid-erably more worn than the perimeter—I found a bicycle shop where a couple of the salespeople were eager map readers and advice providers, and they pointed me east, toward Mille Lacs Lake. (That is, 1,000 Lakes Lake. MEEL-lock, they would say in France—or Quebec—but here it's muh-LAX.)

It was a late-afternoon ride of twenty miles to Garrison, a lakeside resort town, though not an especially fancy one, that had been deserted after the weekend and was notably empty on the day after Labor Day. I checked into a motel and at the lakeside lucked into a majestically tranquil scene. A single dock stretched out for fifty yards into the lake, with two fishing boats moored and bobbing at the end of it, but aside from that, the surface of the lake, deep purple and rippling gently, was empty to the horizon. With the onset of evening, the sky was a slowly darkening azure and the air was glowing amber. On the shore, a flock of white gulls, hundreds of them, were strutting around for a while like a miniature marching band and, on a silent signal, took off all at once in a great flapping of togetherness, the whole body of them rising with the steady urgency of an airplane and angling shiftily this way and that like a tailback loose in the secondary until they simply disappeared over the water in the distance. Gorgeous. The end of summer.

I walked about a hundred yards up the road that hugged the shore and stopped in front of Garrison's most garish attraction, an enormous wooden sculpture of a fish, twenty feet long and mounted on a pedestal maybe ten feet high. It was a walleye—the local delicacy—bronze with a white belly and a barbed shield arced on its back, posed as though breaking the surface of the lake from beneath it, its tail fin swishing fiercely, its mouth open in anger, baring tiny sharp teeth. Three signs were posted beneath it on the pedestal, side by side by side.

The first said: WELCOME TO GARRISON, MINNESOTA.

The second said: LEGEND HAS IT THIS WALLEYE WAS CAUGHT BY PAUL BUNYAN AND BABE THE BLUE OX AFTER A THREE DAY STRUGGLE. PAUL FINALLY WRAPPED HIS LINE AROUND BABE'S HORNS AND BABE PULLED THE FISH OUT OF LAKE MILLE LACS ONTO GARRISON BEACH.

The third said: KEEP OFF THE FISH!

I wish you could see the smile on my face.

My country.

Saturday, September 10, Saint Louis Park, Minnesota

Early Thursday morning I saw something I hadn't seen in weeks.

Because I'm heading east, and because I've put in most of my miles in the morning, the sun has never been low enough in the afternoon to throw a shadow out in front of me. So when my route to the Twin Cities took me due west for a few miles not long after the sun came up, there I was up ahead in silhouette, strolling down the avenue, er, I mean, pedaling away on the shoulder of the road. Cool!

Of course, like the groundhog, I couldn't wait to run from it. Turning south, I left my shadow to the side and slightly behind me, where it belongs. I don't care to see it again until I get home. Eastward ho!

I picked my way through the northern suburbs of Minneapolis, following my GPS through a peculiar mixture of neighborhood streets, park trails, and the sidewalks of busy commercial strips, and spent two cushy nights here in Saint Louis Park, a plush quarter on the southwestern edge of Minneapolis, with an old softball buddy, Rick Gibson. One day, he and I rode around the Twin Cities on their myriad bike paths. I got a kick out of riding through downtown, past the ballpark and the Guthrie Theater, and I found myself wondering what New York City would be like if you could actually get on your bike and travel safely away from traffic to Lincoln Center and Yankee Stadium.

I hadn't seen or heard from Rick since he got married and moved away from New York twenty-five years or so ago. But he wrote to me while I was in North Dakota and offered to put me up for a couple of days if I came through town. I had my own basement room with a television set and a stereo system in a comfy suburban house. Rick and his wife, Cheryl, made sure I ate big meals three times a day; they even lent me their car to get my iPhone repaired at the downtown Apple store and to meet another friend, Glenn Shambroom, who lives in Massachusetts but just happened to be in Minneapolis to visit his brother. All in all, I felt like your average twenty-year-old home from college for the weekend. For a solitary traveler it was an embarrassment of riches.

A handful of news items.

First, Mr. Scorpion is no more. His last post went over the line in disparagement mode—"Stupid is as stupid does" was the line that did it for me—and I called the paper to ask for his actual email address. Here's the note I composed to him:

> Hey dude, I get it. You don't like me. You don't like the bike trip thing. Write all you want about why, but I can't let you call me names on my own blog. One more ad hominem attack and I'll ask the blog guardians to cut you off.
> Your pal, Bruce Weber.

I was too late. The guardians had already nixed him. Bye, old friend.

Next, my ass is finally wearing an accommodating groove in my seat with the yellow stripes, and the discomfort I was living with daily has been reduced considerably. No more numbed netherparts and tender sit bones. I'm back to the bearable and familiar-to-all-cyclists package of afflictions like muscle weariness and chafing.

Also, I bought a plane ticket from Pittsburgh to New Orleans for October 7, four weeks from tomorrow, and from there I'll fly to New Orleans for this wedding of the son of one of Jan's college friends. We spend maybe thirty-six hours in New Orleans, then get on a plane at 5:00 a.m. to fly back to Pittsburgh together, with a layover in Atlanta, where I'll introduce Jan to my brother, who is going to meet us at the airport for breakfast.

Our plan is preposterous, of the so-crazy-it-just-might-work variety. Jan has just bought a collapsible bike that she's going to bring with her. She's going to fly to New York on Thursday the sixth, stay at my apartment, and pack a bag with clothes for me to wear to the wedding and proceed to New Orleans the next morning.

From Pittsburgh we'll ride together for three days, she on her collapsible bike (Will that work? I don't know), at which point she'll rent a car, assuming there's a car to be rented wherever three days from Pittsburgh by bicycle turns out to be. She'll drive to Annapolis to pick up our wedding clothes from a friend of hers who has agreed to schlep them home from the wedding, stop off in West Chester, Pennsylvania, to see her father, and then head back to New York for dinner with her daughters before flying back to Paris the next morning.

By that time I should be about ten days from home. But all of this assumes, of course, that I'll make it to Pittsburgh in time in the first place.

This is pretty exciting. For one thing, it makes some route decisions for me. For another, it's a destination to aim for in advance of my final destination, a finish line before the finish line, one more achievement and one more reward to look forward to. Spurs are helpful.

There's something else, though. What I'm willing to do in order to spend time with Jan is something I'm not sure I'd have done for any of the other women I professed to love. In my life I've shied away from rendezvous plans a lot less complicated than this.

There are reasons I'm fifty-seven and single, and one is that I've often chosen not to extend myself; given the option, I tend to draw the line between a solo life and a coupled one not very far into the gulf between them. "Commitment-phobe" is a term I've heard more than once, and I haven't argued. Have I grown out of this at last? Perhaps I've simply worn out my welcome with myself. Maybe it's that Jan affects me differently than anyone else ever has, making it easier for me to make room for her. Or maybe at this age commitment is less intimidating because it's not as long as it used to be.

As several of my correspondents have pointed out, I arrived in Minnesota simultaneously with perfect biking weather, cool and sunny; yesterday, at last, I had an amiable tailwind, too. The country has endured so much burdensome weather lately that I feel a bit sheepish in admitting I've been smiled on with preposterous regularity so far. The temperature hasn't reached ninety for me in weeks. I've ridden in the rain exactly four times and have been truly soaked only twice. The wind has been predominantly southern, a little irksome lately but not so bad (or good) overall. I'm either due for a comeuppance or I'll bring my good fortune with me to the East.

In the meantime, I'll respond to a few frequently posed questions and oft-stated comments.

1. No, I haven't used my tent and sleeping bag yet, not for their ordinary purpose, anyway, and yes, I could probably ship them home now and save myself a little weight on the back of the bike. But they're earning their keep. As anyone who has suffered from acid reflux will tell you, you should sleep at an incline, with your head and chest higher than your stomach, so the offending acid has to fight gravity, in the manner of salmon swimming upstream to spawn. To effect this, each night I've been shoving my tent and sleeping bag under the mattress. It helps. I sleep through the night without coughing.

2. No, I don't wear headphones to listen to music when I'm riding. Now and then, on a quiet road, especially when I'm climbing, I'll turn on some music on the iPhone mounted on my handlebars—usually

the Beatles or my current favorite country music singer, Trisha Year-wood—to keep me company uphill. But you need to be able to hear cars approaching behind you, and anyway, when you're outdoors it seems silly to shut out the outdoors. I do find myself singing to myself. Perhaps someone out there has a theory for why certain songs repeat themselves in your head in certain situations, as if your brain were equipped with its own idiosyncratic playlist. For whatever reason—maybe because the beats conform to my pedal strokes—the same tunes repeat themselves and have been accompanying me up hills for more than two thousand miles: "Hang On, Sloopy," "Jamaica Farewell" (that's the Harry Bela-fonte classic in which he has to leave a little girl in Kingston town), and a Mozart horn concerto (I forget which one). I have no explanation for the seeming randomness of this.

3. Yes, I've been chased by a few dogs. No harm done (to dog or man). I don't carry mace or onion spray or any of the other weapons I've been advised to keep handy. My strategy? I adopted one reader's advice and, shaking a finger at the barking pursuer, I declare firmly: "Go home!" Seems to work.

4. People ask what I'm reading as though I've got a lot of lonely hours to pass at night. I wish I could say I was reading a lot, but I'm not. I try to keep up with the *Times*, and wherever I am I enjoy reading the local paper. But in the evenings I'm generally too tired to do much besides eat dinner and check in on *SportsCenter*. I did finish *Comedy in a Minor Key*, a short, gripping Holocaust novel about a couple who hide a Jew in their home and must dispose of his body when he dies, by the Dutch writer Hans Keilson, who died himself recently at a hundred and one.

5. So many people have asked about the specifics of my route that I herewith offer a day-by-day log of where I've been. (I haven't indi-cated rest days. Mileage figures are according to my odometer, and yes, a handful of times I accepted rides in pickups—to get over unrideable gravel roads, to get through a construction zone, and twice, in Spokane

and in Itasca State Park in Minnesota, to hang out with friends. The charity rides add up to about forty miles. So shoot me.)

Day 1—Astoria, Ore., to Tillamook, 63.7 mi
Day 2—Tillamook to McMinnville, 64.2 mi (total mileage 127.9)
Day 3—McMinnville to Estacada, 55.8 mi (183.7)
Day 4—Estacada to Troutdale, 24.4 mi (208.1)
Day 5—Troutdale to Hood River, 53.2 mi (261.3)
Day 6—Hood River to Biggs Junction, 45.1 mi (306.4)
Day 7—Biggs Junction to Umatilla, 81.1 mi (387.5)
Day 8—Umatilla to Walla Walla, Wash., 54.7 mi (442.2)
Day 9—Walla Walla to Pomeroy, 66.6 mi (508.8)
Day 10—Pomeroy to Dusty, 34.8 mi (543.6)
Day 11—Dusty to Cheney, 64.2 mi (607.8)
Day 12—Cheney to Spokane, 16.4 mi (624.2)
Day 13—Spokane to Newport, 58.8 mi (683)
Day 14—Newport to Sandpoint, Idaho, 29 mi (712)
Day 15—Sandpoint to Troy, Mont., 67.9 (779.9)
Day 16—Troy to Lake Koocanusa, 44.2 mi (824.1)
Day 17—Lake Koocanusa to Eureka, 43.2 mi (867.3)
Day 18—Eureka to Whitefish, 54 mi (921.3)
Day 19—Whitefish to Lake McDonald (Glacier National Park), 41 mi (962.3)
Day 20—Lake McDonald to Saint Mary, over the Continental Divide, 39.7 mi (1,002)
Day 21—Saint Mary to Cut Bank, 62.8 mi (1,064.8)
Day 22—Cut Bank to Chester, 64.6 mi (1,129.4)
Day 23—Chester to Havre, 58.5 mi (1,187.9)
Day 24—Havre to Malta, 82 mi (1,269.9)
Day 25—Malta to Glasgow, 68.7 mi (1,338.6)
Day 26—Glasgow to Wolf Point, 52.8 mi (1,391.4)
Day 27—Wolf Point to Circle, 51.3 mi (1,442.7)
Day 28—Circle to Glendive, 49.7 mi (1,492.4)
Day 29—Glendive to Medora, N. Dak., 61.5 mi (1,553.9)

Day 30—Loop road, Theodore Roosevelt National Park, 35 mi
       (1,588.9)

Day 31—Medora to Richardton, 58.7 mi (1,647.6)

Day 32—Richardton to Mandan, 75.6 mi (1,723.2)

Day 33—Mandan to Bismarck, 8.3 mi (1,731.5)

Day 34—Bismarck to Medina, 75.9 mi (1,807.4)

Day 35—Medina to Carrington, 43.5 mi (1,850.9)

Day 36—Carrington to Cooperstown, 47.6 mi (1,898.5)

Day 37—Cooperstown to Hillsboro, 64.5 mi (1,963)

Day 38—Hillsboro to Mahnomen, Minn., 60.5 mi (2,023.5)

Day 39—Mahnomen to Itasca State Park, 41.5 mi (2,065)

Day 40—Loop road, Itasca Park, 16 mi (2,081)

Day 41—Park Rapids to Pine River, 56.6 mi (2,137.6)

Day 42—Pine River to Garrison, 64.4 mi (2,202)

Day 43—Garrison to Mora, 60.5 mi (2,262.5)

Day 44—Mora to Brooklyn Center, 69.9 mi (2,332.4)

Day 45—Brooklyn Center to Saint Louis Park, 15.5 mi (2,347.9)

13

Head Games

Sunday, September 11, 2011, Red Wing, Minnesota

*T*en years ago today, I stood in front of my apartment building in lower Manhattan and watched the World Trade Center towers burn. I didn't see either of the planes hit. I was puttering in the kitchen, readying myself to get to work at the keyboard—I had a theater review to write—when my aunt Claire called me from Westchester just before nine.

I thought I knew what the call was about. My father had flown up from Georgia and was staying with her. After eight months of living alone in the cookie-cutter condo where my mother had died, he was ready to take my advice and move to New York, and that day he was supposed to come into the city to look for an apartment. Claire was going to tell me what time his train would get to Grand Central Terminal. But that wasn't it, of course.

"Turn on the TV," she said.

No one knew anything at that point. I hurried downstairs to the street—I live on the eleventh floor—and found an astonished crowd of my neighbors, maybe two hundred people, gathered in the middle of a Greenwich Village intersection, about two miles from what came to be known as Ground Zero. The twin towers were a feature of the neighborhood, looming elegantly over it in the distance; if you looked downtown along our street, they were a fixture of the skyline. This morning, everyone was looking up and watching, aghast, as the north tower, gashed and aflame, spewed smoke into the air, and a breeze carried it toward Brooklyn against a pristine blue sky.

Someone had a radio. The first reports were that the plane was private; a pilot had veered tragically off course. Hungry for more information, I went back inside and was about to step into the elevator when I felt a shudder in the air; the second plane had hit the south tower, which I discovered when I got back upstairs and turned on the television again. Shortly thereafter, I went back down to the street.

This is how it went for the next couple of hours. In and out, in and out. Outside to bear witness, inside to find out what was going on. Outside, shock and disbelief reigned. Inside, sober reality took hold. It was genuinely weird; I couldn't seem to believe my eyes. Only television was able to verify the horror as real.

For my father, the opposite was true. He stubbornly refused to acknowledge—or couldn't—that what was happening in miniature on his screen in Scarsdale was happening with larger-than-life-sized certainty in lower Manhattan, and he called me to complain.

"There are no trains running into the city," he said. "I'm going to miss my appointment with the Realtor. Dammit."

I resisted chiding him for taking a terrorist attack as a personal inconvenience. My father was always someone whose perspective narrowed when he was tense or stressed out, and his decision to start out alone in an intimidating city at age seventy-five had his anxiety dial turned up to max. Now his chosen new home was suddenly under violent assault.

"Easy does it, Dad," I said.

I assured him that the Realtor would understand, that she'd be happy to see him whenever the trains were running again, and that his future apartment was going to be there for him even if he didn't find it today.

"I know," he said, "I know," and I could tell he felt foolish.

"What about you?" he said, after a moment and a breath. "Are you safe?"

*   *   *

Today, ten years later, far from the somber memorial ceremonies at Ground Zero, I started out from Saint Louis Park, following some of the same bike paths I'd ridden with Rick until I crossed the Fort Snelling–Mendota Bridge over the Minnesota River, just above its confluence with the Mississippi. I pedaled south through a tangle of suburbs in the morning and an undistinguished checkerboard of fields and rural communities in the afternoon, at one point ending up on an unpaved road that looked to be a shortcut but wore me out over several miles with camel-hump hills of dust and gravel that made traction going up and balance going down precarious. I could have done a lot better. I'd made one route mistake after another, and I had the feeling, rare on this trip, that I'd wasted a day; with a little more care, a little more planning, some better decisions, I could have had a pleasant, scenic ride. Instead, I had a trying one that I was especially glad was over, and if I was going to feel that way at the end of the day I might just as well have stayed home.

Yeah, I'm a little grouchy for having spent the day in one of America's myriad pockets of unmemorable ordinariness. By now a sense of anonymity hovers over many American places—not the big cities or the small towns, necessarily, or even the older suburbs that started with a slow exodus from an urban center, emerged individually, and created histories of their own. I'm talking about the far outskirts of cities, where exurban landscapes, with their housing developments filled with bland starter homes or frightful McMansions and their shopping malls crowded with the familiar litany of retail names, have evolved the close-to-sameness of siblings. Today that's where I was, and after so many weeks of pedaling through singular places, it pissed me off to be somewhere that didn't strike me as anything new to experience.

As I get older, as I pedal along on this trip, the desire that days be unique—or at least different from one another—is growing more urgent in me, the belief growing stronger that we ought to try and make our days different. It's a hard thing to do, of course, but we ought to be resolute in our determination to live interestingly. Right?

*   *   *

The afternoon of 9/11 I went to the newsroom to help out as a reporter and was sent to the warehouse-sized hangars along the Hudson River in the 50s that were being outfitted as emergency hospital wards for the anticipated flood of casualties. As it turned out, there weren't any. Serious injuries that day were few; nearly everyone who got hurt was dead, and as that realization landed on us—me and the reporters and cameramen from a couple of dozen other news agencies—we began drifting away, feeling our own uselessness on top of the overwhelming dread.

A few days later, most of us in New York felt our dread give way to anger and incredible sadness—or maybe it was sadness and incredible anger—as it dawned on us that life was never going to be quite the same. That's what made 9/11 a touchstone for all New Yorkers, if not all Americans. The event was so unfathomable and so momentous that it felt personal even for those of us who weren't touched personally. How, I remember thinking, would I ever feel anything other than insignificant ever again?

This line of reasoning, of course, describes exactly what my father's had been—perceiving a monumental tragedy in egocentric terms.

I actually recognized my self-pity at the time, though I didn't call it that.

"The reaction on our street could fairly be described as perplexity, which was, as I look back, the seed of the punishing irrelevance that has been plaguing me since then," I wrote in an essay for the *Times* that was published five days after 9/11. "No one knew what to do or which way to move. There was something both compelling and repellent about the incredible event taking place in front of our eyes. I mean that literally; it drew you toward it, it pushed you away. You wanted to race downtown at top speed to bear witness; you wanted to turn your back, to flee.

"Many people were simply held in their tracks, the understanding kicking in that just going to work as usual, just going to the store for the breakfast milk, would be deeply inappropriate."

The essay went on to talk about what it was like to be close enough to a tragedy to witness it but not close enough to be a primary sufferer. Reading it now, I see how narcissistic it is—Yeah, it's awful, but what about me?—but I also think it's perfectly in character. On 9/11 all New Yorkers found themselves contemplating the meaning of our existences, and we all faced the conundrum of whether we stand alone as extraordinary individuals or together as ordinary mortals.

I've been saying New Yorkers as though other Americans didn't go through this, as though the Pentagon hadn't also been attacked and United Airlines flight 93 from Newark to San Francisco hadn't plummeted into a Pennsylvania field. That's another sign of narcissism, isn't it? But it's true that for me—and I think for most if not all of my neighbors—New York City seemed more like the center of the universe that day than it usually does. It's why we live there, of course, because the tug of its importance, its cultural gravity, is immense; it's also why, among other reasons, I'd felt the need to escape this summer on my bike. Anyway, here is the rest of what I wrote ten years ago, slightly edited:

Since Tuesday I've thought a lot about my fellow gawkers on Mercer Street and wondered for how many of them the grotesqueries of the week got closer, more personal, and how many have merely shared my experience of bystanderhood. I heard one network newscaster say that "just about everyone I know has some connection to someone who was involved in this attack," but the reality is that most of us don't. We have been moved to suffer in sympathy. Which, as it turns out, holds a distinct agony of its own. Just about everyone I know felt worse as the week went on.

One of the obvious lessons of terrorism is that it renders people helpless. Americans have understood this, even though up to now we have largely been spared the emotional erosion of living in constant insecurity. On that score our immunity is up.

But the persistent and deepening throb of pain, I think, is caused by something beyond helplessness. I'll speak solely for myself here, but

I've never felt smaller or more insignificant than I have this week and partly this is a terrible irony because I'm among the lucky. As far as I know, I've lost no one close to me. I've lost no property. Whatever images there are to haunt me from the tragedy are the ones that haunt millions who watch television and read the newspaper. Even my personal experience of the calamity is one I shared with a crowd of neighbors.

I have, in other words, no private terror or individuated anguish, the emotional currency of the moment. And though this will sound selfish or chilly or less than magnanimous, I resent having no purchase on sympathy. But I understand. There's only so much sympathy to go around; we're all doing triage with our available feelings.

At the same time, unless you are in certain professions, it turns out there is almost nothing to be done to lend a hand, aside from donating blood (not so easy to do in the chaotic aftermath or, stunningly, so necessary) or money. The business of reassuring out-of-town friends and loved ones of one's own safety doesn't take much time or energy. Compulsively watching television does.

The inability to do much more than keep oneself informed is a terrible frustration. And it is cruelly isolating, at least to me, because of the extraordinary urge I have to be counted among my communities—of New Yorkers, of Americans, and of my fellow men and women. But who knows how to do this right now? The way I'm generally satisfied to announce my presence in the world is through what I do every day.

Whether this is healthy or admirable is another argument, but I won't deny that my profession commands an enormous role in my idea of myself, and as a theater critic I didn't feel any more necessary after curtains went up in New York on Thursday than I did while theaters were dark. How could I find meaning in such frivolousness? I'm thankful to the firefighters, police officers, rescue workers, doctors and others, including my fellow journalists, for responding with such ardor to this catastrophe, but I'm envious of them as well.

I know I'm not alone in this. The fruitlessness of pursuing one's daily life was shared by a spectrum of people who renounced their chosen practices. Professional athletes were among those who publicly expressed disdain for doing what they do, and the shopkeepers in my neighborhood expressed the same thing by closing their shops. Indeed, commerce has rarely seemed so crass; the young man who took advantage of the occasion to peddle American flag bandannas on lower Fifth Avenue on Thursday drew far more glares of disdain than customers, at least while I was watching.

I commend Mayor Rudolph W. Giuliani's declaration that New Yorkers should return to their normal lives, go to restaurants and stores, resume their jobs, in order to keep the economy and the spirit of the city afloat and to send a message of our enduring hardiness to those who would destroy us.

But part of me wants to respond, respectfully: That's easy for you to say. You have a pertinent life to lead.

What about those of us who feel as if we've been robbed of ourselves, who've had no choice but to wait until this all subsides and the world returns to a semblance of something we recognize, something that allows us to go on with our lives without feeling entirely inconsequential?

It seems to me that what terrorists stole from even the most fortunate of New Yorkers on Tuesday may not have been our lives but fragments of them—whole unrecoverable days, an unspecified number of them in which we simply believe we don't matter.

What can we do in the meantime to pretend otherwise? Frankly, writing this essay was all I could think of.

September 11 was a Tuesday. On Thursday, September 13, my father signed the lease for an apartment on the Upper East Side of Manhattan. It occurred to me to bring this to the attention of Mayor Giuliani— *Here's a citizen who believes in the future of our city!*—but I didn't.

He returned to Atlanta for a couple of weeks—my dad, not the mayor. He sold his car, giving up driving for good, thankfully, and packed up the house and Coco, the delicate, feminine, dignified, ageless yellow cat I would later inherit and nickname Brooke Astor. He and Coco were in their new digs by the middle of October.

Just about the first thing we did together was visit Ground Zero, where the cleanup was, of course, still in progress, and the notices of missing people remained posted everywhere. We didn't say much as we walked around; it's remarkable the sobering effect of rubble. Afterward I took him to the theater district in midtown for a comforting lunch, and we had chicken soup and latkes in the coffee shop of the Edison Hotel. I guess I was trying to show him that my New York could be his New York, too, that after his wife had died and after the city had been assaulted, this was still a place for him. I don't deny feeling guilty for my part in our estrangement.

At lunch he told me something I hadn't known about him, that he'd always felt intimidated in Manhattan, that as a child growing up in the Bronx he'd viewed Manhattan as a place the Bronx and its inhabitants revolved around. The sense that he didn't belong here, that he wasn't important enough, never left him, he said. He had been thrilled when I first moved to the Upper West Side; it was no small matter of pride, he said, that his son had felt worthy where he had not.

When I protested that he'd worked in Manhattan for twenty-five years, he shrugged. Every morning he walked from the bus terminal to his office—first in the old McGraw-Hill Building near the Lincoln Tunnel and later the new one on Sixth Avenue—and every evening walked back again. He knew a few restaurants in the neighborhood where he'd gone for a business lunch occasionally—"There was a French place you took me to once when I came to your office," I said, nodding—but he didn't even know if they were still there.

"I always felt like an outsider here," he said, which brought back the memory that, as young boys, my brother and I would often race to the corner of our New Jersey street at dinnertime to wait for my father's bus to arrive and to watch him step off. The realization that I had thought of him daily as a returning hero and that he had thought of himself as a retreating soldier was a poignant shock.

For the nineteen months that my father lived in Manhattan, he had a good time. We saw each other once or twice a week. I took him to the theater with me, sometimes to Off-Off Broadway stuff put on by twenty-somethings in second-floor living rooms or empty garages that left him agog at the creative energy oozing from the city's every crawl space. We took the Number 4 subway to Yankee Stadium or the Number 7 to Shea, or we watched the Giants on television. I took him out for Indian food at a restaurant near his apartment and it was a revelation to him— "Tandoori chicken! Lamb saag! Naan!"—so we ate there frequently. Or he came downtown for dinner at the Knickerbocker, a steakhouse and bar on University Place not far from my apartment, where the owner, Steve Jones, took a liking to him and treated him as a regular.

He began shopping for food in specialty shops, treating himself to the variety and quality he'd denied himself for many years. I finally convinced him to tip waiters and waitresses less grudgingly.

"Dad, let's say you did it my way for a year. How much would it cost you? Three hundred dollars? Four hundred? Would that make a difference in your life?"

"No," he said.

"It would in theirs," I said.

"Ah," he said as the lightbulb went on.

He started going to museums and taking classes and going to lectures at the 92nd Street Y.

"I've been sitting on the steps of the Met all morning," he called to tell me on the phone once. "The girls are unbelievable."

And after a while he joined an online matchmaking service and started dating. I never met any of the women he went out with, but he approached me often for advice. Over dinner one night he said he was perplexed by the emails he was getting from younger women who all said the same thing, that they were looking for a "generous older gentleman." I informed him that *gentleman* means rich and that *gener-*

ous means really rich, and he nodded soberly as if I'd explained to him a murky clause in an international trade agreement.

"But there's this one," he said. "She keeps writing me. And I finally said to her, 'What do you want with an old geezer like me?' And she wrote back and said she's always been attracted to older men because they don't play head games."

He paused, and I wasn't sure what his point was. For a minute I'd lost track of the fact that he hadn't been on a date since 1947.

"Head games," he said finally. "What the hell is she talking about?"

I introduced him to a former girlfriend of mine with whom I'd stayed friends, and the two of them became friends. She lived around the corner from him, and they would meet for lunch now and then at a noodle shop in the neighborhood. He told me he thought she was carrying a torch for me—that was his phrase—and I shrugged. She and I had been together for six months or so, but we were quite different. She worked on Wall Street and was consumed with the details of investment the way I was consumed with the details of language. We couldn't communicate on the subject of either of our fiercest interests, and this bothered me a lot more than it did her. I believed what my father said. I was the one who'd broken off the relationship.

"What do you do if you don't really want to go out with someone again, but she does?" he asked me.

I told him this was an excellent question to which there was no real answer.

"I can tell you this much, though," I said. "The guy you don't want to be is the guy who says he'll call and doesn't call."

"Really?" he said.

"Really," I said.

"You don't mind me asking you about this, do you?" he said. "It doesn't make you feel uncomfortable?"

I told him yes, it made me uncomfortable, but no, I didn't mind.

"But I have to say, Dad, why me?" I said. "Look who you're asking."

"You have a point," he said.

*   *   *

In late December 2002 my father went to the doctor complaining of dizziness and discovered that a cancer in his lungs had migrated to his brain. He was dead in six months.

Through the first part of 2003 I probably spent more time with him than I had as a boy. For a time, while he remained mobile, we continued going out together to dinner and the theater. Later I'd go to his apartment to see him, make sure he had enough food in the refrigerator, take him in a cab to the doctor and take him home again. I brought Coco to live with me.

I'm afraid I resented the obligation, but at least, I told myself, I didn't shirk it. But I was angry—furious, really—because my father had at last been enjoying himself and because he deserved more time. So did I.

After he died, his doctor told me how impressed he was that I was there so often, that it was unusual for a son to do that for a father, and though I thanked him for what I knew was meant as a compliment, it didn't make me feel any less worn-out, or any less guilty for not doing more, for not having done more over many, many years. And I wondered, as long as this was going to be the end no matter what I did, what did it matter what I had or hadn't done? All those other people the doctor was talking about, who couldn't or wouldn't or didn't show up to help their parents live their last days—were they wrong to shield themselves from a grueling and bitter experience?

He finally went into the hospital, and after a few days he was transported to a palliative care facility, coincidentally in the Bronx, where he was born and grew up. I don't know if that ever occurred to him, though it gave me a morsel of solace. He was barely conscious by the time they moved him.

It was pouring rain that day. I sat in the back of the ambulance with him, whispering the things you whisper: "Are you okay, Dad? Anything I can do? We'll be there soon, don't worry. It's a nice place, you'll see. You'll be comfortable."

We drove up the West Side Highway and exited toward the Cross Bronx Expressway. Cars were backed up on the ramp, and as we edged forward to enter the stream of fast-moving traffic, the ambulance was rammed from behind by another car. My father lifted his head, his eyes opened, and he moaned.

This is a joke, I thought, and I actually laughed and said, "Are you kidding me?" It was a moment that made me think of God. Who else would the "you" in that sentence be? I was never a believer, but that was the moment I dispensed with him for good. (I can't even get myself to capitalize the pronouns.) Our lives are in no one's hands but our own.

The accident, it turned out, wasn't serious in any other way. The drivers got out and barked at each other briefly in the rain, but we arrived at Calvary Hospital without further incident and my father lived for a week in the care of kind, skillful people. (And yes, I'm aware of the irony of the name.) The news that he had died came on the phone in the middle of the night.

I thanked the nurse who called and hung up. Coco was asleep at the foot of the bed, and her presence, the knowledge of her heartbeat, was comforting. I've felt sadder in my life, more desperate, more frightened, but never more lonely.

My father's funeral, on a warm day in June two and a half years after my mother's, was held in the same funeral home in White Plains as my mother's, in the same morose room with the stiflingly low ceiling. The same funeral director, with the same well-practiced mien, somber and solicitous both, welcomed many of the same attendees. Robert and I both spoke, as we did at our mother's, after the same rabbi, who had never met either of them, said pretty much the same thing he'd said the last time. (I'll spare you yet another of my eulogies.) We made the same drive to the graveyard in Chappaqua, where we witnessed his casket slide into the mausoleum drawer next to my mother's.

It was all perfectly awful—sad and enervating. And when it was over at last I whispered to my brother:

"Good thing we're out of parents. I can't do this again."

He looked at me with a little bit of shock before he recognized the mordant joke, and he smiled disapprovingly. Robert, who is four years younger than I am, is a friendly, optimistic, responsible guy and there's not an ounce of savagery in him—no bitterness—the way there is in me. It was in both my parents, too. He's lucky that way, though one result is that Robert is missing the sense of grim humor I shared with our folks. In the grand scheme of our DNA, it's not much, a tiny nugget of the family sensibility. But I remember thinking, as we buried our father—well, slid him into his drawer—that he would have understood me instantly and given my remark the appreciative smirk it was meant to elicit.

My dad could tell a joke; well, he used to be able to, before he got really crabby and had a hard time seeing beyond himself. When he was younger, I admired his ability; he knew how to order the details and dole them out, emphasizing this one, casually letting that one escape. He liked shaggy dog stories, the longer and sillier the better, stories he could extend and embellish, building to a punch line that would make everybody groan. There was one about a couple of Italian brothers and two horses they inherited from their father but couldn't tell apart; I won't bother you with that one.

But the one I especially remember he told me when I was a young man and he was maybe the age I am now. It was already an old joke then, I'm sure.

At the time I understood it, but I didn't get it the way I do now. It's about a man in the midst of a midlife crisis. He's got what seems on the surface to be an admirable, successful, rewarding, and happy life. He works on Wall Street and makes a lot of money, lives in a great house, drives a nice car—a couple of nice cars. He's got friends; he plays a good game of golf. He loves his wife, he loves his kids; everyone is well-adjusted.

But as midlife crises do, it has overtaken his sense of well-being and made him feel that everything he has adds up to a big nothing. Driven to despair, he can't fend off the need to strike out on a quest. So he bids his wife and family a difficult but determined farewell and sets off on a trip around the world. He takes an ocean liner across the Atlantic and a train across Europe; he hitchhikes through Turkey and the Middle East and rides a camel across India. At last he finds himself at the foot of the Himalayas, where he engages a team of sherpas for the ascent to the cave of the mystical holy man who, it is said, holds the secret of existence.

Up they climb. It takes days. The temperature dives, the wind howls, and the snow becomes deeper and deeper. The sherpas keep asking the man if he wants to turn back, but driven by his desperate thirst for the ultimate knowledge, he persists. Finally, exhausted but thrilled, he arrives at the holy man's cave and crawls in for his audience.

And there he is, wearing robes and a long beard, sitting cross-legged before a fire. Our hero is so cold, so tired, he cannot speak. But the holy man offers him a bowl of celestial nectar and the man drinks gratefully and finds himself miraculously restored.

"Your Holiness," he says, "I have come such a long way to see you. I left everything I knew behind, my wife and family, my home, my work. I took an ocean liner across the Atlantic, a train across Europe, cars across the Middle East, and a camel across India. I've been climbing these mountains for the past ten days, and all because I want to ask you one question."

"Of course, my son," the holy man says. "What is your question?"

"Your Holiness, what is the meaning of life?"

The holy man leans back a bit and takes a deep breath. A beatific smile lights up his face.

"Listen carefully, my son. Life is a wheel," he says, and falls silent.

The man waits for more but nothing more is forthcoming.

"That's it?" he says. "Life is a wheel?"

"Yes, my son, life is a wheel."

Our hero is suddenly incredulous, and his despair bursts out of him in a flood of exasperated words. As he speaks he gets more and more excited and the volume rises. When he finishes his chest is heaving and his face aflame with passion.

"Life is a wheel?" he says. "That's the secret? Life is a wheel? I leave my wife and family and five hundred thousand dollars a year? I cross the Atlantic on a slow boat, ride a cramped and crowded train across Europe, hitchhike through that miserable desert, ride a camel, for Chris-sakes, through India, and freeze my ass off climbing all the way up here to ask you the question at the heart of my existence and that's all you've got to say to me, that life is a fucking wheel?"

At which point the holy man looks quizzically across the fire at his supplicant. His eyebrows knit in perplexity.

"Life *isn't* a wheel?" he says.

14

∽◡∾

What if . . . ?

Thursday, September 15, Baraboo, Wisconsin

Cyclists revere bike trails. We don't get too many signs from the world that we have a place in it, and bike trails, those routes on which you can get from one place to another without the interference of motorized traffic, well, they tell us we belong on the great transportation grid that caters to the natural restlessness of humankind.

They're growing in number—bike trails, that is, and bike lanes—but even so there aren't enough of them for the growing number of cyclists who don't just re-create but who travel by bike. This is how it must have been for cross-country motorists before the creation of the interstate highway system. The efficient pathways aren't necessarily where you wish they were; you have to arrange your trip just to get to them.

The last couple of weeks, that's what I've been doing, seeking out bike trails and letting them determine my course. From Itasca State Park to here, in central Wisconsin, maybe two hundred and fifty miles of the last five hundred have been off-road. I circumnavigated (more or less) Minneapolis, a city that prides itself on being America's most bike-friendly, which it may be, though Portland, Oregon, stakes the same claim, and it's probably a toss-up.

240

After the unpleasant day that ended in Red Wing, urged on by a number of readers, I aimed for the trails of Wisconsin. This meant riding sixty miles along the Mississippi on the Minnesota side, following the southern branch of Highway 61 to the pleasant city of Winona, and avoiding what several of my correspondents warned me would be a rigorous journey along the Wisconsin bluffs that overlook the river. Highway 61 is a major thoroughfare, some of it a divided four-lane road, but it wasn't too bad. The traffic was bearable, the shoulder wide, and the vantage point frequently high enough to yield views of the river, which in some places is so wide and slow-moving as to be called a lake.

The next morning, sunny with a chill in the air, I crossed the bridge from Winona into Trempealeau, Wisconsin, rode along the edge of a national wildlife refuge and through Perrot State Park, a lovely spot along the river with an American frontier feel; you could imagine a Conestoga wagon rattling up to a log cabin in its flower-dappled fields. From there I picked up the first of the many Wisconsin trails I'd ride much of the way to Chicago.

Last night I stopped in Sparta, a small city that calls itself "The Bicycling Capital of America" on the strength of being one pole of the granddaddy of American bike trails, a thirty-two-mile path established in an old railway bed in 1967 that goes through woods and farmland southeast to the town of Elroy. Like a lot of mid-American places, its size— the population is about ten thousand—Sparta appeared a bit down at the heels, but on this day, with fall approaching in the angled light of late afternoon and early evening, the wooded trail and its surrounding parkland were cheerfully pretty, a place to make a touring bicyclist feel welcome. The bicycle, in fact, is the town symbol; it appears on signage everywhere, clearly an attempt to attract pedalers to Sparta's motels and restaurants (though I wouldn't brag about the ones I sampled). And the local museum, named for an astronaut who grew up nearby, is devoted to the history of transportation. The Deke Slayton Memorial Space & Bicycle Museum, it's called.

The Elroy-Sparta State Trail is actually one of four interconnected trails that took me a hundred miles, from Trempealeau to Reedsburg, which is within a day's ride of Madison. Unlike the Heartland and Paul Bunyan trails in northern Minnesota, which I also used, or for that matter the trails in Minneapolis, the Wisconsin trails are unpaved, mostly packed-down dirt or crushed limestone. That affects the quality of the ride, of course, though it isn't necessarily worse than traveling on pavement. I had glorious rides in Minnesota, but frankly the whole state road system, bike paths included, could use a new application of asphalt. So many roads and shoulders are pocked, potholed, and cracked at regular intervals from cold heaves that I felt that I had speed bumps every twenty yards for five hundred miles.

It's true a bike doesn't roll quite as well on dirt, and the Wisconsin trails were a little lumpy with fallen twigs and leaves; at the end of a fifty-mile trail ride I was more tired than I would be otherwise. But the two-day ride on Wisconsin's trails was a treat. The weather was cool and sunny, the air crisp and bright with the feel of autumn coming on. Alas, the leaves hadn't begun to change, but the greenery was impressive. Woodsy corridors went on for miles, broken up by swampy waterways flanked by immense willows, or by farmhouses, cornfields, barns, silos, and grazing cows that gave me postcard glimpses of dairy land. On the Elroy-Sparta trail, there are three tunnels a cyclist has to negotiate in the dark. (A sign instructs you to walk your bike, but I unpacked my headlamp and got back in the saddle.) The longest of them is well over half a mile long, and with water dripping noisily from the ceiling, sometimes onto your head, and the echoes of your pedal strokes bouncing off the walls, traversing it is spooky, a carnival ride, entertainingly eerie.

For someone who has ridden roads his whole cycling life, the concentrated trail riding I've done lately has been a new wrinkle, mostly a joy but partly disconcerting. Being away from traffic is simply delicious, a whole source of anxiety removed, and of course having a road of one's own is something a cyclist relishes the way a football team relishes its home stadium. On the other hand, as a cyclist, I'm used to finding my way in an unwelcoming world, being the annoying little brother in the vehicular universe. I'm proud of my ability to work around traffic to get to where I'm going. I like to think my skill in negotiating debris-strewn highway shoulders is both earned and useful.

But on a trail, cyclists, particularly long-distance riders, are the home team. We're the popular kids in the lunchroom, the cool clique, and that changes the enterprise. You run into other riders fairly regularly on a trail—that's a change of pace in and of itself—but most of them are local, out for an hour or two of easy exercise on a nice day, and I've been surprised at how they tend to steer clear of me, nervously riding the far edge of the path with their heads down or pointed determinedly straight ahead. I almost always say hello; they almost always don't. For a while I interpreted this as resentment. With my loaded-up bike I was a stranger invading their turf, like a motorcycle gang commandeering the counter at the local diner. But what I've realized is that it's just the opposite; they're the ones who think of themselves as invaders and that they see the turf as mine.

This first occurred to me in Minneapolis, where the complicated network of trails around the city's lakes and through downtown is heavily used by joggers, in-line skaters, and roller skiers as well as cyclists. On these trails bikes are the biggest vehicles, the equivalent of lumber trucks, the things to watch out for, the bullying bad guys. Out here in the boonies, except for maybe the teenaged boys doing tricks on their lowriders, I still represent the dangerous traffic. The tentative riders detouring on the way home from the store with grocery bags in the handlebar basket, the kids on their wobbling training wheels with their parents running behind them, the elderly strollers wearing sun hats, the racewalkers with their heel-toe stride and elbows held high—they stay out of my way, as if the path is my natural habitat and they are trying to borrow it as unobtrusively as possible, the way I keep to the shoulder on the highway.

Do I like this? Well, yes and no. On the long-distance trails, whether paved or unpaved, you can feel pampered, yes, but you also feel sequestered, shut off from conventional—"real"—avenues of transportation. More than once as I rode the trails along a corridor of woods, out of sight and even earshot of a main highway that might be just a few dozen yards away, I had the dreamy sense that I wasn't really traveling but being propelled from station to station like old-fashioned office mail in a pneumatic tube.

That sounds weird, I know—who doesn't like to own the road?—but bike trails are still new to me, as email once was, and I'm just learning to accept them as a legitimate way to negotiate the world as a cyclist.

When I emerged from the Wisconsin trails at Reedsburg, I had to ride the last fifteen miles of the day on a two-lane highway that is the main thoroughfare between two sizable towns, and I was quickly reintroduced to the hazards of cycling in the real world: crowds of harried drivers in a hurry, exhaust-belching trucks, construction. With my motel within a quarter mile—I could see the sign—the road curled around and pitched down, from one pedal stroke to the next the shoulder simply vanished, and for four hundred harrowing yards I found myself riding against a curb with rush-hour traffic whistling by within inches. Yikes!

Still, for most of those fifteen miles, I had a fine time. The shoulder was wide and smooth. The wind, chilly and brisk, was nudging me from behind. The late-afternoon light was golden, and the scenery was a handsome mix of suburbia and farmland. I was pedaling hard at the end of the day, sweating, cruising, enjoying myself and glad to be back on a good old American road.

Monday, September 19, Kenosha, Wisconsin

With its angry waters stretching to the horizon and breakers rolling in, Lake Michigan looks enormous and intimidating on a blustery, gray afternoon. I had my first, awe-inspiring glimpse of it yesterday in Racine, just before the rain began in earnest and gave me a good soaking. For the next hour, I made my way through the city's stately and historic Southside neighborhood along the lakeshore, turned west for a bit through a considerably less stately neighborhood and finally south again into Kenosha, not too far from the Illinois border.

It was a day of urban riding, part of a day, anyway, something I haven't done, really, the entire trip. I was lost, or at least in a muddle, about half the time. After all the pedaling through daunting, wide-open spaces, I'm still getting accustomed to making dozens of turns in a day and keeping my eyes peeled for the one street sign among a million that will point me in the right direction. And after riding bike paths and missing the rough streets, on these rough streets I miss the bike paths.

It's true that there are a lot more people around me now, and I've asked many for directions, but eager and friendly as most of them are, their advice turns out to be accurate only about half the time.

"Sheesh," I want to go back and say to them sometimes, "how long did you say you've lived in this town?"

Besides, as any cyclist can tell you, people who walk and drive don't have a clue what's important to someone on a bike.

"You're about ten minutes away," the deli clerk said to me this afternoon about the road I was interested in; she meant a ten-minute drive.

It also amuses (and amazes) me how often the person behind the counter at the gas station convenience store will ring up my Gatorade and Lorna Doones, look at me in my full bike regalia, including helmet, and ask if I filled my tank outside. It's happened a half dozen times at least.

Still, there's a lot to be said for civilization, and in the last couple of days, as I pedaled east from Madison and turned south in Waukesha, nearly to Milwaukee, and headed down the west side of Lake Michigan, the town centers have been backing up on one another. After weeks of fifty miles between stop signs, traffic lights are annoying, sure, but there's something consoling about being in a region again where you can count on three or four McDonald's a day and a choice of reliable motel chains, each with a guest laundromat.

The best thing about being here in the eastern Midwest, where I went to college and where I was a *Times* correspondent once upon a time, is that I know some of the people here. Visiting with friends over the last couple of weeks has changed the nature of my travels. Until recently, my journey has been a largely solo venture, with little in the way of flesh-and-blood company to look forward to for days or even weeks at a time. I became used to that, even got to enjoy the spine-stiffening self-reliance of it.

Now I may be getting used to the comfort of company again. As I approached Madison the other day, my friends Chuck and Elizabeth Barnhill drove twenty-five miles north out of the city to intercept me. They treated me to my first ButterBurger (unappetizing name, but pretty tasty) at Culver's, a fast-food chain I was unfamiliar with; then Chuck unloaded his bicycle from the car and we rode back together to their home. Elizabeth ferried my saddlebags in the car (a fabulous luxury for me), Chuck supplied the route (an even more fabulous luxury), and we had a terrific, swift ride through Wisconsin cornfields on a bright and beautiful day, witnessing, among other things, a mini-tornado, a vortex of wind about thirty feet high that swirled leaves and corn husks in a mesmerizing spiral for two or three minutes as we watched, before it crossed the road toward us and died.

Jan and I had met the loquacious and witty Barnhills (he a lawyer, she a former math teacher and a nationally ranked amateur tennis player) earlier this year on our bike tour of Provence. (Yes, I've spent an inordinate amount of time on a bicycle seat this year.) They were kicking off a year of celebrating their fortieth anniversary, traveling with their friends Jerry and Amy Nickles, also of Madison, who were also anticipating my arrival. For a day and a half, the four of them saw to it that I ate heartily—Elizabeth's pies!—drank liberally, conversed happily, and slept comfortably. They got me to the bike store to shore up on fall weather gear (a merino underlayer, warmer gloves, and waterproof shoe covers) and pointed me toward the road east and out of town. Jerry, a professor of medical physics at the University of Wisconsin, smashes atoms for a living, and he took me to his lab and showed me his cyclotron. (What's a cross-country bike trip, after all, without a cyclotron?)

All of this companionship has given a bittersweet flavor to getting back on the road alone. I've grown to like waking early, sussing out the weather, consulting my various maps, ritually loading up my bike and rolling out the door of a motel. But leaving a warm hearth and home to pedal into the morning chill—and it's been damp the last few days, too—is, well, a little more difficult. It reminds me, of course, that I have an actual home myself, and an actual life, and they're waiting for me when I return from my quixotic adventure. Several readers have asked me whether the trip has been a joy or an ordeal, and the answer, obviously, is both, some days more of one, some days more of the other. But keep in mind that ordeals can be as satisfying as pleasures, and what I was thinking as the rain began in Racine and I watched the waves of Lake Michigan tumble to the beach was that barring unforeseen incident, I'm about a month from getting back to New York. Maybe it was the direction of the surf, hurtling in from the east, or simply the oceanic dimensions of the lake that made me imagine, well, the ocean. In any case, the closer I get to home the more I'm beginning to wonder: What will I do when I get there?

Thursday, September 22, Racine, Wisconsin

The last few days I've made a loop. On Sunday, after I had my first glimpse of Lake Michigan here in Racine, I trundled down to Chicago, where I spent two days relaxing in a familiar environment—I lived in the city back in the 1990s. I ate well, slept late. I even spent an evening at the theater—Bruce Norris's *Clybourne Park*, a Pulitzer Prize winner, at Steppenwolf, and enjoyed dissecting it over drinks with theatergoing friends.

It was another fine hiatus from my travels—I've been giving myself quite a few breaks lately, I know—except that I kept thinking ahead and was vexed about how to proceed. The lake was in my way, and pretty much every way around it struck me as unpalatable, involving passing through the congested regions in Illinois and Indiana south of Chicago. Paying attention to the suggestions of readers, I wore out several maps, and in the end I decided to turn around and go back up north and take the ferry across the lake from Milwaukee to Muskegon, Michigan. Thus, Racine redux.

Perhaps here is the place to explain to the many who insisted that the best way around Lake Michigan was to the north, through northern Wisconsin and the upper peninsula of Michigan, that that was the route I had followed on my previous trip. There were several highlights I recall: a backyard barbecue on Lake Gogebic, the UP's largest inland lake, with the family of a fellow cyclist I met on the road; bowling in Bruce Crossing, Michigan, a town evidently named for my precise enterprise of the moment; and going through a photo album with the owners of the Mt. Shasta restaurant in Michigamme, where scenes from *Anatomy of a Murder* were filmed.

Why a restaurant on the flats of upper Michigan was named for one of California's highest peaks I don't know. But blowups of the film's stars—Jimmy Stewart, Ben Gazzara, George C. Scott, Eve Arden, and Lee Remick, whom my father loved ("Super Shiksa," he called her), and Duke Ellington, who composed the sensational score—adorned the walls. Here's what I wrote at the time:

My waitress was clearly too young to have been around in 1959 when the film was made, but I was disappointed that she had not even seen it. Diane Billings, who owns the place with her husband, Don, helped me wait out a rainstorm by producing from behind the cash register a sheaf of photographs taken on the set. Mostly they were of townspeople going gaga in the presence of so many celebrities.

The men in town liked to have their pictures taken with Ms. Remick, Ms. Billings said, pointing to a wooden column holding up one corner of the ceiling. The men would ask her to pose with her leg draped around the column, as she did, drunkenly, during one scene in the film. Ms. Billings, who did not own the Mount Shasta then, said the restaurant had been turned into a hotel during the filming, and all the stars stayed there.

All of this delighted me; I had not expected to trip over this piece of Americana. And I was not ready for the addendum.

"All except the Duke," Ms. Billings said sadly. "Back then he couldn't stay here."

That, of course, is Americana, too.

* * *

So I've gone out of my way on this trip not to repeat myself. I don't like the idea of backtracking, or of being in the same place I've pedaled through before. I don't like being in Racine again, especially in the rain. But I do like the idea of the ferry. I've lived on the shore of Lake Michigan, but I've never been out on it. And I like the idea of riding through rural Michigan. My hope is that turning north again will give me an earlier look at fall colors.

I mostly rode bike paths down to Chicago and back to Racine. Going south I followed the Kenosha County path to the Illinois border (perfect timing; it had just been repaved), where it connects to the mostly unpaved, straight-as-a-string Robert McClory trail through Waukegan and other outlying northern suburbs and then to the Green Bay trail, which runs alongside the commuter rail line through affluent Highland Park, Kenilworth, Glencoe, Winnetka, and Wilmette. It's all pretty unscintillating.

In Chicago I spent a sparklingly sunny afternoon in the city's marvelous lakefront park, riding against the wind on the popular bike path from the entrance just south of Evanston to downtown and then gliding with it back again. I bought a hot dog from a vendor and sat in the sun eating it, watching the water and the joggers and cyclists exercising at its edge. A dog owner applauded as his athletic Lab—I think it was a Lab—swam across an inlet.

Is there a city in the world with as lovely a recreational expanse along its waterfront? I hadn't been on the path in a dozen years, and it was a nostalgic occasion for me; great fun, too.

Returning north toward Racine and Milwaukee, where the ferry embarks, and not wanting to follow the same route in reverse, I rode west for a while—endlessly, it seemed—through traffic-heavy streets in Skokie, in order to reach the Des Plaines River trail, a winding path through woods and meadows that cyclists share with equestrians. It's a pretty ride, for the most part, with the odd quality of running through seemingly deep woods that are sometimes only a few dozen yards from busy highways, so the tweeting-bird soundtrack you'd expect from the scenery is obscured; you hear roaring motors instead. From the end of the trail at the Wisconsin border it was street riding, and the city streets of Kenosha and Racine are no havens for cyclists.

All in all, the past several days—I've come to think of them as the Chicago chapter—were a bit more anxiety-making than I'd bargained for. A nice, calming ferry ride seems like just the ticket.

Friday, September 23, Muskegon, Michigan

Someone named Terence from South Bend, Indiana, wrote this to me:

> *I've enjoyed so many of your reports, truly. You're at your best as a writer when you describe the scenery and, above all, the people you meet. As a cyclist, I understand the need to dwell on the bike, your poor legs, and lack of energy, plus the traffic; but what's compelling in your tale is the land and the people. Do more of that; your style soars and you whine less—it's great. For what it's worth, it's exactly what I sense when riding alone in France: my tired legs and squeaky chain may be interesting to a degree, but it's the landscape, the roads, the towns, the assorted people, plus the food, etc. that make the whole thing interesting.*

My first review! It's about a B-plus, I'd say. I'll take it, I guess, but the word *whine* isn't one any writer wants to hear. I suppose that's whining, too. Anyway, Terence had more to say:

> *As for the ferry across Lake Michigan, I trust you'll spend the entire passage on a trainer; otherwise you'd not really be "riding" from coast to coast! Had you thought of that? Better yet, go by way of Gary, Hammond, and Michigan City, and tell of the people and the land and the food along the way. You did it for Montana and North Dakota, so why the exception now? I admit that a calm road is bet- ter than a world of traffic, but isn't that the point of your adventure?*

Skip the boat, stay on your bike . . . and who knows what things—
terrifying, mundane, bizarre, enriching—that you'll meet along the
way. Enjoy and be well.

Ol' Terence is a bit of a scold, isn't he? As it happens, I did consider
the idea of the ferry ride as "cheating," though I dismissed it. After all,
I'm actually adding miles to the trip, not taking a shortcut.

Still, he does raise a point I've been mulling lately, the one about not
being able to be in two places at once, about choices that you make that
obviate other choices. You can't have everything—one of the funda-
mental LCTs. (I'm borrowing the acronym from L. Rust Hills, the late
Esquire fiction editor, my first boss in publishing. LCT = Life's Cruel
Truth.)

This is a mortality issue, of course, not surprisingly brought on by
all the ruminating about my parents and the filial obligations I either
discharged or didn't. At this point, I know an awful lot about being
a son—*their* son, anyway. But I've never had the experience—or the
duty—of looking at the relationship the other way around.

I can't say not having children was a conscious choice, but choosing
not to marry, or at least not to settle down with a woman, strikes me
as tantamount to the same thing. I spent endless hours blathering with
a shrink about women and the revolving door they used in and out of
my life—I chose a female doctor for this very reason—but strangely
enough, in nearly twenty years of therapy I don't think I ever talked
about wanting or not wanting to have kids. I don't remember ever con-
sidering the subject seriously on my own, either, though if therapy
taught me anything it's that it remains buried in my subconscious like
the unfound relic of a scavenger hunt after everybody goes home. Anyway, by now it's like being a soldier, something I've missed for good.

The thing is, I think I like kids, more or less. I was an English teacher
for a few years before I quit to enter publishing, and I enjoyed most of
the work—the performing, the encouraging, the dispensing of door-

opening revelations, even the wheedling and dickering you have to do with reluctant, sullen, grade-grubbing teens—but I was driven out of the classroom by the prospect of a life spent correcting papers. Maybe that reflects badly on me, makes me seem selfish or lacking in stick-to-itiveness or community spirit, or maybe it's just evidence that I'd never have survived as a parent, with all the correcting and explaining *that* job entails. But believe me, you don't even have to read sixty eighth-grade essays on *To Kill a Mockingbird* to suffer an unholy agony. Just carrying them around in your briefcase can bring you to tears from the anticipated tedium.

I know the usual things people say, that your kids (and your kids' kids) are your way of leaving part of yourself on the earth after you're gone, and I buy that, I guess, but that's never been the thing that's made me sorry to be childless. Rather, it's the immediate reward, the satisfaction you can get from your kids while you're still here that makes more sense to me as something not to miss out on, that sets me to wondering "What if?"

I remember the way my parents regarded me, with a particular brand of devotion and affection that I now recognize you can come by only one way. I envied their feelings for me, their proud presumption to ownership of my existence.

Both of them said similar things to me in the weeks before they died, that it didn't matter, it had never mattered, what I had done to anger them or worry them or disappoint them. The love they felt for me overwhelmed everything, they said, only and simply because I was their child.

"My boy," my mother said.

"My son," my father said.

Or maybe it was vice versa. I can't remember, actually. What I remember is being seized, each time, by the notion that I'd never have that feeling and that that was going to end up being a regret.

These days I'm curious about my brother's son, Jacob, who was born the day Mickey Mantle died, and who turned sixteen last month. He's a sweet-tempered and thoughtful boy with a subtle, needling sense of humor and a deadpan speaking style. He enjoys being amused, likes catching people at the moments of their embarrassment, loves finding things to laugh at—or maybe smirk at is more accurate. He's a teenager, after all.

But he has an enlarged worry gene. As a young child, he had an irrational temper, would flip into freakout mode at a slight provocation. He's weathered that. That part of him has evolved into a keen awareness of life's everyday vexatiousness. He knows, perceptively but maybe too self-consciously, that the world he's headed out into is full of knotty problems. This makes him cautious and a little eccentric.

Robert and Lynne are dedicated, loving, and proud parents, and their home life is rich with safety and comfort. It is remarkable, astounding to me, really, how thoroughly their lives are devoted to the household, to the care and feeding of their son, and their family and their home, and every now and then when I go to see them it's a bit of a culture shock as I realize that, in favor of the more solitary life I lead, this is what I don't have, what I've chosen not to have.

My brother tells me that every time I visit Jake talks about me for days afterward, and this naturally fills me with narcissistic pride. But it's true that whenever I'm there I can sense that Jake's antennae have picked up on something—a different way of being an adult than the way his parents are.

This is probably an uncle's role, to be an alternative model, though not too emphatically. For me it's a little frustrating, to tell the truth, drawing the line.

"You were a weird little kid," I said to him during my last visit several months ago. We were sitting in front of the TV, not watching. He doesn't watch much TV—I do—and, much to my delight, doesn't play video games or walk around with an iPod plugged in his ears. His parents were elsewhere.

"Yeah, I know," he said.

"You're still a little weird."

"I am?" he said.

"In a good way," I said.

"I think my parents are weird," he said.

"I'm pretty sure all kids think their parents are weird, Jake," I said. "But trust me, they're so not weird."

He thought about that for a second.

"Really?" he said. "Okay."

The next morning when I left for the airport, I hugged him and said I loved him.

"I like you a lot, too," I said.

He smiled just a little, I think because he recognized I felt awkward.

"Really?" he said. "Okay."

On the phone the other day, Jan was talking about her daughters, Rebecca and Julia, both of them at college now, and recalling how in her mid-thirties, the ache to have a child was so in conflict with her ambitions as a journalist, on the one hand, and with her fear that she'd fail as a mother, on the other, that she had a year of intermittent panic attacks and went into therapy.

"I dreamed I gave birth to a fish," she told me recently.

"Whoa," I said. "What did your shrink say about that?"

"She didn't know what to say," Jan said. "But Becca thinks it explains why she was so interested in aquariums."

I've known the girls their whole lives, though not well. I had glimpses of them intermittently over the years, was suitably impressed each time I saw them at how they'd grown, and heard reports about them from Jan over lunch from time to time. But I wasn't all that interested in them until now. When they were tiny, I was among the faction of single people that voted against allowing the family to be part of a summer house in the Hamptons. Jan says I taught Rebecca to play chess, though frankly I don't remember that. I do remember asking her, when she was thirteen or so, for pointers about buying fish for a beginner's aquarium when I was thinking about getting one myself.

By my lights, both girls turned out just as you would cross your fingers and hope they would—talented, mostly charming, and occasionally difficult. Julia, the younger by a couple of years, is chatty and opinionated with a natural self-possession that belies her work ethic and makes it seem as if she's breezing through life. Rebecca is more of a brooder, incisively and often wittily self-critical with a broad intellectual curiosity that buoys her with the sense that the universe is, in fact, worth exploring. It's hard to make firm judgments about young people, of course, because they're sometimes so impossible that you want to throttle them, but the odds are they're going to be terrific adults, the kind of responsible people who you hope will be running the world in your old age.

Until recently I was always (I think) the tolerable, reasonably engaging friend of their parents, but under the current circumstances that has changed, and they now have to consider my existence in a substantive way. They have to acknowledge my character, such as it is, and react to it, judge it. I can see how they'd perceive this as a nuisance. More to the point, of course, is that now I'm someone to be suspicious of, a symbol of the family breakup. I don't have much to go on at this point, just what Jan tells me, and one dinner we had with each of them when she was briefly in New York, but it's my impression they don't like me very much. They're loyal to their father—a guy who was a friend of mine not so long ago—which is entirely the right thing for them to be.

They're also pretty angry at their mother for moving to Paris, and it's instructive to witness Jan's patience with the casually accusatory barbs they sometimes sling at her. I hear about them afterward, and a couple of times I was in the room during a phone call—how their lives are more difficult now without a cohesive family, how they envy their friends who have a solid and comforting support structure, how they don't know how to think about holidays anymore. What Jan does is listen and sympathize and console, letting blame rest on her shoulders. I told her once that I'm not sure I could sit still for it all without getting angry—or at least defending myself.

"Well, they're beginning to understand that I wasn't happy, and I want them to realize that they can take action in their lives when they're not happy," she said. "And it's good that they still call to talk to me about this stuff, isn't it?"

She added, with sweetness and relief, "They're not quite cooked yet. They still need their mom."

I should say a couple of things. First, there was no romance between Jan and me before she separated from her husband. Second, that said, I've had a crush on her for twenty-five years (unspoken, though all my friends seem to have known about it), and I was pretty disheartened myself when she announced she was leaving the continent for a job at the *International Herald Tribune*.*

I'd known her marriage was in trouble; she let me know before she moved out, and though the news surprised me, that she'd told me didn't. One element of our being friends over the years was a mutual confidant-ship. When we first met, before the girls were born, we'd leave the office and go to lunch once a month at McHale's, a late and lamented bar on Eighth Avenue in the 40s that served huge burgers and surprisingly authentic Mexican food, and talk about our respective experiences in therapy. In my sessions, I told her, we talked about sex, which I was either having or not. In hers, she said, they talked about death, though it wasn't her own she obsessed about. It was her grand-mother's, her parents', and, of course, even though she hadn't had them yet, her children's.

"One of these days, Jan, you're going to have to talk about sex," I often joked, and she always responded, "And you're going to have to talk about death."

Prescient!

This all sounds suspicious, I realize that, but nothing happened, I swear. Here's the timeline:

She left for Paris last September. In February, I made plans to go bicycling with a tour group in Provence and I asked Jan if she wanted to come along. In May, I flew to Paris, where I stayed with her for two

---

*The *IHT,* as it was fondly called for decades, was officially renamed the *International New York Times* in October 2013.

nights—she has a second bedroom—and on a Saturday morning we took the train together to Orange. Over the next week we fell in love. As I said once before, it happened over a long period of time—and all at once.

She had already arranged trips back to New York in June and July, and on the first of them she told Rebecca and Julia about us. Julia asked if anything had been going on before she left for Paris, and she seemed to accept it when Jan said no.

Rebecca's reaction was hilarious, acid—and piercing in too many ways to count.

"Well," she said to her mother, "if it doesn't work out, don't come crying to me."

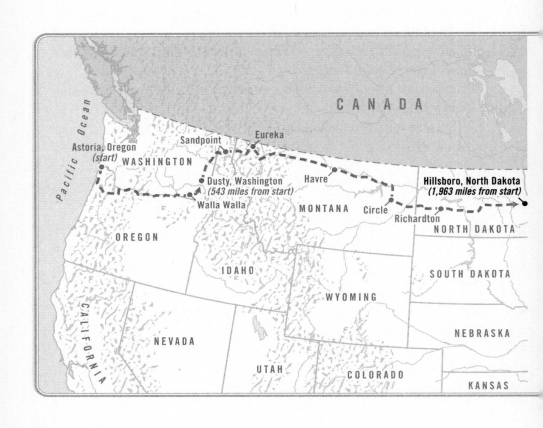

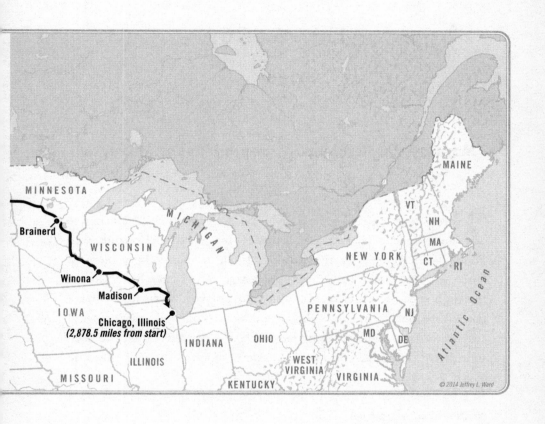

MAINE

VT

NH

MA

NEW YORK

CT

RI

MINNESOTA

Brainerd

WISCONSIN

M I C H I G A N

Winona

Madison

IOWA

Chicago, Illinois
(2,878.5 miles from start)

PENNSYLVANIA

NJ

MD

DE

INDIANA

OHIO

Atlantic Ocean

ILLINOIS

WEST
VIRGINIA

VIRGINIA

MISSOURI

KENTUCKY

© 2014 Jeffrey L. Ward

15

∽∾✺∾∾

The Wet Guy

Monday, September 26, South Haven, Michigan

*T*hree thousand miles into my trans-America bicycle journey—
my odometer clicked over Saturday, just north of Holland—I've
finally been stymied by the weather. I had an exceedingly pleasant
(and guilt-free—take that, Terence) passage across Lake Michigan on
the high-speed ferry from Milwaukee to Muskegon, during which I
made occasional forays on deck to stand up to a cold and assertive wind
that seemed capable of slinging me overboard. But since then I've been
pinned by that same wind to the eastern shore of the lake, heading
south.

It has also been raining, so my last two days in the saddle have been
relatively short and very damp.

Well, a day and a half, actually. Saturday morning it drizzled off
and on, but I stayed mostly dry on the ride south from Muskegon on
Lakeshore Drive—which does run along the lake though you're really
riding through wooded residential areas—and I even had some company. A local bike club was out for a ride, and a couple of their more
leisurely minded members escorted me to Holland. There I followed
Ottawa Beach Road along a peninsula to the state park, a vast sandy
expanse that was almost deserted on a chilly, threatening day, with a

260

striking, bright red lighthouse (known locally as Big Red) standing sentry at the end of a strait separating Lake Michigan from Macatawa, an inland bay. It got a little chilly out there, so I rode downtown for lunch in a fancy diner frequented, evidently, by students from Hope College when their parents are visiting.

The weather was looking a little sketchy, and I could have stayed in Holland, probably should have, but I pushed on another twenty miles or so to the town of Saugatuck, an upscale quaint village (that's a bit of an oxymoron, but you know what I mean) specializing in art galleries and harborside restaurants. I didn't see much of it because I rode the last dozen miles or so through open fields in a pelting downpour and bolted straight for the Best Western.

Riding in wet weather can be discomforting—usually is, in fact—partly because with slippery terrain and limited visibility (especially if you wear glasses, as I do) it can be dangerous, and partly because being soggy and cold is an added physical tax to an already taxing enterprise. But there is something rewarding about it, too—namely, the ruggedness you feel while you're doing it, the damn-the-torpedoes attitude that accompanies forward movement through a cloudburst.

The views over Lake Michigan from the eastern shore, the angry clouds, and the forbidding water meeting way out on the horizon are pretty thrilling in the rain, I have to say. Just south of Douglas, I took a little detour off the main road and found a two-lane path in front of some Victorian-style mansions on a high bluff along the water. As I rode by, I noticed a woman to my right standing quietly with her back to me, looking out over the water and holding an umbrella, leaning it on one shoulder so that it sheltered her from the rain and hid her head and shoulders from me. It was a painting in real life, and I stopped and looked closely at the scene—the misty air over the eerily calm water, the steely sky, the bushes like clumps of long grass growing on top of the bluff, the umbrella woman standing on a wooden deck and gazing out at the vast empty space, I supposed, like the French lieutenant's woman. It was really lovely.

After a few seconds, the woman moved, turning away from the water. I think she was startled to see me there watching her, but I asked her, before she went back into the house she'd obviously come from, Would she return to her place with the umbrella over her shoulder so I could take a picture? And she did.

She left after a little while, abruptly pivoting on her heel, and never said a word to me as she crossed the road into her front yard, opened the door to the house, and was gone.

*　*　*

That was the high point of yesterday, which I cut short here after just two hours and twenty-five miles. It poured much of the way and the drops laced my face like hailstones in the blustery east wind. I can't go any farther south unless I want to end up back in Chicago, but the rain persists this morning and the wind has grown only stronger. I'm frustrated and eager to put some miles behind me—I've got a date in New Orleans in less than two weeks and a flight to make in Pittsburgh—but thunderstorms are forecast for the next few hours and to ride on purpose into a fifteen- to twenty-mile-per-hour blow strikes me as foolish, or worse—no fun.

Anyway, this is an agreeable town with a handsome harbor, a resortish stop for boaters located in the northwest corner of a county known for its blueberries. Not a bad place to be stuck, actually, with a variety of places to eat, a bicycle shop (where I think I'll take advantage of a rainy morning to get a tune-up), and a first-run movie house where admission, a tub of popcorn, and a bottle of water cost me $8.50—a miracle to a New Yorker. I saw *Moneyball*. (Some nice performances by Brad Pitt and Jonah Hill, and a sweet, thoughtful coda, but otherwise a bit of a drag: long-winded, conventional as a drama—the renegade is told no by the powers-that-be—and not very instructive about baseball.) The point is, I can think of many places on my journey where I'd have been far less well off stranded for a couple of days, and I've spent some of my time here ruminating on luck.

Mine has been astonishingly good. Flat tires, accidents, heat stroke, a tornado, being stranded, hospitalized, ill: The list of disastrous things that haven't happened to me would be a long one. (Now there's an exercise—make a list of the calamities you've avoided. So far.) And innumerable moments come to mind when, grinding along on one difficult stretch of road or another, I worried about conditions taking a turn for the worse, but instead they turned better. The rumble strips on the shoulder suddenly disappeared, or the wind died down, or I crossed a county line and the potholed road I'd been rattling over was suddenly smoothly paved. To complete a trip like this you need things to go your way more often than they don't, and I can only hope I've got three or four more weeks of the kind of fortune I've already had.

Speaking of good fortune, as I've been writing this there has been a break in the weather. The forecast says I've got a five- or six-hour window before the next downpour, enough time, I think, to get that tune-up and bolt to Kalamazoo, about forty miles away. There's a trail from here to there.

And look at that! Out the window, a rainbow!

Wednesday, September 28, Montpelier, Ohio

Feeling a little pruney here.

For several days now—from Kalamazoo through lower Michigan, the northeast corner of Indiana, and into western Ohio, pretty much since I wrote about how lucky I've been with the weather—the skies have been broodingly gray, the air has been heavy, the wind has been contrary and chill, and for a few hours each day I've been rained on. A couple of the days I could have stayed put, I guess, but at this point I'm relishing the momentum I've built with daily rides, and my legs pretty much start pedaling in the morning whether I'm on the bike or not. Anyway, rain is hardly catastrophic, and now that the Yankees are in the playoffs, I want to be home for the World Series. (Am I confident they'll make it? Not really. As everyone knows, they don't have the starting pitching.*)

You get used to being wet. You get used to peeling off your soggy clothes at the end of the day and leaving them all in a pile on the bathroom floor like a melted wicked witch. You get used to concentrating on protecting the important things: cell phone, maps, cookies. Besides, I'm happy to report that my gear is performing, so inside my saddlebags my stuff is staying dry—including the iPad I'm typing this on—and aside from my head and my hands (the allegedly waterproof gloves I just bought aren't anywhere close), for the most part so am I.

Well, that isn't exactly true. Wearing a rain-repelling Windbreaker may keep out the weather, but it holds in your body heat, so after

---

*The pitching held up okay, but the Yanks lost anyway in the first round of the playoffs, three games to two, to Detroit.

fifty or sixty miles, I'm pretty well drenched anyway. And in this kind of relentless weather, moisture finds every pore in every surface, and you're just going to be a sponge even if you're better equipped and a lot smarter than I am.

Regarding being not so smart: Late Wednesday afternoon I crossed the border into Ohio from Indiana. A few miles in, the road bent downhill and flattened into a perfect basin, and at the bottom it was underwater for a stretch of maybe fifty feet. The water overflowed the road, and the grassy shoulder was submerged, too. I couldn't go around.

I was tired, and my GPS had led me on a wild-goose chase to a ghost motel; the place where the Ramada was supposed to be was a lonely farmhouse in the middle of a vast soybean field. I was several miles from a shower and something to eat. A drizzle had just thickened into actual precipitation, beating a steady thrum on my helmet, and as I stopped before the puddle and watched the drops dotting its surface, I made a hopeful, lazy bet that it was only three or four inches deep.

That being the case, rather than removing my shoes and walking my bike across, I figured I could coast through it, holding my pedals parallel to the ground and still keeping my feet above the surface. But I lost the bet in eight inches of water. Both my feet were submerged as the bike nearly came to a stop halfway through the puddle, and I had to pedal through the rest, leaving me to ride with soaking feet the last hour of the day.

After a few hours in the saddle on a wet day, I tend to take on a soggy identity. Wet outside, wet inside: I'm a wet guy. That's how I think of myself. It's how I present myself to the motel clerk when I finally arrive at a destination, rolling my bike into the lobby and dripping on the decorative tile.

"Yes," I announce, "I'm wet."

Motel clerks are often sympathetic and helpful—they generally recognize that a first-floor room is preferable, and one upgraded me to a room with a hot tub—but rarely gifted at repartee.

"Yes sir" is the usual response.

My recent path has taken me through Michiana, as they call it here, the farming region that exists on either side of the Michigan-Indiana border, and I've been able to find local maps and local citizens to guide me through rural counties on roads where the traffic is mostly limited to tractors, the mailman, and an occasional FedEx truck. They're good roads to ride, though they do have a propensity to turn to dirt for stretches of a mile or so, a bit sluggish in sodden weather. Horses and cows and even the occasional llama, grazing just an arm's length or two from the roadside, nosed up close to me behind their fences and shied away when I stopped to say hello.

The scenery has been bucolic—lanes with overarching trees, farms with tall cornfields, yellowing pea patches, and gardens of pumpkins or melons. Leaves are beginning to turn—they seem to be a bit behind schedule this year—but in the dank air and against the battleship skies, the yellows and reds are muted. The roads are littered with twigs, leaves, buckeyes, and fallen apples, a genuine cycling hazard that I hadn't considered. But the quiet is more than worth it.

This is territory I'm familiar with only from behind the wheel of a car. When my GPS threw me a curve on Wednesday and sent me a few miles out of the way, I ended up crossing the Ohio Turnpike three different times on three different overpasses. It's a road I've driven dozens of times, and I was able to imagine myself in a car on the highway watching myself crossing over it on a bike.

"Who's that guy on a bicycle in the rain on the overpass?" I'd ask myself from behind a windshield on the highway. Even in the rain I would be able to say: "Sure wish that was me."

Monday, October 3, Wooster, Ohio

Eighteen years ago, the ride from the Golden Gate Bridge to the George Washington Bridge took seventy-five days. Yesterday was day seventy-five of my second transcontinental trip, and the distance I have yet to travel from here to Manhattan—four hundred seventy miles by car, probably another hundred on a bicyclist's more meandering path—is one way to measure how I've aged. Another is that my knees are stiff and sore; every morning I feel a little more like the Tin Man pleading squeakily for his oilcan. (Okay, enough already with the *Oz* allusions. But thank you, L. Frank Baum.)

This is no surprise, of course. As a thirty-nine-year-old I was a more vigorous fellow than I am at fifty-seven (fifty-eight in a month, *arrgh*), physically stronger and capable of more sustained daily exertion. I was also more impatient. One thing I've noticed about myself on this trip is that I'm in less of a hurry, with a greater propensity for stopping to take pictures and to enjoy the scenery. I'm more willing to call it a day before I've pushed myself to the brink of exhaustion. Counting days off, I averaged more than sixty miles per day in 1993; this time it's under fifty. (The 1993 trip was forty-six hundred miles; so far this one is thirty-four hundred.) As the years go faster, I'm slowing down: another LCT.

Comparisons like these are taking up more room in my thinking lately. How many ways are there to measure the passage of time? As I get closer to New York, which also means closer to returning to the obituaries desk, I can't help thinking how nice it's been for the past couple of months to wake up and think intensely only about the day ahead of me and not the sum total of someone's life.

Obit writers differ from other reporters in a number of interesting ways. We don't have to come up with story ideas, for one thing, and there aren't any follow-up stories, for another. We're the only reporters who spend most of our time reporting on the past. There is, after all, only one piece of news in an obituary, and it's the same news every time. An obit begins at the end of the story.

All this sounds a bit glib, I know, but it's actually sort of profound, a whole other imperative for a writer.

I arrived at the obits desk following a circuitous tour of more conventional journalistic enterprises.

After my cross-country trip in 1993, I covered the theater for the *Times* as a reporter, then was sent to the metro desk for a stint on general assignment, writing about the fiftieth anniversary of the United Nations, the world chess championships, and the Woody Allen–Mia Farrow connubial strife, among other things. In 1997, I was posted to Chicago as a cultural correspondent, traveling all over the country for stories about the arts (what a fabulous gig that was!), and I wrote a kid's book with the tap dancer Savion Glover. In 1999, I was brought back to New York and became a theater critic, and then, after four years left the arts section and became a kind of lifestyle reporter covering recreation. (In twenty-five years at the *Times*, I think I've had four bylines above the fold on the front page, and one was for a story about the national baton twirling championships.) In 2006, I took a leave from the paper for a couple of years to write a book about baseball umpires.

So that's the résumé—another way to measure time.

When I came back to the *Times* in 2008 I joined the obits desk, and for good or ill, it feels like a final resting place, journalistically speaking. (Though I hope it's not; one of the reasons I got on my bike this summer was to tell a story that looks forward and not back.)

In any case, over the last three years I've written more than three hundred obits, rendering, as entertainingly and informatively as possible in a handful of hours before deadline, the lives of scientists, inventors, writers, actors, musicians, historians, politicians, lawyers, jurists, filmmakers, impressionists, cartoonists, athletes, adventurers, and journalists in concise blocs of six hundred, eight hundred, or a thousand words that generally appear deep in the B section of the daily paper. You get accustomed to acknowledging mortality in a casual, less than awestruck, not even solemn way. We have a file in the department, people who we've heard are seriously ailing, called "Circling the Drain." Every morning I go to the office and ask, sometimes literally, "Who's dead?"

It's a job that accommodates list making and name dropping.

To wit: I did a guy who hijacked an airplane and a guy who helped find Hitler's will. I did a founder of the Heritage Foundation and a defender of the Chicago Seven. I did a Black Panther (two, actually) and a South African white separatist. I did the model for Lois Lane and the model for the Dustin Hoffman character in *Rain Man*. I did a Swiss yodeling champion, a British snooker champion, an American Ping-Pong champion, a boxing world champion, an Olympic gymnastics champion, and a judge whose ruling allowed girls to play Little League. I did the founder of the Gap and the creator of *Hazel*. I did an eleven-year-old who appeared in *The Lion King* and a one-hundred-and-four-year-old who laid claim to having written "The Hokey Pokey." I did two Golden Girls and two Redgraves (three, if you count Natasha Richardson). I did George Carlin, David Foster Wallace, David Levine, Greta Waitz, Duke Snider, David Nelson (brother of Rick, son of Ozzie and Harriet), George Blanda, David Carradine, David Broder (a lot of Davids, for some reason), Jimmy Dean (the country singer and breakfast sausage maven), Peter Falk (a.k.a. Columbo), and Marilyn Chambers (the porn star who was also the Ivory Snow girl).

Then there's the matter of advance obits, writing about the dead while they're still living—the future dead, as it were. We do a lot of that, too, an element of our macabre enterprise that seems to tickle people as especially macabre, though it's a purely pragmatic thing. Let's say Jesse Jackson or Barbra Streisand dies in the middle of the afternoon one day; you just can't research and write a thorough obit for someone like that in time for the next day's paper. (Actually, you need to be faster than ever now; word of the deaths of well-known people finds its way to the web before it gets to the funeral home.)

The nightmare that my boss, the obits editor Bill McDonald, lives with is the sudden and unexpected demise of someone famous and accomplished—think Michael Jackson or Tim Russert—who isn't in our advance file. So he's become a mortality troubleshooter, keeping close tabs on the waning lives of celebrities in dozens of wide-ranging fields and assigning writers to their not-yet-complete life stories. In a way, Bill is journalism's equivalent of an actuary, though he'd be the first to tell you that there's no real science involved, and there's no formula for deciding when to assign an advance. It's just guesswork. Frances Reid, a ninety-five-year-old soap opera actress, actually died while I was working on her advance—good call, Bill!—but I've written about thirty others that are just sitting there waiting for the moment they're released from journalistic limbo: Yogi Berra, Stephen Sondheim, Mort Sahl, Ruby Dee, Jean Stapleton,* Roger Bannister, Elaine Stritch, and Russell Johnson, who played the Professor on *Gilligan's Island*, are among them. The *Times* doesn't like to be public about the names, but really, what's the big secret? Like these people don't know they're going to die? I don't even see the problem with showing people their obits. Let them request changes, insist on them, even. Generally that's anathema in journalism, but in this case it'll make them feel better, and how are they going to know when it turns out you've ignored them? (I'm joking.)

---

*Jean Stapleton died on May 31, 2013, and my obituary for her was published in the *Times* the next day.

Anyway, we've got advances on hand that are five, ten, even fifteen years old and that are going to need rewriting or at least updating when the time comes, and every now and then we print one posthumously, where the writer died before the subject did. Mel Gussow on Elizabeth Taylor, for instance, just a few months ago. (This is nothing I aspire to, just to be clear.)

How healthy it is to think about death in this quotidian way—as an unexceptional reality for someone or other, and therefore nothing to be too glum or concerned about—I'm uncertain. Every so often it has happened that, as a reporter, I'd met the subject of one of my obituaries, and each time it happens—that is, each time I have to write about someone I've previously encountered in the flesh—my mind does the same thing, goes back to the moment of the meeting and imagines that there's a frisson of recognition on both our parts, an eerie, telepathic message that lets us in on our future connection. In the Ingmar Bergman film version of this tale, I'm the guy in the black robe carrying the scepter. But what would it be like to be the other guy, to realize that by chance you've just shaken hands with your obituarist, someone who, at some uncertain future time, will consign you to history? It's actually the case that once or twice I've run into someone whose obituary I've already written; not too long ago I sat across the aisle from one of them—okay, it was Tony Bennett—at a Broadway show. So far I've resisted the mischievous, troubling impulse to let them know.

The *Times* doesn't abide the euphemisms for death and dying, and I feel well instructed by that policy, so in our pages (and in my mind) nobody passes on or passes away or ascends to heaven or goes to a better place. They just die. They're just dead. That sounds like a cold thing, perhaps, but it's one way that writing obituaries has unromanticized death for me, if it ever seemed romantic. For the sake of argument I'll even stipulate the possibility of an afterlife, but that still leaves people on earth susceptible, in the wake of a loved one's death, to agonizing loneliness, lingering, unendurable pangs of grief, and the inconsolability that comes with an irrecoverable loss.

Granted, for that kind of suffering we damn well should be rewarded with an afterlife, but I'm not counting on it. And given the fact of the deaths of those around me the last few years, I think my job has made me feel more fundamentally connected to other people in general. You can't talk to grieving relatives day after day and not recognize how the universality of death contributes to our sense of a shared human condition. If there's an especially gratifying thing about writing obits, that's it.

Maybe it seems odd to bring up politics at this juncture. But the poison in our public intercourse lately—the red state/blue state divide, the venomous antagonism between liberals and conservatives—has certainly cheapened the idea, or mocked it, anyway, that people do share a condition as we live on the earth. I don't think I'm alone in feeling a kind of despair over what sometimes seems like an enveloping malevolence in the world—or in feeling a kind of guilt for now and then participating in it. My views are, for the most part, politically liberal, and when I listen to Limbaugh, Hannity, and Coulter and their ilk maintaining their reactionary brand by spewing ugly disdain at people like me— Why do I listen at all? That's a good question—the rage they stir up in their devotees on one side and in me on the other makes me think that we might as well be different species in mortal combat over the fate of mankind.

It's a lousy way to feel, and weirdly enough, writing obituaries assuages it a little bit. So does riding a bike, I think, because it is among the least aggressive, least contentious of activities. You ride into a strange town on a bike and no one's suspicious of you; everyone's curious. No one sees a long-distance cyclist as a threat; a nut, maybe, but a benign and interesting one. And the cyclist—tired, alone, homeless—is needy in a way that appeals to people's better angels and allows strangers to be generous without having to try very hard. They invite you for a meal, offer a bed for the night, dispense directions, fill your water bottles at their kitchen sinks, stop for you when you're stuck on the side of the road, applaud you when you reach the mountain pass, and encourage you, encourage you, encourage you.

You don't even have to meet them. The messages I've been getting online lately, from people who have no bone to pick and no earthly reason to write except to urge me on, are thrillingly consoling:

"Keep up the good work!" wrote someone named Jim. "I am keeping track of you from way down in New Zealand during our fresh springtime. A cross country bike trip has been on my agenda for the last 30 years after talking to a fellow US citizen in NZ back in the early 80's who went from Chicago to the West Coast. It sounded great then and it still sounds like something I want to do someday. It has been in the back of my head ever since then and continues to live there. Ahh, someday . . . Good on ya! Keep the story telling up, I look forward to it."

"I know many people have been inspired by your awesome trip," Shane from Massachusetts wrote. *"Wishing you all the best for a fantastically slow, but exciting, rest of the trip."*

"Bruce, greetings from the Champlain Valley of VT," wrote David. *"Enjoying this second ride of yours immensely—reminds me of a trip I took with my family 11 years ago, mostly on the Old Lincoln Highway, Route 30, VT to SF. You've got better knees than me, young feller. Be well."*

"It will be very sad for us when your trip comes to an end," Sarah Wiley wrote from Midland, Michigan.

Maybe there's a human gene after all.

For a week I've been riding the county and town roads that you can discover only on local maps; they crisscross the landscape like netting—narrow lanes through corn and soybean fields, past suburban-style farmhouses, formidable barns and silos, and a remarkable number of small cemeteries. In Wauseon, Ohio, I noticed the mailboxes for the houses across the street from the graveyard were alongside the grave-yard, as though the occupants beneath certain headstones are still get-ting their phone bills.

The challenge is finding your way through the maze of roads, trying to avoid the more heavily trafficked direct routes between population centers like Sturgis, Michigan, and Mansfield, Ohio. I zigzagged to stay on the empty routes, passing through villagey places like Centreville, Michigan; Orland, Indiana; and Centerton, Ohio, where horses were likely to be grazing in side yards. In slightly bigger towns—Whitehouse, Ohio, for example—signs for local political candidates were everywhere, stabbed into front lawns, signifying the fall election season. Interest-ingly, in what I assume is part of red state America, I saw no banners or bumper stickers for any of the Republican presidential hopefuls.

In the blustery, rainy weather that beset the region for about ten days, leaves and twigs and split-open buckeyes were all over the pavement. (Smashed on the ground—as a Michigan Wolverine, I have to say that's how I like my buckeyes.) All the ball fields and basketball courts were empty. I was riding largely during school hours; I saw almost no children.

I enjoyed myself, mostly, though I was wet a good deal of the time, and cold occasionally, too. A couple of days, the temperature barely made it out of the forties. The riding days were relatively short; my average mileage has dipped a bit lately. That's another thing that's different from 1993. On my last trip, I picked up the pace as I got closer to home, eager to have achieved completion and triumph. Oddly enough, it turned out I was a little bit sad when I did, in fact, finish, and maybe that's why the same sense of urgency to get to the end of the road hasn't taken hold of me this time. Perhaps I'm old enough now to recognize the end of an adventure for what it is: one less adventure ahead of me.

Thursday, October 6, West Homestead, Pennsylvania

Several days ago, a reader tipped me off to the Great Allegheny Passage, a.k.a. GAP, a bike trail on a former railroad bed that heads southeast from Pittsburgh for about one hundred and forty miles to Cumberland, Maryland, supposedly passing through lovely woods and skirting western Pennsylvania's relentless hills. It's off the direct path to New York—pretty much out of the way, actually—but it solves the problem of where to ride with Jan. I've been worried about how much she can handle on a fold-up bicycle—or how much the fold-up bicycle can handle with her on it—and I think (I hope) three days on flat ground of less than fifty miles a day should be okay. That still sounds like a lot, I know, for someone who hasn't been riding all day every day this summer, but we had at least one fifty-mile day in Provence in May, with persistent winds and plenty of climbing, and she finished with energy to spare.

I got here yesterday, to Pittsburgh and a little beyond, on one of the first sunny afternoons I've had in weeks. West Homestead is southeast of the city, a former home to brickworks and other manufacturers and businesses in the orbit of the steel industry. Now it seems to be reinventing itself as a suburb. The Marriott Courtyard, where I'm staying, is on the south bank of the Monongahela River, within the limits of a vast, just-about-brand-new shopping mall with a full complement of upper-middle franchises, including a twenty-two-screen multiplex and a parking lot the size of some counties.

I chose the hotel because the trailhead of the GAP is within half a mile or so, and strange as it is to be ensconced in Comfy Consumerland, I'm enjoying it. For one thing, there's almost nobody here, acres of places in which to spend money and very few people spending it. The lobby of the theater was entirely empty when I checked on the movie times before dinner last night. Parents were using the vacant expanses of the parking lot to give driving lessons to their teenagers.

I ate a mammoth early dinner at the bar in an overpriced seafood restaurant and then went shopping for a sweater (Hmmm, the Gap, J.Crew, or Banana Republic?) because the one I've been carrying with me has grown, at last, unwearably gamy. I wore the new one (the Gap) to the theater, where I watched a political thriller, *The Ides of March*, directed by and starring George Clooney. It wasn't bad; halfway through I realized I knew the story. I'd seen the play it was based on, *Farragut North* by Beau Willimon, in New York. That was in 2008—I looked it up later—only three years ago, but I didn't recognize it as familiar until it was half over. I worry about my memory sometimes, but once the recollection hit me, it seemed vivid and close by. I remembered how the play ended, where the theater was, where I sat, who I was with.

Only three years ago and I didn't recall it right away? Or wow, three years ago and I recalled all that? The way we process the passing of time—it's profoundly perplexing (not to mention perplexingly profound).

*   *   *

A long bike ride delivers you from one set of conditions to another. For almost a year—well, okay, ten days, but it felt like a year—I was riding in the damp and cold as a crummy weather front arrived over lower Michigan and Ohio and sat there. More than once I played the alternate universe game with myself: Would I trade a steady rain and a chilling wind for the heat and rolling hills of the Palouse in eastern Washington? How about for the endless prairie of Montana? A cyclist can appreciate all those challenges and enjoy meeting them, including the rain, but after a week or so of being soggy to the bone, the answer to every trade possibility was yes.

When the sun finally came out late on Tuesday afternoon, I was entering the northern panhandle of West Virginia, a toothpick of terri- tory wedged between Ohio and Pennsylvania. (I never noticed it before, but Ohio is shaped sort of like a molar.)

I'd passed through the Mennonite settlements of eastern Ohio, where the pleasant clip-clop of horses drawing covered wagons was a welcome change from the grind and whir of automobile engines (though the droppings on the road made for a unique cycling hazard). I'd reached the foothills of the Appalachians, a wholly different kind of riding from what I'd encountered before on this trip. In the West, the hills are long and relentless but even in the Rockies are graded less steeply than they are here in the East, where no road builders, it seems, have ever heard of a switchback. The ascents are shorter—you don't have any four- or five- or six-mile climbs—but they stand up straighter, like spikes driven into the flat ground. To get to the top, you crank down into your granny gear and try to find a comfortable pedal stroke even as your quads, ham- strings, and glutes are sending similar messages to your brain—Hey, what the hell is this? There were occasional rewards at the top: views of valleys with the seasonal colors beginning to change, and when the roadbed wasn't too chewed up, an exciting plunge down the other side. But overall it has been slow going. I've had about a hundred miles of it now, starting in eastern Ohio, not long after I crossed I-71, which makes me look forward to the GAP as a welcome respite.

Tuesday I started in the quiet and quaint village of Bolivar—rhymes with Oliver—and landed on the western shore of the Ohio River just below Wellsville, a dour-looking town hemmed in by geography, a wall of imposing hills to the west squeezing it against the water. It wasn't an overly long ride, fifty miles or so, but it was enervating, up and down, up and down, in and out of soaking showers, on roads that had probably needed repaving for a long time. By the time I stopped for a midafternoon lunch at McDonald's, my wrists were sore and my fingers stiff and gnarled from the rattling. The sun was breaking through by then and my clothes were reasonably dry (though my shoes weren't), but I felt glum and pretty bedraggled.

It wouldn't get much better, either. To get across the river, I had to ride six miles or so upriver to East Liverpool, and the only road was a high-speed four-lane highway; its shoulder was wide enough for safety, but it was littered with debris and fed me into the crowded center of town where—preposterously, because it's really not a very big place and you'd think my sense of direction would be pretty well honed by now—I got lost looking for the bridge and spent fifteen minutes making wrong turns down residential streets of weathered row houses and commercial strips pocked with empty storefronts.

When I finally got over the bridge, I had to ride seven miles or so downriver on the West Virginia side from Newell, where the Holiday Inn was unaccountably full, to find a place to stay. It was another terrible stretch of road, dangerously narrow, pocked and busy, and at the end of it a meager reward: the Mountaineer Casino, Racetrack & Resort, a brassy adult amusement park of a place where they gave me an awful, tiny ground-floor room with a window opening so close upon the parking lot that I could just about reach out and polish the grille of the nearest Buick.

I did a load of laundry, ate too much at the buffet, and fell asleep with the Yankees whipping the Tigers on television. I suppose it was balm for the rest of the day, but my personal, doom-inclined crystal ball

finding the way to my hotel. I crossed several bridges, rode several sidewalks, and found myself in more than one construction zone. The last
stretch of the day began with a brutish climb up Greenfield Avenue
from the river to the borough of Squirrel Hill. Then there was a nasty
descent on a rutted sidewalk to the Homestead Grays Bridge—named
for the old Negro leagues baseball team—which crossed high above
the Monongahela and brought me to one more dangerous intersection
before depositing me at the shopping mall and the motel.

As I checked in, feeling one hundred percent safe for the first time
in a few hours, I found myself thinking about Scott Fisher, the owner of
the Fort Laurens Antique Trading Company, in Bolivar, a regular stop
on the eastern Ohio antiquing trail. I had met him, and the manager
of his store, Allen Miller, at the bar of an Italian restaurant, where I'd
stopped for dinner two nights earlier and they were having an argument about the Cincinnati Reds. (I don't remember the exact bone of
contention, but I did give them the name of the player they were looking for: Tom Seaver.) It was raining that night—it had rained all day—
and to reward me for solving their problem, Mr. Miller promised me
better weather the next morning.

The two of them were a little out of sorts; for the past week their
store had been commandeered by an independent film crew, and they
were caught between being the proud proprietors to whom the mov-
iemakers were being entirely solicitous and having nothing much to
do. The movie, they said, was called *Old Fashioned*, and it is about the
traditional courtship between an antiques store owner and the young
woman who moves into a flat above his shop.*

The next morning, I visited the set and walked through the appeal-
ingly cluttered store. Mr. Fisher, a wry, friendly man, is an American
history buff who spoke knowledgeably about the region, which was
the far western front of the Revolutionary War. With other like-minded
devotees, dressed in full colonial army regalia and carrying a musket, he
once walked seventy-five miles to Bolivar from Beaver, Pennsylvania,

---

* As of January 2014, it hadn't yet been released.

reenacting a march by General Washington's infantry. Based on his experience, he told me, I'd have hills to climb until I reached the Pennsylvania border, but then it would be more downhill. (On balance, I'd say he was right. In any case, his prediction was better than Mr. Miller's—it rained all morning and into the afternoon.) He told me he liked New York but wouldn't be able to live there. I said I felt the same about Bolivar. He laughed.

"No stoplights," he said. "That's kind of the motto of the old-timers in town: 'I moved here because there's not a damned stoplight to be found.'"

16

Life Is an Etch A Sketch

Sunday, October 9, West Homestead, Pennsylvania

Years ago, when I first thought of writing for a living, it was fiction that appealed to me, novels and short stories. In my college creative writing classes, I learned the importance of writing with authority—that is, with knowledge of your setting and subject and conviction in your observations and opinions. At the same time, I thrilled to the magical idea that a fictional character might come alive in a writer's mind and act with seeming independence, propelling the narrative on his own—the creation animating the creator rather than the other way around.

Absorbing the cognitive dissonance within those tenets—relishing it, in fact—is a job requirement for a serious fiction writer; it's the only way to establish a world for the reader to live in that is both persuasively real and entirely made up.

And I could never do it. For ten years or so, I tried, but I always managed to violate the literary equation one way or another. Mostly I wrote stories with protagonists who shared a number of my experiences (though I remember one that was about a guy playing minor league ball in Abilene, Texas, something I hadn't done and somewhere I'd never been), but either it became evident I didn't know what I was talking about or, more often, the characters were never fully enough imagined to steer the stories on their own, leaving me to rely on the desperate tactics of a puppeteer—dredging up clichés or, probably worse, explaining what actually happened to me—to sustain any kind of narrative momentum.

In 1981, I got my first job in publishing, as an assistant fiction editor at *Esquire*, and one of my tasks was to read the slush pile—the stories that arrive unsolicited with their unsung writers' hopes attached. There were about a hundred of them a week, thousands in a year, and they provided for me an intense seminar in recognizing bad writing. After a few months it got so I could usually tell within a page, sometimes a paragraph or two—a sentence, if it began with "Once upon a time" or "Long ago and far away"—whether the writer had the mastery and the imagination that warranted a close reading to the end. I spent two years at *Esquire*, and I think we published one slush story.

Of course, I recognized my own amateurism in a lot of what I read, and it became clear to me that the last thing the world needed was another semi-okay fiction writer. So I gave up on short stories and started working on personal essays, criticism, and, eventually, reported pieces. A journalist, I've sometimes said since then—glibly, but sort of seriously—is a writer in search of something to say.

New Orleans went by in a rush. Jan and I met at the airport baggage carousel, found a taxi, and, like a couple of kids, pretty much didn't let go of each other for thirty-six hours, until 4:00 a.m. Sunday, when we got up after three or four hours' sleep to make our plane. At that point we were too groggy to even hold hands, and later neither of us could remember much about our layover breakfast with Robert, Lynne, and Jake at the Atlanta airport, except that Jake asked Jan if she'd ever met any of the other girlfriends I'd introduced him to.

It was all sweet, but the sweetest moment was the first. As it happens sometimes (or always) in airports, the gate was at the opposite pole from the baggage area, and I plodded through the bland corridors for what seemed like a mile before I poked my head around a corner and there she was, sitting with one leg crossed over the other, her foot wagging in worry or impatience. She saw me as she made an idle turn of her head and did a double take and her eyes widened, she seemed to sob, and her face looked suddenly relieved and grateful.

Seeing her see me, I was deeply self-conscious. She looked girlish and compelling—like someone I'd fall in love with at first sight if I'd never laid eyes on her before. But weirdly enough, I felt as if I might seem physically strange to her. I knew I'd lost weight. My face was thinner and my jeans were hanging from my hips, and it made me shy. I stood there with a goofy, stubborn, terrified smile, hesitating, but Jan just ran to me and we kissed. And as satisfied as I've been with myself these past weeks, as impressed with my perseverance in solitude, my physical prowess (such as it is), mental toughness, and emotional resilience, as proud of my self-sufficiency, in an instant I understood what I've been missing.

*   *   *

I didn't see much of the city this time. It was a fancy wedding, and there were buses to take us from the hotel in the French Quarter, where the rehearsal dinner took place on Friday night, to the church in the Garden District for the ceremony on Saturday afternoon, and back to the Quarter for the wedding feast at Antoine's. For a number of the guests, I was a secondary feature, like the newsreel before the movie, nowhere near as interesting as the young couple, of course, but I was making my debut as Jan's boyfriend in front of many of her oldest friends and I had my teeth and hooves examined pretty thoroughly. I didn't mind it; I could tell I was being approved of, mainly because when I was watching Jan and watching her friends watch her, and it was shamelessly evident that she was blissful.

We didn't spend a great deal of time alone, but we had a chance to walk around on Saturday morning; I wanted beignets and chicory coffee at Café Du Monde, but the place was overflowing with tourists so we had breakfast at Restaurant Stanley, a friendly bistro nearby on Jackson Square, and afterward bought baseball caps from a street vendor selling them to benefit breast cancer research. She suckered us, but charmingly so, and the hats had a cute logo.

I have a strange history with this city, much of it, oddly enough, revolving around weddings. Catherine's brother got married there; well, it was in Baton Rouge, actually, but afterward Catherine and I drove to New Orleans, where we broke up for the eighth or ninth time.

The first time I arrived there, in 1991, was on a bicycle, in fact, after a three-day ride from Jackson, Mississippi, where my brother had gotten married. I was still a fledgling bike traveler at that point, and for a New Yorker in the deepest South it felt like a brave journey. I anticipated adventures in culture clash—cotton fields, willows, sleepy Main Streets, and suspicious, big-bellied sheriffs wearing opaque sunglasses leaning on their cars on the side of the road, chewing toothpicks and watching me, making sure I proceeded out of town with dispatch. Of course, there was none of that—well, maybe a few willows. It was a pleasant and not very eventful ride, a couple hundred miles through rural Mississippi fields, mostly, in my memory, untilled and empty, as if waiting for people to come along and pay attention. Now and then an isolated building—a motel, an adult bookstore, a warehouse, an auto body shop—underscored the impression of a human outpost on a distant planet.

As I entered Louisiana and got closer to the water, there were bogs and a soggy wildlife park, and then the isthmus between Lake Pontchartrain and the Gulf, and finally a surprisingly long, trafficky lead-in to New Orleans itself. Looking at the map now, I see I must have ridden just above, if not through, the Lower Ninth Ward, the eastern region of the city that I next saw after its obliteration by Hurricane Katrina in 2005. I remember that first passage into the city fuzzily, the area seemingly down on its heels and a little ramshackle but stubbornly upright—modest shotgun houses whose front yards were scrubby and burnt yellow from the summer heat, flanking a main drag with a grassy center island that needed mowing. A struggling American place, an undistinguished American place that would later be made memorable by its destruction.

I went straight downtown to the train station, packed up my bike and shipped it back to New York. Then I met my parents for a couple of days of good eating, the only time I ever went to Commander's Palace, the celebrated restaurant in the Garden District, where I had my first Sazerac and, I'm pretty sure, the only bowl of turtle soup I've ever consumed. I remember my parents were happy, one son married, the other with them on vacation, both of them seemingly distracted from their usual burdens. That was a rare thing. It's a good memory.

I reported from New Orleans twice, once when the excellent art museum was celebrating the French painter Edgar Degas, who had an uncle and a couple of brothers in New Orleans and visited for several months in 1872 and 1873, painting one of his acknowledged masterpieces, *A Cotton Office in New Orleans*.

It turned out the Degas family history in New Orleans was rife with juicy controversy. It had been only a dozen or so years earlier that a historian of the city unearthed the fact that although Degas's brother René was a prominent member of a racist political group, the Crescent City White League, a branch of the family was descended from a black woman who had six children with the brother of Edgar and René's grandmother. In addition, René had been a serious cad who left his blind wife for a neighbor. He brought the neighbor back to France, where he started a second family, scandalizing everyone and causing a rift in the clan—the New Orleans side changed its name from Degas to Musson, René's first wife's surname—and a battle over inheritance that lasted for generations.

Anyway, the house they all lived in was on Esplanade Avenue, a boulevard of lazy opulence that forms the northeastern boundary of the French Quarter and runs for three miles from the Mississippi River to the steps of the museum, which is located in City Park. A signature address in New Orleans, it was a symbol of the city's distinct visual aesthetic, its lovely sense of hothouse dilapidation, the "atmosphere of decay," as Tennessee Williams fondly described it. Esplanade was known especially for the magnificent live oak trees that lined its median strip, their branches spreading out over the avenue to form an elaborately webbed green awning.

I wrote about the street the last time I was in New Orleans, right after Hurricane Katrina. The high winds that accompanied the storm killed some of Esplanade's trees, tore off myriad branches and defoliated others, ripping gashes in the shady canopy as though a vindictive model had taken a knife to a painter's canvas. It was heartbreaking to behold at the time; New Orleans overall lost more than eight thousand trees, and City Park, among the nation's largest urban parks—a gorgeous greensward of thirteen hundred acres that includes a golf course, a botanical garden, a football stadium, and a children's amusement park as well as the museum—looked bulldozed.

Of course, there was worse to witness. My three weeks in New Orleans after the hurricane were the saddest of my journalistic life, which, as journalistic lives go, has been a pampered one. I've never been a war correspondent or seen up close the ravages of famine or the aftermath of a volcano eruption or a tornado or a nuclear accident. But arriving in New Orleans in the fall of 2005, five weeks after the storm, I found much of the place buried in detritus. Towers of garbage and muddy cars that would no longer start lined the streets, whole blocks of houses were marked by waterline stains, the lawns in front of them deathly gray, spongy to walk on. It was a lesson for me in disaster, namely that ruinousness isn't simply shocking, which is what comes across on television, the gasp-inducing images creating a potent visual aesthetic of calamity that can be appreciated for its terrible beauty. When you're in the midst of it, it's a whole other thing. In New Orleans after the storm, I was simply sickened. So much of it was ugly, revolting, the sense of waste overwhelming. On more than one afternoon, I drove through the most devastated areas, the Lower Ninth and beyond, through miles and miles and miles of what can be described only as a former civilization, neighborhood upon neighborhood, shopping center upon shopping center deserted, grotesquely soiled and horrifyingly lifeless. I've never been in another landscape, in the city or the country, entirely without a heartbeat and I never wish to be again.

This weekend I didn't get a chance to ride up Esplanade, visit the art museum, or check on the resurrection of the Lower Ninth (which remains, according to what I've read, a sparsely populated, largely unrestored urban wilderness, a dumping ground for old tires and unwanted cats and dogs amid swaths of jungly undergrowth). But the recollections of my previous visits to the city came streaming back to me as the wedding events unfolded. I almost said flooding, but that would have been inaccurate as well as unseemly, because the memories returned one at a time, each following on the previous one's heels, a narrative of my New Orleans history, connecting the little blips of personal experience that add up to my knowledge of the place.

It's the local version of what I'm doing with America this summer, a passage through time instead of space but, still and all, gathering knowledge a blip at a time, scratching out my own skinny little path in the silvery dust of the grand scheme of things. The world is but an Etch A Sketch.

Thursday, October 13, Cumberland, Maryland

Jan just left. She packed her Brompton folding bike in the trunk of a rented Ford Malibu and disappeared onto a highway cloverleaf. She's on her circuitous way back to Paris via Annapolis, the Brandywine Valley in Pennsylvania, and Manhattan. It's good I still have three hundred miles of pedaling to pay attention to because watching her drive away was dispiriting. I've spent a lot of my romantic life in long-distance relationships and enough is enough. This is one thing I *am* too old for, no argument.

One reason I began riding cross-country in midsummer was so I could be on the road as the seasons changed. I had some chilly, autumnal weather before it was actually autumn, but the foliage has been slow to turn this year. It's only in the past week or so that the colors have taken on the burnt yellows and burnished reds that we associate with fall, and I was lucky enough to be in the woods when it happened, and lucky enough not to be alone.

Back in Pittsburgh on Sunday, we had a goofy afternoon exploring the mall and slept well at the Marriott. On Monday we woke up early and found the Great Allegheny Passage at the far end of the parking lot, at that point an undistinguished-looking bike path along the Monongahela. Early on, it wasn't much of a ride, passing through industrial and commercial sites in Homestead and Duquesne, paralleling railroad tracks for a while and then following the sidewalks and city streets of McKeesport.

But shortly thereafter the passage, the GAP, sidles up alongside the north-flowing Youghiogheny River (pronounced, I think, yock-uh-GAY-nee) and accompanies it through a gorgeous, seeming wilderness, crossing over it now and then and yielding, from bridges that once were railroad trestles, fine views of fast-flowing white water and the excitement of being suspended above a gorge. After a hundred and twenty miles or so, the path reaches its apex of elevation, 2,375 feet above sea level, at the Eastern Continental Divide (separating the Atlantic watershed from the Gulf of Mexico watershed), and the last twenty-two miles are a steady cruise downhill.

The towns along the trail—Connellsville, Ohiopyle, Confluence, Meyersdale, and others—are slowly yielding their longtime identities as coal and rail towns and embracing bike travelers. Bike shops are doing business in most of them; bike racks are standard features in front of stores and restaurants. Bed-and-breakfasts catering to cyclists have sprung up along the trail. In Connellsville we stayed in one owned by a Czech couple who had hung a glass vitrine on the wall above our bed. Inside was what looked to be a *mittel*-European folk dance outfit but that we learned was actually the husband's grandmother's wedding dress.

Quite aside from my delight in Jan's company, it was a marvelous few days, a supremely seasonal experience. The weather was mostly overcast when it wasn't wet, but the air evoked that early fall, glad-to-be-outdoors-as-long-as-I'm-dressed-properly feeling. You could ride all day without overheating. The trail bed—mostly packed, crushed limestone and built on abandoned rail lines (the grades from one end to the other are very gentle)—was carpeted in fallen leaves, and the trees were subtly aflame. Now and then the trail opens onto mountain panoramas, and they were so rich with complementary colors that the hillsides seemed to have been crocheted in velour.

"We could wrap ourselves in this," I said to Jan.

Since Catherine, there have been a few women I've been hopeful about—or tried to be hopeful about, I should say—and a few more toward whom I behaved badly in one way or another, usually just vanishing at the first sign of attachment. Or maybe the second sign. There were a few who behaved badly toward me, too—it has been a fair fight overall, I'd say—but in any case the idea of thinking forward about a love affair with not only hope but confidence is brand new to me.

A couple of days ago when Jan and I were resting on the trail, she said: "Do you know when I knew I loved you?"

She recalled the exact moment. It was in Provence, on the second day of our trip, and she was still getting used to her bike, still a little shaky, and we were riding on a busy road.

"You came up behind me and said you were riding to my outside," Jan said. "'Don't worry, the cars have to go around me,' you said. And I felt so taken care of."

I remembered the moment, too. And I remember being conscious of precisely the same thing, of wanting her to know that I want to take care of her. Now, after three days of riding together on the GAP, feeling as though we might well have a life together, it pleases me no end that such a turning point for us took place on bicycles.

This is a little silly, maybe, but my history of bicycling with girl-friends is catastrophic. A couple of them weren't interested. A couple wanted to take short recreational rides with me, but they weren't capable riders, and it was, for me, a bore—except that I was constantly on the alert lest they wobble their way into traffic. One, who was a decent athlete, though not a bicyclist, and very competitive, was intent on proving she could keep up with me, which she couldn't. We went out for afternoon rides a few times. If I rode ahead and set my pace, she felt neglected and angry; if I rode behind and let her lead, she felt pandered to.

Catherine was always uneasy about my wanting to take long rides alone. No matter how much I explained about rejuvenating solitude and about wanting to push myself without having to worry about anyone else, no matter how many times I told her that every time we rode together I spent my mental energy looking after her, she took it personally when I didn't want her along. So we took a handful of trips together by bike and fought bitterly, without fail, on each one.

Jan's a talented rider, which is to say she's reasonably fit, with strong legs and the right temperament. She has patience and tenacity and relishes rather than resents making the effort. That's the test, really, sticking it out through fatigue and discomfort.

I knew this from our ride together in Provence, but this one on the GAP was different. We weren't being looked after. We didn't have guides to mark the route ahead of us, make the hotel arrangements, and carry our baggage in a sag wagon; we didn't have other cyclists around us, sharing our ride and our meals and our hotels and mitigating the intensity of spending whole days of riding together.

In three days we had a day and a half of rain. The second day was sixty miles, a lengthy stretch for anyone. We rode a solid pace over long intervals, didn't push it speedwise, really, but late afternoon passed into early evening and it was nearly dark when we arrived at our B and B and finally got off our saddles. Now and then she asked to rest, and now and then I asked. She made it easy for me. We pedal beautifully together.

17

⌒〜◇〜⌒

Time and Distance

Friday, October 14, Cumberland, Maryland

S o if you can be said to be hurrying on a cross-country bicycle trip, from Chicago I hurried to Pittsburgh. I had to push through some dreary weather in Michigan and Ohio, climb the roller-coaster foothills of the Appalachians and battle traffic and chewed-up roads as I entered the city. But I was meeting a deadline.

From there, though, with the end of a ride that began almost three months ago looming, I slowed down and started on an oblique route home.

For three days, instead of plunging ahead eastward toward Manhattan Jan and I veered to the south, eventually crossing the Mason-Dixon line (there's a sign!), the wrong way for someone in a hurry, though of course it was the right way for us. In retrospect our ride along the GAP, with the scenic wild rivers alongside it—the Casselman picks up where the Youghiogheny leaves off—was pure avoidance, my subconscious (or maybe not so sub-) informing me that I'm not quite ready to be home with my feet up on the coffee table and my knees swaddled in ice.

The temptation is to race to the finish, especially now that I'm alone out here again and feeling my aloneness rather acutely, and to imagine

294

it even before I get there. That's certainly how my previous continental crossing ended eighteen years ago; I was thirty-nine, a young man eager to feel a conqueror of the country and to accept the plaudits of friends and colleagues. This time, while I won't say that I won't be ready for the trip to end when it does, I'm feeling the different pleasures of delayed gratification.

I'm feeling the pleasures of contrariness, too. Why is everyone trying to rush me?

People have been telling me that the tough part of my cross-country bicycle journey was behind me, or that I was almost finished, or that the rest would be easy—or some related sentiment—ever since I crossed the Continental Divide, and several friends and readers wrote to express the absurdly wrong idea that all the climbing was behind me. When I reached the Mississippi River at its source in northern Minnesota, a grocery clerk made sure to inform me that I was closer to the finish than the start. In Minneapolis, in Madison, and again in Chicago, the friends I met up with offered congratulations, as if I were already taking a victory lap.

When I began my ride on July 20 in Astoria, the continent was sprawled enormously in front of me, but from the outset what people (noncyclists, generally) always seemed to be interested in was when it would be over: "How long's it going to take?"

I understand the impulse; it's a way of encapsulating an enterprise that doesn't exactly fit in a capsule. After all, an endless journey is a little intimidating, a little scary—Columbus sailing off over the flat edge of the world—but a journey that ends you can put in your pocket.

Still, the actual day-by-day doing of the trip—the hours-at-a-time riding, the countless pedal strokes and huffing and puffing up hills or into the wind, not to mention the daily deciding on a route, the finding of places to stay, the maintaining of the bike, and the consuming of sufficient calories—has been so fraught with effort that I've never been able to project convincingly and see myself any farther east than, say, the Holiday Inn Express across the county.

This isn't to say I don't dream about crossing the George Washington Bridge with my arms raised in triumph (and then putting away my bicycle for a winter's hibernation). I do. But my visions aren't terribly persuasive; they generally engender despair, causing me to sigh out loud and give off a lament for the long list of things that have ended and things that I'll never do again. It makes me more than a little nervous to write about this now, a few hundred miles from Manhattan. It may be easy to expect that someone who has already pedaled well over three thousand miles can do three hundred or four hundred more with his eyes closed, but I don't think so. In order to own those miles, I have to expend my energy on them; in order to live those days, I have to work through all their hours. I'm as daunted by the next four hundred miles as I was on Day 1 by the first thirty-six hundred.

I've often told people—and I've said so here—that traveling by bicycle isn't the contemplative, mind-meandering activity that it is generally presumed to be. Rather, it's concentration-enhancing. When I'm cycling I tend to be focused on cycling, keeping a close eye on the road, keeping tabs on the messages my bicycle and my body are sending me. But one thing that *has* diverted me all across the country is the relationship between time and distance. I've measured my progress with both of them: closing in on four thousand miles and thirteen weeks.

It interests me that both time and distance are concepts in the abstract, but that both are more often used in specific terms—a particular span of one or the other—and can be described similarly as long or short. On a tiring afternoon I'll habitually monitor my odometer and do the math—twenty-three miles to go, two hours if the wind doesn't turn; I'll be in my motel by five fifteen. This suggests that time and distance are inextricably related, but that isn't so. If I stood still on the shoulder of the road, five fifteen would come and go on the shoulder of the road. I said twenty-three miles in two hours—11.5 miles an hour. For a cyclist that's not especially speedy—it's pretty much a crawl, in fact. Thirteen weeks might describe a lot more than four thousand miles for someone stronger or more zealous, but I'm the cyclist I am.

In sum, for time to be meaningful, it needs to be filled by distance; for me, 11.5 miles generally fills up an hour pretty full. For distance to be meaningful, it needs to fill an appropriate measure of time. A long trip like mine—timewise, I mean—requires a lot of distance, even at a slow roll, to make the whole experience rise above standing on the roadside. You have to pedal and keep pedaling.

Perhaps you sense my favorite metaphor looming ahead. Good for you, because here it comes again. I decided to make this trip in the first place because I felt my résumé for adventure wasn't keeping pace with my advancing age. Unlike my last trip, which I viewed, somewhat contradictorily, as both a young man's errand and a farewell to youth, this one, at age fifty-seven, has been about my encroaching mortality, no doubt about it, and when I compare the two journeys I recognize in the current one the frailty of age. I'm slower. I'm less eager to ride long days and long hours or to ride with the sun going down. I'm much more concerned about finding a place to stay and knowing early in the day where I'll be spending the night. Never an especially intrepid down-hiller, I now ride the brakes on a steep incline like a grandfather. And though I've been thinking all across the country that there is simply more auto traffic than there used to be, and that roads that felt safe eighteen years ago are now riddled with hazard, it occurred to me recently that I'm simply more attuned to cars on the road and no longer blithely unconcerned about them. To put it bluntly, I'm more of a chicken.

All that acknowledged, my decision to ride cross-country again was a great one. Not because I've staved off anything grim, but because I've found a new way to think about my life—as a self-powered ride. What is distance, after all, but experience?

Sunday, October 16, Mifflintown, Pennsylvania

When I crossed from Ohio through a sliver of West Virginia and soon pedaled into Pennsylvania, I entered the East—that's how the state line declared itself in my mind—and a subliminal current ran through my thoughts: *You're back in familiar territory. This coast-to-coast bike ride is no longer exotic. The great days of pedaling are behind you, in Oregon, Montana, North Dakota, Minnesota, remote places with overwhelming dimensions and landscapes that a city dweller like you thinks of as occupying another part of the world.*

Still, a bike trip, like a ball game, as Yogi may or may not have said, ain't over till it's over. It turns out I was wrong about the grand riding. For one thing, Jan and I had those three great days on the GAP.

When she left, I had a down day, a little mopey; I didn't have Pittsburgh and New Orleans to motivate me anymore, and now I was waking up to the same damn bike ride and thinking about nothing but being a returning hero to my friends, a former cross-country bike rider. But what do you know? Over the weekend I had the best two days of riding of the entire journey.

Actually, in Cumberland I'd felt a little hemmed in, emotionally because I was suddenly lonesome, and physically because the city is in a river valley amid the Appalachian foothills, and as I learned from the guys at Cumberland Trail Connection, the local bike store, climbing on trafficky roads was the only way out of town if I wanted to head toward New York, north and east. The alternative was the Chesapeake & Ohio Canal towpath, often called the C&O, a rugged trail that dates to the first half of the nineteenth century and circumvents the mountains. It runs generally east and then southeast, all the way to Washington, and on Saturday I followed its first sixty miles to Hancock, Maryland, wriggling with the Potomac River along the Maryland–West Virginia border.

It was a thrilling, daylong carnival ride on a muddy track. After a stretch of wet weather, the sky was deep blue and the air was polished clear, the kind of fall day when the world presents itself in high def. A stiff, cleansing wind was blowing from the southwest, whistling and occasionally roaring through the treetops but rarely affecting the ride—I was protected by the woods. The Potomac, winding gracefully and companionably alongside me with the autumn sun angling off its surface, was simply beautiful.

The trail was another matter. Packed dirt with patches of embedded stones, it offers a rattly ride in the best circumstances, but after two days of rain, there were intermittent puddles up to a few inches deep, mud that caused my wheels to slide, and forest debris—piles of leaves and tossed branches—that made my bike buck and rear like a temperamental stallion. Near Paw Paw, West Virginia, a tunnel more than half a mile long leaves you in darkness, walking your bike, hugging the tunnel wall.

For reasons I can't entirely explain, I loved it. My riding focus had never been more intense, and the obstacle course of the trail felt to me as if it had been designed for the pleasure of a challenge, as if it were an amusement park attraction. My bicycle performed splendidly. When I brought it in, splattered in mud and grit, to be cleaned and tuned at the bike shop in Hancock, the mechanic couldn't find anything he needed to tune. The last twelve miles, I took a paved, parallel trail, and the smoothness underneath my wheels was pure luxury. A massage. Dessert.

That evening, having acted on a whim and driven all afternoon from New York, my friends Bob Ball and Maria Kastanis joined me for dinner. Among other pleasures of that visit, it was titillating to realize that I'd gotten to within a day's drive of home.

Still, I hadn't seen Bob since Billy's funeral, and before our reunion turned jolly, we had some sober moments of recollection over drinks.

Death trails you wherever you go, right? And for me, at least, especially at this age, its shadow is generally pretty apparent. We all have our appointments in Samarra, an acknowledgment of which was one of the big reasons for the bike trip in the first place. I wanted to escape the daily plodding toward the grave in the obituaries department, and it's probably a healthy thing that for several weeks I haven't been thinking much about dead people in general. But I was a little disappointed in myself to realize I hadn't done much thinking about Billy in particular since I'd flown out of Los Angeles. Bobby said he'd been haunted with memories of the weekend the two of us spent with Billy before he died, when he was suffering so terribly, and the vivid memory of his anguish came to me in a painful stab.

Bobby suddenly laughed.

"I found this," he said, and from his pocket he took a piece of paper and unfolded it on the table, a copy of an old photograph I hadn't seen in decades. In it, Billy was about eighteen, and he was running, a full and graceful sprint. Leaning forward, his arms pumping, he sped across the campus of Clark University, in Worcester, Massachusetts, where he and Bobby had met. Though the picture was taken from the side, you could make out his facial expression—it was gleeful and mischievous—and he was carrying something in the crook of one arm, maybe a bundle of clothes. Aside from sneakers and sweat socks, he was naked. Streaking, we called it then. I don't know that I've ever seen a more joyous, animated, vibrant portrait of anyone, the embodiment of meaningless daring, an adrenaline rush, and happy rebellion.

Talk about time and distance.

*   *   *

This morning I was back on highway asphalt, leaving behind (somewhat reluctantly) the Washington-bound towpath and pointing myself and my friends toward New York City. Happily, Bob and Maria had brought their bikes, and they alternated, one of them riding with me, the other driving the car, into which—my support wagon for the day!—I loaded my bags. The weather was splendid again, and as we headed northeast the wind was behind us. Hancock is in the slenderest part of the central Maryland neck, so we were back in Pennsylvania early on, climbing up along ridge roads where Hollywood might have arranged the view, the hills in the distance painted in deep fall colors. At noon, we were riding through the village of Hustontown, where the VFW was holding a community buffet lunch for the benefit of the volunteer fire department, and we joined maybe two hundred people for a hearty meal. (Homemade German chocolate cake! Whoa!)

For most of the rest of the day, as the sky clouded, we sped through farm-rich valleys, followed streams afizz with white water through the woods, and rose and fell along steep, rolling hills. Horses and cows appeared as ornaments on the landscape as if placed there by a decorator. At one point on the side of the road, we passed an enclosed pen full of turkeys, and they crowded to the pen window to watch us, their gobbles and squawks sounding pleading and panicky. I didn't blame them; it's only a month until Thanksgiving, after all.

Perhaps it was having company, perhaps the heartening tailwind, perhaps being reminded of what riding is like without the burden of saddlebags, but my legs felt springier than they had in weeks, and I had the longest day of my journey—ninety-two miles.

Bob and Maria both had to be at work in New York City the next day, and they left me in a cheesy motel here in Mifflintown, astonished, really, to be so close to home that I could have climbed in the backseat with them and slept in my own bed three hours later.

The skies opened as they left, and I watched them pull out of the parking lot in a cloudburst, which cut down on my dinner possibilities.

There was a Burger King across the parking lot, and I bought a fish sandwich, a double cheeseburger, a large fries, and an enormous lemonade, scarfing the whole thing down on the soft, lumpy mattress in my room. I felt absolutely great.

Wednesday, October 19, Jonas, Pennsylvania

Rain and a gusty headwind kept me to a half day's riding today, slowing my progress home, though I'm not entirely bummed about that. It's pretty here. I'm about a hundred miles from Manhattan, having climbed some roller-coaster hills and wound a woodsy path through Hickory Run State Park.

The little inn here is inviting but rickety, the kind of place where they keep the keys to the rooms upstairs behind the bar and you can order fish and chips and a cheeseburger and mushroom soup but not much else. It feels remote, at least for a cyclist pedaling in a cold rain. The woods are pretty deep and they don't expect too many strangers is my guess, not in the middle of the week when there aren't likely any hikers or hunters needing a place to stay.

During my ride this morning, just beyond a crossroads at the foot of a brief but punishing climb into the state park, I came across the Tannery Depot General Store, a homespun establishment with a roofed-over porch, a bit of shelter I took advantage of as the heavens suddenly opened. I was shivering out there and must have looked miserable—more miserable than I was, though I've been more comfortable in my life. The owner of the place, a woman named Bunny, popped her head out and told me not to be foolish and to come in for a cup of tea, which struck me as reasonable. We chatted amiably for ten minutes or so. It was she who pointed me here to Jonas and the inn, and I left happily fortified as the rain diminished to a drizzle, though by the time I got to the top of the hill it was pouring again. The last fifteen miles of the day were a chilly bath.

A table of blue-haired ladies was finishing lunch when I parked my bike under the eaves and walked in, soaked and bedraggled. The bartender and hotel proprietor, a woman about my age wearing a kerchief and an apron, took immediate pity on me, handing me a towel and letting me wheel my bike through the barroom and up the back stairs. There I moved into a tiny room with a single bed, a plastic stall shower, and a toaster-sized black-and-white television with a wire coat hanger serving as the antenna. With my bike wedged in a corner, there wasn't much space to move around, and by the time I spread out my wet stuff to dry, hanging my shorts and shirt on the handlebars and my socks from the knobs on the dresser, it was comical and cozy in equal measure. I took a hot shower, went down to the bar for a bowl of chili, and then took a nap until it was almost dark, when I went out for a walk. The air was damp but the sky was clearing, the gray clouds breaking up as daylight waned.

I followed a road into the woods for about a mile until it opened up into the beginnings of a housing development, and it occurred to me that I'd had a terrific day for reasons I couldn't really explain. What came to my mind was a passage I'd written at the end of my 1993 trip, and when I got back to my room I looked it up. The place had Wi-Fi. Who would've guessed?

"One thing I learned on my journey is that there are two kinds of people in the world," I wrote, "those who instinctively understand the appeal of a trip like mine and those who never could."

Then I explained:

> In Hardin, Mont., on the Crow Indian reservation, a young guy in a pickup found out what I was up to and asked, genuinely perplexed: "What would make you want to do that?" he asked. Some 1,200 miles later, in Odanah, Wis., on another reservation, another guy in a pickup offered me a ride. It was a kindness. He was going out of his way. It never occurred to him I might be riding my bike because I wanted to.
>
> A couple of weeks after that, I stopped to visit some cousins near Detroit, people I hadn't seen since a bar mitzvah more than a year earlier. I told these two stories over a raucous dinner table, concluding that there was something in Native American culture that judged me a nut.

"The Indians don't seem to understand," I said.
"I got news for you," one of my relatives said. "Neither do the Jews."

Friday, October 21, Teaneck, New Jersey

This is where I grew up. As I did on the last day of my trip in 1993, today I rode past my old house and took a few pictures, shaking my head at how the neighborhood had and hadn't changed. Then I took a room at the Marriott less than a mile away that hadn't existed when I lived here. It's right on the entrance ramp to Interstate 80, at the base of the Palisades that line the Hudson.

Tonight is the last night before my reentry into life as I once knew it—that is, in the spring. Yeah, it's about time to be back in my own bed like a settled adult and in the newsroom like a reporter with a real job. But it will be difficult to say good-bye to this three-month interlude of enlightening exercise, to trade in the outdoors, the physical expenditure, the unpredictability of every day, the adrenaline pump that has been propelling me through cycling's inherent hazards for the daily repetition of home and office, home and office.

I can feel a period of brooding coming on, a big melancholy, but for the moment I'm excited and to celebrate—and amuse myself—I'm taking a little inventory, counting stuff up, making lists.

For instance, I've imagined all the dinners of the trip on a big buffet table in front of me. Dinner has been the big meal of the day, and it's usually been really big, its contents determined by the cuisine of the restaurant closest to the motel. I've eaten a number of steaks, a sackful of pork chops, maybe a dozen chicken fajitas, several portions of lasagna, three pizzas, more than a few takeout egg rolls and wontons, and a variety of fish: snapper, salmon, tuna swordfish, trout, walleye. I ordered sushi once, in Cumberland, Maryland. Wasn't so bad.

Without looking at the map, I'm trying to remember the towns I passed through: Seaside, Cannon Beach, Manzanita, McMinnville, Estacada, Troutdale, Hood River, The Dalles, Biggs Junction, and Umatilla, Oregon; Touchet, Walla Walla, Starbuck, Pomeroy, Endicott, Saint

John, Dusty, Cheney, Spokane, and Newport, Washington; Rathdrum, Spirit Lake, Priest River, Sandpoint, Colburn, Naples, Bonners Ferry, and Moyle Springs, Idaho; Troy, Libby, Kootenai, Rexford, Eureka, Whitefish, Saint Mary, Browning, Cut Bank, Chester, Havre, Malta, Rudyard, Hingham, Harlem, Dodson, Wolf Point, Circle, and Glendive, Montana; Beach, Sentinel Butte, Medora, Belfield, Hebron, Glen Ullin, Dickinson, Richardton, Mandan, Bismarck, Medina, Carrington, Cooperstown, and Hillsboro, North Dakota; Ada, Mahnomen, Zerkel, Park Rapids, Hackensack, Pine River, Brainerd, Mille Lacs, Onamia, Mora, Minneapolis, Eagan, Red Wing, and Winona, Minnesota; Trempealeau, Onalaska, Sparta, Norwalk, Elroy, Reedsburg, Madison, Cottage Grove, Waukesha, Racine, Kenosha, and Milwaukee, Wisconsin; Waukegan, Lake Forest, Highland Park, Skokie, Evanston, Chicago, and Des Plaines, Illinois; Muskegon, Saugatuck, Holland, Grand Haven, Douglas, South Haven, Kalamazoo, Centreville, and Sturgis, Michigan; Howe and Orland, Indiana; Montpelier, Wauseon, Whitehouse, Fostoria, Mansfield, Hayesville, Bowling Green, Tiffin, Wooster, Bolivar, Carrollton, Wellsville, and East Liverpool, Ohio; Newell and Chester, West Virginia; Monaca, Alipquippa, Caraopolis, Pittsburgh, West Homestead, Duquesne, McKeesport, Ohiopyle, Meyersdale, Shade Gap, Orbisonia, Mifflin, Mifflintown, Mifflinville, Sunbury, Danville, Bloomsburg, Hazleton, Jonas, Kunkletown, and Portland, Pennsylvania; Cumberland and Hancock, Maryland; Columbia, Blairstown, Netcong, Rockaway, Denville, Wayne, Paterson, Rochelle Park, and Hackensack, New Jersey. (Two Hackensacks!) I've left some out, I know, and I'm pretty sure they're not exactly in order. But they're musical to me. Someone should memorialize them in song.

I used my tire pump regularly and an Allen wrench a few times to adjust my seat and handlebars and check to see that all the crucial screws were secure, but otherwise my tools, such as they are, stayed in their cases.

The trip was hard on my chain, and I had it replaced three times, but I let bike store mechanics do that. The biggest equipment problem was my cell phone. I dropped it on the road in Montana and cracked the crystal, and ended up replacing it in Minnesota. I left it in gas station restrooms twice and had to hustle back to get it. Happily, I still have my wallet.

I did lose some stuff, and inexplicably almost all the things I lost, I lost twice. Two toothbrushes. Two razors. (I didn't just lose the toilet kits; the toothbrushes and razors were all separate incidents.) Two of those cheapie bike locks. (I really don't understand how I lost even one bike lock.) Two little change purses, probably with a few dollars of change in each. Two socks. Okay, one pair. Maybe that doesn't count. Still, this seems like a pattern worth interpreting, doesn't it?

Amazingly, I had no flat tires. Well, shit, one. Yesterday, can you believe it? And it was my own fault. I overinflated the rear tire at a gas station pump and thirty miles later—*bang!* I'm delighted that I didn't have to spend an hour or so every couple of days unloading the bike at the side of the road, turning it upside down and replacing or patching a tube. The last time I crossed the country by bike I had twenty-four flats. But I'm troubled by the symbolism, a flat that screwed up a perfect slate, brought on by carelessness at the very end of the journey. It's not like it spoils everything, but that little taint on my triumphant reentry just bugs me, like a bunt single in the ninth that undoes a no-hitter. I'll always remember it.

The sun is going down now. In the grainy gold light from my window on the fourteenth floor I can see the row of apartment buildings that line the Palisades on the Jersey side of the Hudson and, beyond them, the spire of the Empire State Building. The George Washington Bridge is not even three miles from here, though it's straight uphill. Tomorrow I'll sleep late, have a hearty hotel breakfast, and climb through the familiar suburbs from my childhood, Leonia and Fort Lee, to the bridge, where several friends and colleagues are planning to meet me at noon.

Eighteen years ago on the same occasion, the welcoming committee was my parents. I'm not sure how they got to the middle of the span, where they parked or how my father managed to wheel my mother in her wheelchair onto the walkway—it's not so easy, especially from

the Manhattan side—but there they were, above the Hudson at mid-river, where New Jersey and New York share a border and the cat-enary cables hanging from the bridge towers on either side are at their lowest, so you can almost leap up and touch them. My aunt Claire was there, too, and she took some memorable pictures. There's one of me holding hands with my mother, me looking amused, she ecstatic. There's another of me with my father; he looks impatient, like such a sourpuss! Jeez, looking back, I loved the two of them monumentally then, being so emphatically who they were and making it their busi-ness to be around for that moment of their son's triumph, even though they thought I was a kook for making the trip in the first place. In the end, they understood.

One of the things that makes me feel as though this bike ride was like my life is that it has been long enough in both time and distance that I can't remember everything about it. (One of the things that makes me feel as though it isn't like my life is that it'll be over tomorrow. But that's only marginally pertinent.) Scenes from the West keep running through my head, but I have to remind myself again and again that these were my experiences, that I'm not remembering photographs or a movie, and that indeed the twisting path up the Columbia River gorge, the glorious ascent to—and descent from—Logan Pass, the passage through vast sunflower fields in North Dakota, and the fog-shrouded ride past small-town Paul Bunyan statues in northern Minnesota are part of the same path that I'm still tracing in the direction of home.

Details, for example, from my several days' ride through the Mon-tana Hi-Line are hazy, the towns I stopped in mixed up in my head. Was that meal in Chester or Malta? The picture I took of the silos and the passing freight train—was that before or after I took a rest day in Havre? It's hard for me to believe that the bike ride I'm on now is the same one I was on then.

But of course it is. The other day, in eastern Ohio, I turned a corner from a lonely country lane onto a better-used thoroughfare, a two-lane highway with a yellow center stripe and a very slender shoulder with a raggedy edge that dropped off dangerously into a cornfield. There wasn't much traffic, and it was the sort of road I've been on a lot, but it always makes me a little nervous to share a lane with drivers who don't expect a lot of company and hurtle by at high speed.

The moment I made the turn I had a vision, the kind of flash before your eyes that people call déjà vu. Maybe it was the time of day, late afternoon with its pretty, angled sunlight. Maybe it was the fact that there was sunlight at all; I'd been riding in wet weather for several days. Maybe it was the precise height of the corn or the precise width of the shoulder. Maybe it was the sense of anxiety at having to trust the drivers coming up behind me after happy hour had begun. Maybe it was my level of exhaustion. Whatever the stimulus, I saw in my mind's eye a road outside McMinnville, Oregon, that I'd ridden at the end of the second day of my journey. I suddenly recalled that whole day's ride with utter clarity, from the Oregon coast on a rainy morning, along the twisty, forested bank of the Nestucca River, and out into a sunny valley with the foothills of the Cascades in the distance. I love the idea that the bike trip, in and of itself, has its own vanished but recoverable memories, things that might come rushing back to me.

Like Billy streaking across campus. Or Catherine in front of my apartment building waiting for a proposal that I never made. Or my father in his blue Superman pajamas. Or my mother as a young woman, walking.

Saturday, October 22, New York City, north of Houston Street

The final numbers are in:

Day 46—Saint Louis Park, Minn. to Red Wing, 71.7 mi (2,419.6 total miles)
Day 47—Red Wing to Winona, 66.9 mi (2,486.5)
Day 48—Winona to Sparta, Wis., 68.1 mi (2,554.6)
Day 49—Sparta to Baraboo, 76.8 mi (2,631.4)

Day 50—Baraboo to Madison, 46.1 mi, (2,677.5)

Day 51—Madison to Waukesha, 72.0 mi (2,749.5)

Day 52—Waukesha to Racine, 44.3 mi (2,793.8)

Day 53—Racine to Chicago, Ill., 72.7 mi (2,866.5)

Day 54—Chicago lake route, 12.0 mi (2,878.5)

Day 55—Chicago to Racine, Wis., 74.1 mi (2,952.6)

Day 56—Racine to Milwaukee/Muskegon, Mich., 29.3 mi
    (2,981.9)

Day 57—Muskegon to Saugatuck, 28.0 mi, (3,009.9)

Day 58—Saugatuck to South Haven, 21.4 mi (3,031.3)

Day 59—South Haven to Kalamazoo, 43.1 mi (3,074.4)

Day 60—Kalamazoo to Howe, Ind., 52.5 mi (3,126.9)

Day 61—Howe to Montpelier, Ohio, 60.8 mi (3,187.7)

Day 62—Montpelier to Bowling Green, 70.6 mi (3,258.3)

Day 63—Bowling Green to Tiffin, 61.1 mi (3,319.4)

Day 64—Tiffin to Mansfield, 55.0 mi (3,374.4)

Day 65—Mansfield to Wooster, 39.8 mi. (3,414.2)

Day 66—Wooster to Bolivar, 43.1 mi (3,457.3)

Day 67—Bolivar to Newell, W. Va., 61.1 mi. (3,518.4)

Day 68—Newell to West Homestead, Pa., 54.7 mi. (3,573.1)

Day 69—West Homestead to Connellsville, 58 miles (3,631.1)

Day 70—Connellsville to Meyersdale, 55.6 mi. (3,686.7)

Day 71—Meyersdale to Cumberland, Md., 33.7 mi. (3,720.4)

Day 72—Cumberland to Hancock, 70 mi. (3,790.4)

Day 73—Hancock to Mifflintown, Pa., 91.9 mi (3,882.3)

Day 74—Mifflintown to Danville, 51.9 mi. (3,934.2)

Day 75—Danville to Hazleton, 40.2 mi. (3,974.4)

Day 76—Hazleton to Jonas, 39.7 mi. (4,014.1)

Day 77—Jonas to Netcong, N.J., 72.4 mi. (4,086.5)

Day 78—Netcong to Teaneck, 48.5 mi. (4,135)

Day 79—Teaneck to Greenwich Village, New York City, 17.2 mi
    (4,152.2)

*   *   *

The last leg of my bicycle journey was spurred by thoughts of home, of completing a task, of being welcomed back. It was a brisk final chapter, both exciting and sad, as endings tend to be.

So I wrote in 1993, and though I expected some similar feelings this time around, when I arrived home on Saturday I experienced no such inner conflict.

It's true I've been reflecting on the impending end of my trip for a few weeks now, and for a while I slowed my pace to accommodate my fear of reentry. But as I crossed the Delaware River and left Pennsylvania behind, an eagerness for completion surged over me. I sped through New Jersey (as far as I can tell, the nation's least bike-friendly state), negotiating a zigzaggy route through suburbs that I shared with zillions of drivers in a hurry and that took me, among other places, through downtown Paterson and past several landmarks in my hometown—Louie's Charcoal Pit, the Wigwam Tavern (though it isn't called the Wigwam anymore, it's the Cottage Bar & Restaurant), and the building that once was Longfellow Elementary School (now it's the True Light Presbyterian Church). I hadn't seen the house I grew up in or the old neighborhood since I made the same pilgrimage at the end of my last cross-country ride, and though the names of my neighbors— the McDermotts, the Kopfs, the Hansens (two Hansen families, actually, next door and across the street), the Ferraras, the Tells, the Asadorians, the Blacks, the Levitans, the Luskins, the Kellys—came parading back to me, visually it had all faded in memory. Trees are in different places than they have been in my mind. Our backyard, which supplied the football stadium of my childhood, is smaller than half a tennis court.

It was a nostalgic, slightly disconcerting detour, made a little more poignant by the memory of my folks greeting me. But this time, a few hours ago, when I was met on the bridge by a cheering gaggle of friends and a bottle of champagne, I wasn't thinking about the last trip or my parents; I felt nothing but exhilaration, and the memory that came back to me was of another unambiguously gratifying occasion, further back in the past.

My first job after graduate school was teaching English at a private academy in the Bronx, and in my third (and last) year as a teacher, the senior class dedicated its yearbook to me. That was thirty-two years ago. (My God, I've been an adult that long!) It was a fiercely thrilling honor, no less spirit-rousing for being not especially deserved. At the school assembly where they made the announcement, I was called up onto the auditorium stage, and the kids gave me a standing ovation, which is an experience I wish everyone in the world could have at least once.

There's nothing more humbling, more unadulteratedly ego-bolstering or more weirdly embarrassing, nothing that makes you feel more appreciated in the world, than people on their feet applauding you with vociferous sincerity, and among other things, it made me understand the manic drive of actors and athletes and politicians who feed so nakedly on that kind of lionization. Greeted by my friends on the George Washington Bridge—Mia, Donald, Dan, Allen, Avery, Carole, Bob, Amy, Eric, and two Steves, all of whom were exultant on my behalf, giggling, clapping, and taking pictures and videos, which they then dispatched by email to Jan in Paris—I felt that sensation for the second time in my life.

*   *   *

Sitting here at my desk, working on my home computer with a glass of bourbon for company, I'm still feeling the residual sparkle, grinning my head off in a way I doubt I did in 1993. For one thing, I'm thrilled to be wearing something other than a fetid merino undershirt, rain pants, and snug shorts with a pad between my legs, and after months of erratic motel showerheads to be reacquainted with my own bathroom.

For the last hour or so I've been thinking with satisfaction about the hair-raising moments of my journey—riding the dangerously chewed-up truck route into Whitefish, Montana, for instance; sharing the interstate shoulder with detoured traffic in North Dakota; cruising into Baraboo, Wisconsin, during rush hour, on a four-lane highway whose shoulder suddenly stopped short; being marooned on a cement island outside of Pittsburgh, forced to sprint across the road and leap over a divider with my bike on my back.

Survivor's pride is powerful; I prevailed.

Okay, I'll say it: Hurray for me! I feel, for the moment at least, extraordinary.

And very, very American. Among other things, my path through the nation has made me far more admiring of the nation.

I'm not speaking only of the scenic highlights, though the Columbia River gorge, Glacier National Park, Theodore Roosevelt National Park, the headwaters of the Mississippi River, and the Great Allegheny Passage in the full flush of autumn are more than enough to make a patriot out of a cynic.

This was a journey by a New Yorker who became more of an Oregonian, more of a Washingtonian, Idahoan, Montanan, North Dakotan, Minnesotan—you get the idea—as he went along. By virtue of absorbing upwards of four thousand miles of thrilling landscape, inch by inch, I learned more about topography and how it figures in the identities of thousands of localities and millions of citizens than I had ever understood.

Is there any way for a cyclist, especially one from a vertical metropolis, not to be awestruck by northern Montana? It took me two weeks to cross its astonishing expanse, from the dauntingly immense Rockies in the west to the endless, wind-whipped flatland of the east, where the towns are dots on the highway dozens of miles apart, pulsing on the prairie like blips on a colossal oscilloscope. As I sit here, it feels like there are more lightbulbs in my apartment building than there are in the entire state.

Easterners, city dwellers, and certainly Manhattanites tend to view the West with a kind of dismissive interest in its vastness and little interest at all in its variations. But it was striking to me how equally remote regions are hewn by different forces. In the Palouse of eastern Washington, where the golden wheat fields were so blanched by the summer sun that they seemed to reflect the light, life revolves around the heat and the harvest. A month after I left there, I passed through the flood-riddled plains of eastern North Dakota, where crops had been compromised and grazing land for sheep and cattle submerged, and everyone joked unhappily about a cloudburst gathering beyond the horizon. Worrying about storms is something we rarely do in New York, where threatening weather is relatively anomalous,* but I got the sense of what it must be like to always have one eye cast fretfully upward, even on sunny days, scanning the heavens for the next bad news.

In the heartland—Minnesota, Wisconsin, Michigan, Ohio—day after day I traversed enormous farms, and the sheer acreage of corn and soybeans, not to mention the huge grain silos and mammoth tractors and hay trucks, testified to the unending labor of farmers. They were always out working in the rain, and as I rode by, sodden myself, they always waved.

---

*Perhaps I spoke too soon. Almost exactly a year later, Hurricane Sandy brutalized much of the mid-Atlantic region and clobbered New York City, flooding the subway system and several road tunnels, causing massive power outages, and destroying more than one hundred homes in the Breezy Point section of Queens.

*   *   *

We New Yorkers can be so enamored of our high cultural advantages that we lord our sophistication over the rest of the population. An island off the coast of America—so goes the smug definition of Manhattan. Here is what I have to say about that after not being home for three months. New York City remains the national center of conversation; one thing I missed on the road is the kind of verbal dexterity that you can find in any Manhattan bar. (New York is also where restaurants know how much mayonnaise to put on a sandwich—not much.) But one thing we could use more of in the city is the inclination toward benevolence.

By the lights of my experience, in most of the country, the default temperament is decency. Okay, there were a few beer cans tossed at me out the windows of pickup trucks, but the total hostility amounted to what I'm used to on the subway on the way to work in the morning.

Strangers went out of their way for me regularly, to give me a lift over a construction site or unrideable gravel, to help me find a place to stay when none were evident, to help me out with simple favors when there was no actual reason to do so except the inclination to be kind. Ellen in Montana, remember her? The woman in the sheriff's office who found me a motel room in Chester, way out on the prairie, and offered, if I was struggling, to send a police cruiser out on the highway to ferry me into town?

There was a motel owner in Medina, North Dakota, who didn't have a room for me but who did have a cousin with a spare cabin on her property and called ahead on my behalf. I spent a night in relative luxury in that cabin, listening to the contented bleating of well-fed sheep in the pens out back.

And Scott Zoet, the proprietor of Rock 'n' Road Cycle in South Haven, Michigan, who opened his shop on his day off to perform an expert and much-needed tune-up in time for me to get out of town ahead of a storm.

It's hard not to be grateful for that collective attitude.

Finally, one more thing that enhanced the journey, an advantage I didn't have the benefit of the last time around and couldn't have predicted: the outpouring of goodwill from the readers of my blog and those who followed my ride on Twitter. I've been hugely grateful that so many people found a way to identify with the experience of this bike ride and took the time to tell me so. That those myriad good wishes helped me along is undeniable.

Of course, from coast to coast, I didn't have a single political discussion, minimizing whatever enmity was out there to be had, a happy result that makes a point that collective discourse is no substitute for people encountering one another in individual circumstances, and another point about the powerfully circumstantial nature of relationships in general.

I remember having the same reaction at the end of my ride in Vietnam in 1995, near the end of which I met a man named Than Minh Son, with whom I discussed the war and its aftermath. A retired government driver, Mr. Than had moved to the south in the late 1970s, but he had served on the side of the Communists, driving a supply truck along the northern reaches of the Ho Chi Minh Trail. Here is what I wrote about him:

> *A friendly man with a shrewd, wry manner, he described, through an interpreter, perilous journeys of 30 or 40 miles a night, driving on barely discernible roads, with lights mounted only beneath the truck so as not to be spotted from the air.*
>
> *"We were attacked frequently by American planes," he said. "If 10 out of 100 trucks arrived safely, that was a great victory. If a bomb hit in front of us, we drove through the forest and made a new road. Sometimes, revolutionaries in the villages saw that a truck couldn't move and they helped dig the new road through the jungle."*
>
> *He lost a brother and two cousins in the war, he said; he was wounded when bomb shrapnel took a chunk from his scalp.*

"When I smile or laugh a lot, I get a headache," he said.

Asked how he felt now, with Americans visiting Vietnam as tourists, he responded philosophically.

"As Uncle Ho said, wartime is one thing but peacetime is quite another."

Saturday, October 29, New York City, north of Houston Street

If I'd left Astoria, Oregon, to start my trip across the country a week later than I did, on July 27 instead of July 20, I'd be crossing into Manhattan today, in a raging snowstorm. It's really blowing outside; the forecast is for a foot or more. The Halloween blizzard, they're calling it.

I suppose I should feel fortunate, but I can't help wishing I'd had the chance for such a dramatic finish, plunging across the bridge in zero-visibility icy fog, trailing a slushy path downtown along the Hudson, tires sliding and brakes barely gripping, and crossing the finish line into my apartment lobby with my fingertips frozen and burning and tiny icicles clinging to my eyebrows.

The stories that make up our lives don't always unfold how we want them to, of course, and though you can will yourself an adventure, you can't necessarily make it turn out the way you've planned. Ah, well, life is long. Maybe on the next trip I'll get the exciting climax I missed out on by a week this time.

You laugh. But I didn't anticipate a second trip after the first one, so who's to say? I was forty before I had the escapade of my life in Vietnam, a place I would once have done anything never to have seen. I was fifty before I wrote a full-length book, and by then I thought I'd never write one, much less two.

And then to fall in love with a woman I'd known for twenty-five years, someone who belonged in a whole different compartment of my life—where the friends and colleagues are, where the people who raised families are—well, life has to do a lot of meandering around corners and into landscapes you can't imagine in order for that to happen.

Life is short, too, of course.

This morning I went to the gym and pedaled the exercise bike for an hour, a habit I'm determined to keep up through the winter. I don't much like riding on city streets, truth be told, but I'd like to keep my legs and lungs somewhere close to the shape I just whipped them into, and I like being this thin. My appetite hasn't slowed down, and now that I'm not working out all day every day, the weight I lost is bound to return. It's only been a week and I've put back two or three pounds already, but I can at least try and stall the inevitable.

Yes, I recognize the irony of stationary bicycling: all time, no distance. As I was pedaling this morning, cranking up the resistance so that I was working hard and breathing heavily, I began counting my pedal strokes, monitoring my calorie count, checking the down-ticking timer on the screen of my iPod as it shuffled through a couple dozen songs by the Rolling Stones—all different ways of being impatient with the clock.

Jan called a little while ago. I told her about the snowstorm, and she pouted, wanting to be here.

"I hate missing weather," she said.

She'll be back in New York in about a month, for Thanksgiving. We talked about our plans.

"I can't wait," she said. "Can you?"

"Well . . . ," I began.

How many mundane ways do I encourage later to arrive sooner? My housekeeper comes every two weeks, and the last few days I'm antsy over my own untidiness. I'm bored in the second act of a play and want it to be over. I'm writing something that's troublesome—an article, an essay, a journal entry, a book about a bike ride—and envision, with an ache of longing, the final sentence.

Here's something I understand now that I didn't eighteen years ago, and that I hadn't quite figured out yet in July. Even when you're far from home, exhausted, coughing, missing your girlfriend, and grinding uphill in the rain, where you are is where you belong. Never wish away distance. Never wish away time.

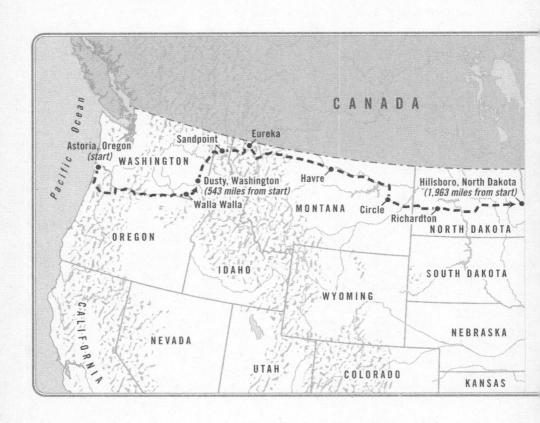

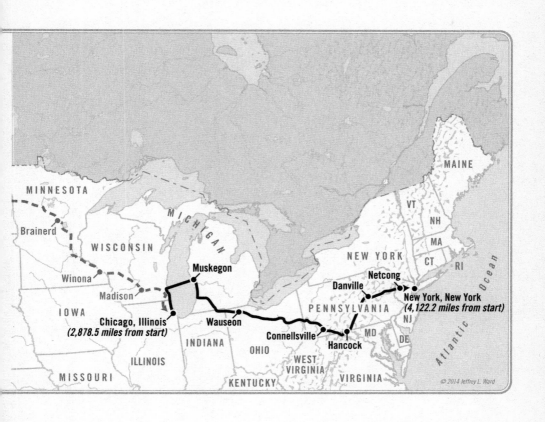

MINNESOTA

Brainerd

WISCONSIN

M I C H I G A N

Muskegon

Winona

Madison

IOWA

Chicago, Illinois
(2,878.5 miles from start)

Wauseon

INDIANA

ILLINOIS

MISSOURI

OHIO

WEST
VIRGINIA

KENTUCKY

Connellsville

Hancock

MD

PENNSYLVANIA

Danville

Netcong

New York, New York
(4,122.2 miles from start)

NJ

DE

VIRGINIA

MAINE

VT

NH

MA

NEW YORK

CT

RI

Atlantic Ocean

© 2014 Jeffrey L. Ward

Epilogue: An Actual Thing

~o~

Dear Bruce,

As a poet I should know all about the heart, but this mitral valve is news to me. Does it have anything to do with falling in love or gazing at a sunset?

—Billy Collins, age seventy-two, to the author,
    August 10, 2013

Old really has nothing to do with any of this. You're not, in any terms, old; you're just not too young for this. And that signifies a new authorship of your own life, based on the recognition that it could easily end. So you should act—however you're moved to—accordingly. "I could die tomorrow." This statement (which you could've made most any time in the last 50+ years or longer) now has new gravity.

—Richard Ford, age sixty-nine, to the author,
    August 21, 2013

Monday, Sept. 23, 2013, New York City

On July 31, two years to the day after Billy's funeral, just a few weeks after I turned in the manuscript of this book (and fifteen days before Jan was to return to New York for good), I was on Eighth Avenue near Twenty-Third Street in Manhattan, riding a bicycle uptown to the office, when I felt an unusual tightening in my chest, a stab of discomfort that I thought, at first, was heartburn. Pedaling the next several blocks, I felt my breathing become noticeably shallower, and when I reached the New York Times building, across the street from the Port Authority, I was conscious of the rapid *tom-tom* of my heart. I was drenched in sweat, way more than I'd ordinarily be, even on a warm midsummer morning.

Out of a precautionary instinct (I was more wary than alarmed), I called my doctor, Catherine Hart, from my desk. I expected her to ask a few questions and tell me I should probably come in for a checkup in the near future. What she said, however, with a drill sergeant's emphasis, was to get to her office pronto. This was a Wednesday, not quite eight weeks ago.

A couple of hours later, after Dr. Hart had given me an exam that included an electrocardiogram—it was normal—her tone was considerably less urgent but still cautious as she sent me back to work with an appointment on Friday for a stress test and an echocardiogram with a cardiologist. I felt like I'd done the right thing, getting myself checked, and didn't feel terribly worried, but almost as soon as I left Dr. Hart's office I began feeling feverish, and a mild cough that I had attributed to a reflux flare-up suddenly grew worse.

By midafternoon, legitimately ill, I left the office and went home. For two days I lay in bed alternately shivering and overheating, guzzling water and canned soup and sucking on cough drops in a largely vain attempt to keep my cough at bay, and on Friday morning, I called the cardiologist's office to cancel my appointment. I couldn't possibly take a stress test feeling this way, I said, not if it involves strenuous exercise. (It does.) But the woman who took the call, Dr. Jacqueline Mayo, a colleague of the cardiologist, told me I sounded awful and made the logical remark that being sick was no reason not to go to the doctor. Good thing she was sensible and concerned; good thing I saw her point.

I was right about one thing. I was in no shape to take a stress test. However, the echocardiogram—a sonogram of the heart—was evidence enough that I had a serious problem. I needed surgery. Dr. Richard Fuchs, the cardiologist, announced the results this way: "The good news is that I know exactly what's wrong—and we can fix it. The bad news is that you have to go to the hospital."

"Today?" I said.

"Today."

I was dumbfounded.

"So this is a thing," I said. "This is an actual thing."

"This is an actual thing," he said.

The diagnosis was flail mitral valve, which, in English, means that the gate that controls the blood flow between two chambers of the heart had essentially come off its hinges.

Blood is supposed to flow in one direction, from the left atrium—which receives it from the lungs via the pulmonary vein—through the mitral valve to the left ventricle, which pumps it out to the body through the aorta. I'd long had a common and unthreatening condition called prolapse, a mild flaw in the valve that allows a trickle of blood to leak back toward the atrium. (The sound this makes, a whooshing that can be heard with a stethoscope, is known as a heart murmur.)

But when the valve ruptures, as mine had, and its arms are flailing, the normal flow of blood is interrupted as an unhealthy amount is regurgitated back through the valve, like an undertow meeting an incoming wave. Blood flow out of the heart to the body is thus hampered, and the heart, seeking to compensate, can become dangerously overworked. In addition, blood may back up into the pulmonary vein, forcing fluid into the lungs—this is what was causing, or at least exacerbating, my cough.

In the hospital, things happened both fast and not so. I got there on Friday afternoon, August 2, but the surgery didn't happen until Thursday the eighth. During the days in between, as the doctors tried to figure out exactly what they'd find when they opened my chest, a parade of them came through my room, all asking the same questions, and a dozen or so nurses took turns siphoning blood from my forearms, leaving tracks worthy of a dope fiend. Often the doctors were trailed by students, several of whom were instructed to place their stethoscopes on my chest and have a listen—because, as Dr. Fuchs had informed me, my heart murmur was "world-class."

"Even a second-year med student can hear it," he said.

The doctors were puzzled by a couple of things. My intermittent fever indicated an infection, either in the heart or possibly on the mitral valve itself, the existence of which would complicate the surgery, among other things making it likely that I'd need a valve replacement and not simply a repair. But blood tests conducted throughout the weekend—this is why the nurses were so busy poking at my veins with needles—all came up negative.

Also, though a cough is often a symptom of mitral valve problems, mine was far worse than normal, a repetitive dry heave that left me in an occasional fit of retching and pleading with each doctor in the parade that trailed through my room to medicate it somehow. They finally prescribed codeine, which helped marginally. The cough seemed to get worse at night, keeping me awake through the wee-hour infomercials for skin-care products and exercise machines. (It also kept my roommate awake. He was a Russian about my age, also awaiting heart surgery, who had learned shortly before I arrived that his mother had died; he was trying to get the funeral arranged before he went under the knife. Poor guy.)

After the first weekend, the doctors ordered a test called a transesophageal echocardiogram, essentially a sonogram of the heart conducted from inside the body. This is a completely dreadful procedure in which a transducer is attached to a thin tube (not so thin, actually, just about the width of a finger) and inserted down the throat and into the esophagus, where the proximity to the heart's upper chambers and valves affords a more detailed view of them than can be obtained otherwise.

To snake the transducer into position, they have to numb your throat. You gargle twice with a thick jelly that tastes like burnt rubber. They make you swallow it once—really awful. To defuse the gag reflex, they paint the back of your throat with an acrid spray from what looks like an aerosol can. After each spritz, the nurse pokes a tongue depressor deep into your throat to see if you gag. If you do, you get another spritz. I took four, by which time I was nearly in tears.

I was coughing, too, through all this, and it was uncertain whether I could control myself with a tube in my throat, even with an anesthetic that didn't quite put me out. Every cough, after all, would jostle the transducer enough to blur its transmissions.

As I opened my mouth for the tube and felt it inch its way inside me to what felt like the middle of my chest, I remember lying on my side, curling up fetally, breathing through my nose and trying not to whimper. I would judge the whole procedure as the worst hour I've ever spent.

They did manage somehow to get the pictures they wanted. They still found no infection, which surprised them, but it was good news.

The next day, I underwent another test, a heart catheterization, which might have been less bearable if I hadn't had the previous day's ordeal as a standard for discomfort. The doctors slid a couple of probes into blood vessels in my upper thigh, up inside my torso and into my heart. They injected dye into the probes, which made the coronary blood vessels visible on an X-ray and showed that I had two occluded arteries. In addition to the repair or replacement of the valve, I needed a double bypass as well.

I'm writing this six weeks or so after the operation, well into my recovery. I'm up and about—Jan and I have been to the movies and the theater—my appetite has come back, and I'm getting to the gym regularly, riding a stationary bike, and climbing stairs.

My chest hurts where they cut into it; the most fearful moments of the day are the instants before a sneeze. The wound, though losing its angry visage as it begins to fade, remains sensitive and throbs, a regular reminder that I'm still a patient. I'm also coping with powerful, intermittent fatigue, a sudden, overwhelming lassitude that demands I nap a couple of times a day.

But all in all, not so bad. I feel lucky. I'm mending.

My cough, miraculously, is gone. It makes no sense to me—what happened to my chronic reflux?—but I'm vastly relieved. Dr. Fuchs theorized that the unusual severity of my cough before surgery was a consequence of the wear and tear in my throat and trachea caused by stomach acid, that I was already so raw and sensitive owing to years of reflux that any additional provocation to cough was going to have nasty results. But I don't know. As instructed, I've been eating and drinking with relative abandon the last few weeks (I left the hospital having lost twenty pounds) and I haven't needed a cough drop or a cup of hot water with honey for a month.

On the other hand, Dr. Fuchs tells me it's very possible, even likely, that the bouts of coughing and retching I suffered on my cross-country ride were signals of an incipient heart problem. I told him there had been an especially grueling afternoon during my ride—it was on a rest day in Havre, Montana—that my relentless spells of coughing in the hospital made me recall. The hours-long persistence and harshness of the spasms were similar, I said, and there had been no other like episode in between, a period of two years. Could it be true that I was having heart issues on my bike ride?

He thought it probably was. Making my heart work so hard no doubt increased the blood flow through the mitral valve, he said, potentially exacerbating its already imperfect mechanism and causing an increase in the regurgitation of blood back through the valve.

There was something chilling about this revelation: What if my heart had been on the verge of failing while I was on the plains of Montana or the flats of North Dakota and not within blocks of a hospital with a first-rate cardiac staff?

That's one of the things I think about these days. Another is my time in the hospital. I've been trying to reconstruct my days there, two weeks that are something of a blur. For a good deal of the time I was heavily dosed with painkillers—Dilaudid and Percocet and probably a few others—not to mention that the anesthesia from surgery lingers in your body for a while, so my memory, never a forte, is especially hazy. For instance, I simply don't recall the visits of several people who came to see me, though Jan and my brother, Robert, and my good friend Allen Steinberg were especially stalwart, and I remember them. I remember

I had difficulty sleeping; I remember the shuffling walks I took around the ward in the days after the operation and the breathlessness that caught up to me as I climbed back into bed; I remember being unable to eat because nothing appealed to me, certainly not the execrable hospital food, but not even the sandwiches, pizza slices, and desserts my visitors brought. (There is a picture of me with an icepack on my head, sucking on a lime FrozFruit and smiling, so I must have enjoyed at least that.)

I remember, after the heart catheterization, the indignity of nurse after nurse checking under my hospital gown, usually with Jan looking on, to make sure the incisions high up on my right thigh, "in my groin area," as they put it, were closing up properly. I remember Jan's joking that she wanted to object and tell them "Watch it, honey, that groin is mine," and I remember joking myself, remarking that at this point any woman on the Upper East Side of Manhattan might as well be invited to come in and inspect my junk.

I did cough for ten days or so after the surgery, clearing the residual liquid from my lungs, and I remember squeezing a pillow against my fresh surgical wound and steeling myself against the agony of each hack, the sudden convulsion in my chest that made it seem about to burst open at its newly sewn seam.

Mostly I remember being keenly alert to the isolation of hospital life, of living inside an illness, being unaware of not just the news—the New York City mayoral primaries were heating up and Syria was convulsing (the infamous sarin gas attack took place on August 21, six days after I got home)—but of the most mundane aspects of a life outside: the weather, email messages, and my Facebook account, even the Yankees' vain pennant chase. I didn't care about any of it; they seemed irrelevant.

Rather, I peppered my doctors with questions. As it became clear to me that they didn't want to cut me open until they were sure they wouldn't be surprised by anything, I began to envision the operation: the incision, the cracking of the breastplate, the disconnecting of the heart from the body and the connecting of the body to a blood-pumping machine, the pulsing innards, the circle of doctors and nurses in their surgical masks and gloves, the somber passing of scalpels and forceps, the locating of the minute infirmities that were making me miserable, and the hands of my surgeon as he performed, inside my heart—my only heart—in circumstances with the highest stakes, the tasks of an artisan seamstress or the sail-rigger of a ship in a bottle. His name is Leonard Girardi, and he was, I was pleased to learn, the son of an auto mechanic. Handsome and solid-looking, he had the brusque confidence of a fighter pilot and a manner that let me know he would take good care of me, if only because it would reflect badly on him if he didn't. I met him only four times before I put my life in his hands, and I paid specific attention to his hands, which felt uncallused when we shook, and thought (or perhaps only wished) I recognized the magnificent steadiness and, in the casual movements of his fingers, the dexterity and finesse he'd need to make me whole again.

In any case, I saw the entire operation in my mind before it happened. I wonder if it actually looked like that.

What else? Like a captive with Stockholm syndrome, I became consumed with curiosity about my nurses: Randi, Rebecca, Colene, Chen, Carolyn, Jewel, Po, Derek, and a dozen others, well-informed, well-trained, and concerned people from all over the globe—the Caribbean, China, Guyana, the Philippines, Ireland, Long Island—who showed up at my bedside one at a time to perform one invaluable service or another. I wanted to know more about them—their backgrounds, where they went to nursing school, when and why they came to live in New York City—to understand how our paths happened to cross at this particular time and place, in this particular circumstance. Since I couldn't get on a bicycle and sketch a path through the world, the world seemed to be sketching a path toward me. Maybe that's a little facile, but it's what I thought and it kept me occupied.

In fact, being sick was interesting enough that I didn't think much about dying, maybe not at all until the surgery was imminent. Even after that awful transesophageal thing, I wasn't despairing; though I don't remember it, Jan said I returned to the room not fearful or debilitated but sputtering in angry disbelief at the torment that had been inflicted on me. Strangely enough, it's fair to say that I thought more about death on my way across the country on a bicycle than I did on my way to a heart operation. Death, not necessarily my own, but death, its specter, the idea of it, and, of course, its actuality in Billy's case, rode along with me, all the way from Astoria, Oregon, to New York. On the other hand, in the hospital, as close to death as I've ever been, I put it easily out of my mind.

Except for one night, the night before surgery. I was sick and coughing and vulnerable and frightened. I didn't think I would sleep at all, and I didn't relish the idea of several hours alone with my thoughts, awaiting the morning when I'd be put forcefully to sleep and, who knows, maybe never to wake up again. You think that way when your heart is about to be stopped for it to be fixed. When you imagine what's going to happen to you while you're anesthetized and oblivious, it feels like a desperate, impossible predicament, like only a miracle could make things go the way they're supposed to, the way the doctors have assured you they will. Anyway, even the best-case scenario—the *best*— was that I would wake up confused, weak, intubated, catheterized, and in pain, with a five-inch gash in my chest and tubes running in and out of my gut and my neck, unable to shit or wash myself and facing weeks of feeling, as my doctors had warned me, more tired than I'd ever felt before in my life.

Jan was there. She'd dropped everything in Paris and arrived at the side of my bed less than twenty-four hours after I climbed into it. The first night she slept in a chair in my room, and for most of a week had tried to get me to eat, monitored my visitors, pestered the nurses to bring my meds on time, made sure the doctors explained things clearly, and guarded my comfort, such as it was, all the while keeping her monumental worry to herself. She stayed with me until after my surgery, went back to Paris for three days to rush through her final obligations and returned to New York and the hospital in time to bring me home.

I'm not someone who is accustomed to being cared for. I'll take the blame for that; I've pushed away a lot of caring over the years, but for Jan's presence, her ministrations, her demonstrated palpable love I was

332 Epilogue: An Actual Thing

grateful in a way I can never recall being grateful. Late in the evening the night before my surgery, she was getting ready to leave, to get a few hours' sleep before returning to follow me to the doors of the operating room.

"What time should I be back tomorrow morning, do you think?" she said, and I felt myself panicking.

"You're leaving?" I said, weakly.

"Would you like me to stay?"

"Yes," I said, and started to cry. She stayed.

Jan and I are living together now, cramming our two lives into the one-bedroom apartment I've inhabited alone since 1989. I've cleared out some bookshelves for her books, cleared out some drawers for her sheets and towels, cleared out some closet space for her clothes, cleared out some kitchen space for her dishes, and taken some of my favorite photographs and posters and ornaments down to make space on the wall for some of her favorite photographs, posters, and ornaments. We're throwing out my couch and buying a new one.

Against the base of one wall, I had had a decent-looking but actually rather cheesy cedar chest with a lid that was sealed, like a pirate's locker, with a rusty bolt. We've replaced it with one of Jan's prized belongings, a solid and handsome cabinet—unvarnished pine, I think—that probably began life in a farmhouse in young America. It stands two or three times as high as the cedar chest did, and I initially thought it was too big for the room, but in fact it's not; it's an improvement, though it means that we had to rehang a large map of the United States that I'd situated above the chest.

It's not exactly sophisticated interior design—the map, I mean—but on it I've marked the paths of my two cross-country bike rides with pushpins, pink ones for the trip in 1993, the 2011 one in blue. It gives me great pleasure to look at the map, a pushpin in each town where I stayed overnight, and to recall (or at least try to) the scenery, the people, the events, and the physical effort that each pin represents.

I offered to put the map in storage, to hang something else, something of Jan's, in its place, but she said no. She liked looking at it, too, she said, and besides, it made her proud of me.

When I finished the second ride, one of the things many people said to me, partly joking but partly as if it were a natural thing to ask, "So when are you going to do it again?"

This happened quite often. I would say a dozen times, until it began to seem like a reasonable query, as if another trip were a foregone conclusion and riding a bicycle across the country were the defining activity of my life, something that every so often was expected of me. What I always said in response, partly joking and partly annoyed, was, "Twice isn't enough?"

But as Jan and I were rehanging the map, I flashed on the events of the past month and a half. I turn sixty in a few weeks, and you could say I've had a change of heart.

I pointed out to Jan that as a purely visual thing, the map seemed off-kilter, incomplete. Both of my trips, after all, traversed the northern part of the country, and the whole south was empty, naked of pins.

"If you go, I'm going with you," she said.

Twice isn't enough?

Maybe not.

Acknowledgments

In a way, Life Is a Wheel is a book-length acknowledgment of the many folks who propelled me across the country. If your name is mentioned anywhere in the text, you can be sure you have my gratitude.

Other people helped in other ways. My friends Allen Steinberg and Avery Corman (the author, incidentally, of *Kramer vs. Kramer*) read early versions of the manuscript and offered valuable commentary. Another writer friend, Bob Shacochis (*The Woman Who Lost Her Soul*), didn't have anything to do with this book, but I never thanked him for his contributions to my previous one, *As They See 'Em*. Among other things, he lent me an excellent tape recorder that served me through dozens of interviews and that I subsequently lost before I could return it. Sorry, Bob.

I'd like to thank my stalwart editor, Colin Harrison, and my stalwart agent, Amanda Urban, for their stalwartness. Thanks, in addition, to Katrina Diaz, Colin's highly competent and exceedingly pleasant assistant, who made the issues of book production less of a burden than they usually are.

At the *New York Times*, Susan Edgerley was the editor who heard my idea for a blog about a cross-country bike ride, declared it a good one, and found a way to make it happen. She connected me with Danielle Mattoon, then the editor of the paper's Travel section (now the culture editor), who gave me valuable space in her section and, along with other editors on her staff, namely Rachel Saltz and Dan Saltzstein, the wise counsel that kept me on the proper narrative path. Special thanks to Rachel Lee Harris, a personable and clever young woman clearly overqualified for the tiresome task of handling my expense reports.

Bill McDonald, the modest and underappreciated obituaries editor of the *Times*, and his indispensable deputy editors, Jack Kadden and Peter Keepnews—really smart guys, all of them—fully supported me on this venture, even though my absence from the newsroom left them short-staffed. Which brings me to my obituarist colleagues—Doug Martin, Margo Fox, Paul Vitello, Dennis Hevesi, and William Yardley—who carried an additional load while I was gone, both during the bike trip in 2011 and in the weeks after my surgery in 2013. I know how hard they work; if you read their stuff, you know how good they are.

Given recent events, I'd be colossally remiss if I didn't acknowledge my debt to my doctors—especially Catherine Hart, Richard Fuchs, and Leonard Girardi—and to the nurses of the cardiac unit and the intensive care unit of New York–Presbyterian Hospital. Excellent work, all! Wow, am I grateful.

As for the friends who came to see me in the hospital and at home during my recovery—well, you reminded me (or maybe taught me for the first time) how important friends are and friendship is. I've mentioned some of you already—Allen, Avery, Bill, Doug, Colin—but happily, there are many others: Rick Woodward, Joyce Wadler, Lew Grossberger, Donald McNeil, Erik Eckholm, Carole Stuart, Jean-René François, Bob Bazell, Margot Weinshel, Steve Jones, Chris Calhoun, Janny Scott, Mia Navarro, Jim Sterngold, Rebecca Rohrer, Steve Greenhouse, John Schwartz, Alex Ward, Bob Ball, Alan Dynerman, Dave Bernstein, Glenn Shambroom, Nina Righter, Joyce Fitzpatrick, Jorge Luis Perez Flores, and Mike Frank. I hope I didn't forget anyone. I'm really lucky, friendwise.

Brotherwise, too. Thank you, Wobbit, I mean Robert. You're a mensch and I love you.

Finally, Jan. For everything.

About the Author

❧

Bruce Weber, an obituary writer for the *New York Times*, has worked for the paper in various capacities—as a magazine editor, reporter, and theater critic—since 1986. His work has also appeared in *Esquire*, *Sports Illustrated*, *Sport*, *Harper's Bazaar*, *Mademoiselle*, and *Vogue*. He is the author of *As They See 'Em: A Fan's Travels in the Land of Umpires* (2009) and *Savion!: My Life in Tap* (2000) with the dancer Savion Glover, and he was the editor of *Look Who's Talking: An Anthology of Voices in the Modern American Short Story* (1986). He lives in Manhattan.